D1218120

# TOXIC TRUTH

# TOXIC TRUTH

*A Scientist, a Doctor, and the Battle over Lead*

Lydia Denworth

Beacon Press
Boston

Beacon Press
25 Beacon Street
Boston, Massachusetts 02108-2892
www.beacon.org

Beacon Press books
are published under the auspices of
the Unitarian Universalist Association of Congregations.


Printed in the United States of America

11 10 09 08 8 7 6 5 4 3 2 1

This book is printed on acid-free paper that meets the uncoated paper ANSI/NISO specifications for permanence as revised in 1992.

Text design by Yvonne Tsang at
Wilsted & Taylor Publishing Services

Library of Congress Cataloging-in-Publication Data

Denworth, Lydia
Toxic truth : a scientist, a doctor, and the battle over lead / Lydia Denworth.
p. cm.
Includes bibliographical references and index.
ISBN-13: 978-0-8070-0032-8 (hardcover : alk. paper)
1. Patterson, Clair C. 2. Needleman, Herbert L. 3. Lead—Toxicology—United States—History. 4. Lead poisoning in children—United States—History. 5. Lead based paint—Toxicology—United States—History. 6. Lead abatement—Law and legislation—United States—History. I. Title.

RA1231.L4D46 2008
615.9'25688—dc22 2008021017

*For my father, Ray Denworth,*
*who left the world better than he found it,*
*and for my mother, Joanne Denworth,*
*who still works every day to improve our environment.*
*They set inspiring examples.*

# *Contents*

# *Introduction*

This is a book about a process of scientific discovery and about the dramatic clashes that resulted when industry disagreed with science about the significance of those discoveries. Lead was at the heart of those clashes, and it is at the heart of this book. But this is also a book about people, and it began with them, specifically with Herbert Needleman.

An unsung hero—that's how Dr. Needleman was first described to me. I was given only the bare bones of the story: He was the one who showed that lead, even at low levels, was bad for children; the lead industry attacked him; he fought the industry for years.

For a journalist like me, the idea that someone has a worthy tale that hasn't been properly told is compelling enough. But I was also a new mother, and like most new mothers, slightly obsessed and puritanical. I had recently moved into a Victorian brownstone in Brooklyn that was one of the roughly twenty-four million homes in the United States that still contained lead paint. The dangers of lead were real to me every time my baby reached for the windowsill. So I was also outraged. It seemed a simple enough equation to me. If something is bad for kids, we shouldn't use it. Somewhat naively, I wanted to know: What took so long? Why did Needleman have to fight so hard?

I began to look into the history of lead. Almost immediately, another name popped up: Clair Patterson. On the face of it, they didn't have much in common. Patterson was a geochemist; Needleman was a pediatrician and psychiatrist. Patterson was on the West Coast, Needleman on the East. Patterson traveled from Greenland to New Zealand, from Samoa to Antarctica making minute measurements of trace metals in rock, water, ice, and rain. Needleman went into schoolyards and homes in Philadelphia and Boston and measured children's attention and IQ.

But they were both studying lead. What they shared was more critical than what they did not. Each did seminal research in his area of expertise. I found following the process of their scientific discoveries thrilling. Their personal stories were fascinating and encompassed the Manhattan Project, the age of the earth, the Vietnam War, urban race relations, polar research, the early environmental movement, academic intrigue, and political and legal battles. Each was attacked by the lead industry, and each risked his career and reputation to pursue what he thought was right. Neither suffered fools gladly (or even non-fools who happened to disagree with them) and that sometimes cost them, but they were certainly never dull. The individual threads of scientific knowledge that Needleman and Patterson pursued, once woven together, revealed a startling and important pattern: humankind was systematically filling the world with a toxic substance that was doing irreparable harm to everyone, especially children.

Clair Patterson and Herb Needleman were not the only people who contributed to current knowledge of this environmental hazard —far from it. Many others have done important studies, and many others fought hard in conferences, hearing rooms, and courtrooms on this issue. I have included as many of them as possible in this book. Humanity owes them all—named and unnamed—a debt of gratitude.

But Patterson and Needleman stood out. I saw that by putting their stories together—although it meant jumping around in time a little—I could tell a larger and more important tale. Coming at lead from their two different disciplines provides a wide-angle lens that makes for a clearer picture of lead itself—of its history and use and of the arguments that have been marshaled for and against it. That history and those arguments have much to teach us about other toxins and about our own priorities and values.

"Lead is at the leading edge of the toxicity picture," Herb Needleman told me. The laboratories in which scientists measure toxins, the clinical approach to them, the importance accorded to their biochemical effects—all of these owe something to the study of lead. Another researcher described it as "the quintessential toxin." And so it has been. Since the time of the ancient Greeks, humankind has been removing lead from the rock in which it is found and putting it to use. Over the centuries, humans have dispersed millions of tons of lead into earth's environment—far more, for example, than mercury and arsenic, two other toxic trace elements. Lead also had a huge head start on the chemicals that industries began producing in great amounts in the twentieth century. From the beginning, lead was known to be toxic. In fact, it is now the toxin best known by scientists; thousands of scientific papers have been written on the subject. Yet the practice of dispersing it freely into the environment was not questioned seriously until the 1960s. Vigorous battles ensued, and the process of taking it out of the environment commenced in the 1970s. Now the arc of its story is nearly complete.

To fully understand how and why lead was toxic, scientists had to develop a whole new body of knowledge on its role in the environment. Roughly in concert with growing concerns over radioactive fallout and pesticide use, we learned that lead painted onto a wall doesn't necessarily stay on that wall, that lead used to seal a soup can may end up in the soup, and that lead in gasoline does not dissipate harmlessly into the air. Once put out into the world, lead travels. Where lead traveled, Clair Patterson and his colleagues followed. They studied its "sources" and "pathways." Disturbingly, the path led to us, to our bodies. By delineating the way lead worked its way into people, Patterson helped to redefine what was meant by a "contaminant." Lead didn't contaminate only water or soil or animals; it contaminated us. Concern about the environment was inextricably linked to concern for public health.

What did it mean that lead found its way into our bodies? What did it do once it got there? Even in ancient civilizations, observers recognized that a lot of lead could make a person very sick. But just how much did it take? And what about smaller amounts of lead? Did they accumulate in the body over time? If heavy exposure could kill you, what would long-term low-level exposure—a slow buildup over many years—do to you? To even ask that question, as Herb Needleman did, and then painstakingly parse the answer meant redefining disease. It's easiest to grasp the changing rationale if we put environmental toxins in the framework of medicine. Some researchers use cardiology as an example. In the 1950s, doctors treated heart attacks. Today, they look at cholesterol and blood pressure and other precursors of heart disease. If they waited for the heart attack before they took action, they would most likely be found guilty of malpractice.

With these new understandings of contaminants and disease to work with, there was one more area that needed to be rethought: public safety. What would it take to keep people safe? How far did we have to go? How much risk could we accept? There's no better case study in redefining an acceptable margin of safety than the steady ratcheting down of our official "level of concern" for lead, which was set by public health officials to tell doctors when to worry and when to act, and directly reflected the rapidly changing state of knowledge on toxicity. Acceptable levels of lead went from 80 micrograms per deciliter of blood in the 1950s to 60 micrograms, then to 30 and 25 and finally to 10 micrograms in 1991. As the level of concern dropped, a countervailing effect emerged. In the 1970s, a blood lead level of 75 was an emergency, but a blood lead level of 25 was commonplace. The realization that 25, not to mention 10, was dangerous ushered in a whole new kind of problem: far more children were above the line.

Such dramatic changes in our national approach were not without cost. Lead was big business in America. The metal was a component of literally hundreds of products beyond those with which it is most often associated—paint and gasoline. Industry dug it out of the ground for use. By the start of the twentieth century, the United States was the world's largest producer of lead. Lead was an integral part of the American economy.

Obviously, companies benefiting from lead had a lot to lose if the country reduced its dependence on the metal. They couldn't countenance the shifting views of lead as it went from being considered a boon to civilization to environmental enemy number one. (And those were the Republicans talking.) "To business leaders the environmental movement was hardly understandable," wrote Samuel P. Hays in his comprehensive history of environmental politics. "At first it was looked on with fascination, but as its influence increased in the late 1960s and early 1970s, this perception turned to incredulity and fright." With very few exceptions, environmental concerns were at odds with business concerns of material production and profitability. Lead was not the only battleground, but it was one of the fiercest.

As scientists and activists pushed back the boundaries on health effects of lead, industry ceded no ground without a struggle. Any delay in regulation was considered a victory. When they weren't trying to weaken new standards, they were launching public relations campaigns in support of their product. Although disappointing, perhaps it's not surprising that industry amassed such a poor record on environmental health. Beginning in the 1970s, in a series of interesting though troubling experiments concerning the sale of a drug that had been shown to be dangerous, a business school professor found that groups who believed their primary responsibility was to their company, such as corporate boards, consistently based decisions on economics rather than public health. The results surprised even the participants, who made different decisions if they came at the problem from a noncorporate perspective. (In the real-world case on which the experiments were based, it fell to the Federal Drug Administration to ban the drug in question after the company refused to stop selling it.)

With lead, as with other toxins, everything depended on the science. That is why the questions of who funds science and who evaluates it are crucial. In the first half of the twentieth century, industry —the companies who mined lead, manufactured lead additives, sold paint or gasoline, or the trade associations that represented them —controlled the science on lead. They repeatedly said there was nothing to worry about. "The wrong people were looking at the problem—the people who were producing it," says North Carolina toxicologist Paul Mushak, who served as a consultant on lead to the Environmental Protection Agency and to Congress. "Leaps forward were prompted by who was looking at lead and how they were doing it."

When upstarts like Patterson and Needleman questioned industry's cozy arrangement with the science and presented new data and new interpretations of it, industry changed tactics. It didn't stop producing its own studies, but it devoted considerable resources to attacking the critics and their science. In Patterson and Needleman, however, industry met determined opponents. "No matter where Patterson turned, you had a sense that his science was sound," says Mushak. "By God, he wasn't going to back down. You couldn't break him with a hammer. And Needleman, well, he was reluctant to relent."

As much as the history of lead is a story about the power of individuals to change the world, it is also a story about the power of government. Noticeably absent or impotent in the first half of the century, the federal government, once roused into action—though more slowly than many would have liked—was formidable and effective. Lead was the pollutant on which government made the most progress toward eradication. "EPA, to its credit, operates as the arbiter of discourse," says toxicologist Ellen Silbergeld, who won a MacArthur Fellowship for her work on lead both as a scientist and as an advocate. "We were there with the better science, and we prevailed." As historian Hays notes, it was "an intense debate between those who argued that regulatory action should proceed once tendencies in evidence indicated 'reasonable anticipation of harm' and those who argued that it should wait until 'conclusive proof of harm' had been established." Industry was, of course, in the latter category.

Conveniently for industry, the nature of environmental science is such that causality is almost impossible to prove. (The only exception is the link between tobacco and lung cancer, now considered irrefutable.) "Critics are asking for more proof than the discipline of epidemiology can deliver," says Needleman. "You can't give lead to kids and see what happens. What you can do is attempt to show robust associations that are trustworthy." Even Needleman agrees that one or two lead studies, no matter how striking the results, would never be enough. The answer, he says, is to also go to the laboratory and look at animal research. Then go to the geochemists and look at lead in the environment. Lead exemplifies the need to see a toxin in totality—to consider biochemistry, pathology, toxicology, and epidemiology as well as economics, sociology, and politics.

From the big picture, with industry's historic failure to respond to health concerns looming in the background, a simple but urgent message emerges: pay heed. Because we haven't gotten rid of it entirely, lead periodically comes back to haunt us—or rather those of us who like to think it's not our problem. It lives on in the walls that surround us, still poisoning many poor inner-city children as well as many not-so-poor children who are most often exposed during home renovations. In Brooklyn alone, there are thousands of old brownstones like mine, and hundreds of thousands of children. I was horrified to discover while working on this book that some house painters illegally use lead paint, which is still available for limited exterior use, on interior walls. "We always do this," one painter told a friend of mine, a homeowner who discovered the switch. "It goes on better."

The flurry of toy recalls in 2007 was an eerie case of déjà vu for those who know the history. In a turnaround for lead paint, once a high-end product, Chinese toy manufacturers used lead paint because it was cheap. And, of course, American toy manufacturers use Chinese factories because they are cheap. When the Chinese-made toys slipped through poor inspection processes in both countries, lead paint ended up in the hands of millions of children. More than ten million toys had to be recalled by Mattel alone. But lead in toys is an old, old problem. As early as the 1930s, one of the U.S. government's few actions on lead was to distribute a brochure that included the recommendation that parents choose nontoxic paint for toys and cribs. When parents asked where to find such paint, however, the government didn't know. According to public health historians David Rosner and Gerald Markowitz, a 1957 study of painted toys found that 25 percent of those made by Mattel (yes, Mattel) had dangerously high levels of lead paint. There is absolutely no reason other than low cost for lead to be present in toys today.

Lead poisoning is something humans brought about. And it is absolutely preventable—no lead exposure, no lead poisoning. As this book will make clear, we have come a long way, but it is easy to go backwards if we are not vigilant.

Over the last decade, the battle between the lead industry and its critics has focused on accountability. State attorneys general, environmental and children's health advocates, and public health historians have argued in court that the companies, particularly the makers of lead paint pigment, knew their products were toxic but refused to stop their distribution. They claimed that these products constituted a "public nuisance." The companies said they had done nothing wrong. Their products were legal, they noted. They said that the responsibility for ensuring safety lay with landlords, parents, and others who came into contact with lead.

For a time it seemed the "public nuisance" legal strategy would succeed. In February 2006, a Rhode Island jury became the first in the nation to find against lead paint manufacturers. The court ordered three companies—Sherwin-Williams, NL Industries (formerly National Lead), and Lyondell (makers of Glidden)—to help the state pay for the cleanup of hundreds of thousands of homes containing lead paint, remediation that might cost billions of dollars. Other states, including California, New Jersey, Illinois, and Ohio, filed similar suits.

But in July 2008, the Rhode Island Supreme Court overturned the landmark jury decision on the grounds that "public nuisance law simply does not provide a remedy for this harm." The decision was a bitter disappointment for the plaintiffs, who had hoped that the Rhode Island case would usher in a new era in lead paint litigation, one in which paint manufacturers would shoulder some responsibility for the damage done by their product. (So far, none of the other lawsuits has succeeded either.) There was little consolation in the fact that Rhode Island's justices did not dispute the severity of the harm caused by lead. They wrote in their ruling: "Our hearts go out to those children whose lives forever have been changed by the poisonous presence of lead."

The questions with which I began—What took so long? Why was the fight so hard?—may have been naive when I originally asked them, but they are no less valid to me today. It should not take so long and it should not be so hard to rid our environment of toxins. We shouldn't put them there in the first place if we can possibly help it. Yet we are probably doing just that every day.

In 1998, the Environmental Defense Fund began to look at what was known about widely used chemicals. Of the roughly nine thousand chemicals then being manufactured and released into the environment (equal to more than 2.5 billion pounds), some thirty-eight hundred were considered "high production volume chemicals." What the organization found was that less than half of the thirty-eight hundred had been even minimally tested for toxicity to humans. Only 10 percent had been tested specifically for their effect on children. Since then, the environmental group has joined with the EPA and industry associations to sponsor a "challenge" to companies to take responsibility for filling in the gaps in our knowledge of these chemicals, and progress has been made. But should we discover that any one of them is particularly dangerous, there will be no possibility of putting the genie back in the bottle. The chemicals are already in the environment.

The effects of low-level exposure to lead, and of other toxins for that matter, are indeed like high cholesterol and high blood pressure—a warning that all is not well, that trouble is brewing, in our bodies and in our environment. And unless we as a nation heed that warning, we may be as guilty of malpractice as are doctors who ignore the major warning signs of heart disease.

How much proof do we need? Many would say we have enough.

The same question holds for global warming, the effects of mercury and pesticides, the environmental causes of cancer, and nearly every other environmental issue of our day. It is worth looking back at the story of lead to be reminded of how we approached this question and others in the past and what the cost of those approaches has been.

# *Prelude*

BROOKLYN, NEW YORK: SUMMER 1951

It was July when two-year-old Celeste Felder started crying and refusing to eat. At first, her parents thought she was jealous of her baby brother, who had been born June 5. When the crying didn't let up, her parents called the family physician. He diagnosed intestinal grippe, prescribed penicillin, and told them not to worry.

But Celeste got worse. As the weeks went by, her crying turned to screams, and what little food her parents could get her to eat, she couldn't hold down. The family doctor insisted she would improve.

By Monday, August 20, her father, William, a thirty-four-year-old subway clerk, was beside himself. He took her to see another doctor, who said that Celeste had a viral infection—nothing to worry about.

On Tuesday, Celeste "went out of her head" before lapsing into unconsciousness. William Felder rushed his daughter to Kings County Hospital, which wasn't far from their home on Macon Street in Bedford-Stuyvesant. The doctor who saw her there said it was an upper respiratory infection. Felder pleaded that she was too sick for that, but the doctor gave him more medicine and told him to take Celeste home.

On Wednesday, Celeste began having convulsions—they shook

her small body all day. In desperation, Felder called the police, who sent an ambulance that took Celeste to Bushwick Hospital. There, a doctor examined Celeste and said she had a bad case of tonsillitis. Take her home, let her rest, and give her medicine, she advised. "You don't understand," William Felder cried. "My baby's dying." But the doctor told him it "would be foolish and a waste of money" to admit Celeste for further observation. "Take her home," the doctor repeated.

Back home on Macon Street, the convulsions and periods of unconsciousness continued. So Felder, unable to believe what he'd been told, took his daughter to yet another hospital, the third in as many days. At Brooklyn Eye and Ear, the doctor, who was the fifth to see Celeste since she had first gotten sick, agreed with Mr. Felder. Although the little girl did have inflamed tonsils, that didn't explain how sick she was. This doctor had another idea: "It might be lead poisoning."

Felder said that that was possible because his daughter had a habit of eating "anything she could get her hands on," including dirt, plaster, putty, and paint. But Brooklyn Eye and Ear wasn't equipped to treat lead poisoning, so Celeste was transferred to Cumberland Hospital, where doctors agreed with the diagnosis and began treatment to try to rid her body of lead.

But by then it was too late. Celeste Felder died at 4:15 a.m. on Thursday, August 23, 1951.

CHAPTER ONE

# *Every Conceivable Source*

University of Chicago, 1949

The small laboratory was quiet, just as chemist Clair Patterson liked it. When he needed to think, he couldn't abide noise or distraction. Intent on his lab notebooks, he paid no attention to the students crossing the quadrangle outside his window. All six feet four inches of him focused as sharply as an arrow on the problem before him, with his chin pointing at the neatly inked columns of numbers. Each was a measurement of a minute amount of lead from a piece of granite, but what they were telling him didn't add up.

Patterson had been as careful as he knew how to be, and that was saying something. Although he was only twenty-seven, he was masterful in the lab; chemical solutions were the magic potion that turned his Iowa farm-boy awkwardness to grace. "Pat has beautiful hands," a colleague once said of his technique. The work he was considering now was critical. It would determine the awarding of his doctoral degree in chemistry.

He had started looking for lead in a piece of granite that came from Ontario, Canada, near a place called Essonville. In its natural state, lead is a dull blue-gray metal. It's one of ninety-two trace elements in the earth—the elements that make up chemistry's Bible, the periodic table. Because it's so soft, lead usually combines with other elements. Its most common form is galena ore, but it's also found alloyed with silver and zinc. Initially, lead suffered by comparison with the far flashier silver and got dumped on the waste piles of ancient mines. But it didn't take long for mankind to reconsider lead's merits. It is heavy, malleable, and resistant to corrosion. The Romans used it to line water pipes and wine casks. (The words "plumber" and "plumbing" come from the Latin word for lead, *plumbum*. It's also the source for the chemical symbol for lead, Pb.) During the Civil War, the Union Army mined galena in New York to make bullets. In the nineteenth century, it was appreciated for the pure color it provided to ceramic glazes and paints. Beginning in the 1920s, it famously proved useful as an antiknock gasoline additive. Over the centuries, it has had a few other uses as well: in battery cases, bearings, building materials, and burial vault liners; in crystal glasses, cable covering, caulking, and computer monitors; in makeup, pots, pans, and pewter; in radiation shielding, solders, and soundproofing; and in television tubes, television monitors, weights, and windows.

But it begins its life chemically bound up with other elements in rock like the Essonville granite in Patterson's lab. Patterson had very specific requirements for his samples, and this one met them. It had to be from the Precambrian age—among the oldest rocks on Earth. It could not have been altered or recrystallized, but ought to be moderately radioactive. It had to contain some lead and at least average amounts of the accessory minerals zircon, apatite, sphene, and magnetite.

The granite had been ground up, and Patterson had separated its minerals. He was particularly interested in the zircon crystals, which looked like "stout prisms" about one millimeter long. These he ground to a fine powder. He dissolved the samples with acid, concentrated them with chemicals, then fused and evaporated them—sometimes to near dryness, sometimes to a "moist cake." Then he mixed in more reagents, heated and cooled again. Like a finicky chef developing a complex recipe by touch, smell, and instinct, he moved around the lab with innate skill and an intuitive understanding of his chemical ingredients. There had been some trial and error in the process—and always a danger of blowing up his "kitchen"—but he thought he had solved all the problems. When he finally had the samples ready, he transported them to a high-security laboratory where they could be measured in a state-of-the-art mass spectrometer.

It had taken him a year to get to this point.

Now, he looked out the window at the students scurrying across the quadrangle, and then looked back at the results in the lab notebook in front of him. He knew the age of the Essonville granite, and he knew how much uranium was in the zircon. With those two pieces of information, he had predicted roughly how much lead there should be. But his results didn't fit. "Not right, Patterson!" he said to himself in frustration. There was too much lead, far more than there ought to be.

Now the question was why. Where was the lead coming from?

He looked around the lab at the benches and hoods and distilling racks—all standard issue for the chemistry department of the University of Chicago in the late 1940s. From the outside, the building had a gothic grandeur that bespoke serious intellectual pursuit; the words "Kent Chemical Laboratory" were carved in heavy script over the double wooden door, and ivy clung to the walls. But once through the doors, the surroundings rapidly turned more grubby than grand. His laboratory was down the hall to the right, just before the auditorium where the campus communists met. The lab had been created when the building was erected in 1894, and it showed its years. Paint was peeling from the walls; the floor was stained and ugly. The wooden drawers and benches were scuffed and scratched. Dust seemed permanently lodged in the corners.

Could the lab be the problem?

Until that moment, the dirt and dust hadn't mattered much to Patterson; it seemed of little consequence given his excitement at being at the University of Chicago. He was in heady company. Just downstairs was Harold Urey, the physical chemist who discovered deuterium and won the 1934 Nobel Prize in chemistry for his work on isotopes. In another nearby lab, Willard Libby was in the process of working out the principles of carbon-14 dating, which revolutionized archeology. (He, too, would receive a Nobel Prize.) Patterson's lab was a few blocks from the spot where, in December 1942, Enrico Fermi had conducted the first controlled nuclear chain reaction, in a squash court near the university's stadium.

For a young chemist, Patterson was in the right place at the right time. He had come to Chicago after working on the Manhattan Project during World War II only one year out of college. The necessities of war had ushered in the atomic age and led to significant advances in chemistry and atomic physics such as the completion of the periodic table and the development of mass spectrometers. After the war, scientists were eager—even relieved—to take the ideas and techniques developed during the war and apply them to basic science again. It was a golden age, and the University of Chicago was at the center of it. Much of the seminal research in nuclear physics and chemistry occurred there. "All of these ideas that had been cooking around in [scientists'] minds during the war came to fruition as goals," Patterson said later. Scientific knowledge was so new that in his classes Patterson had mostly mimeographed sheets for reference—the textbooks were being rewritten.

As a Ph.D. student in chemistry, Patterson had spent his first year at Chicago immersed in classes. Then he met Harrison Brown, an assistant chemistry professor in the Institute for Nuclear Studies. Brown was a silver-tongued idea man who was making a name for himself as a dynamic and creative thinker willing to take on the big questions in chemistry. As one colleague said, "[Brown] had a remarkable instinct for the right problem at the right time."

To some extent, Brown and Patterson were opposites. Brown had flair. He was always nattily dressed, although his shock of brown hair sometimes disobediently flopped onto his forehead. He had a worldly nonchalance that impressed his students to no end. Patterson, on the other hand, had far more intensity than style. "No matter the weather, he wore the same tan windbreaker, head down, charging ahead," says his wife, Laurie Patterson, describing her abiding image of him from their college days. All his life, he kept his hair in the same close-cropped cut and wore a pair of thick-rimmed glasses. He walked with striding but ungainly purposefulness; his shoulders bunched up around his ears in a manner that managed to make him look simultaneously lanky and hunched. When he got caught up in what he was saying, which was often, he wheeled and waved his long arms for emphasis.

When the two men met soon after Patterson arrived at Chicago, Brown realized that this direct young scientist with an evidently fierce intellect and persistence, as well as considerable wartime experience in the lab, might be just the man he'd been seeking. Brown excelled at talking people into things, but Patterson wasn't hard to convince. He found the older professor's vision inspiring. "He never wanted people to attack solid, reassuring problems infused with an aura of certainty that acceptable solutions would be ground out if the crank were turned," Patterson wrote years later. "Instead, he enticed people into striving for splendid new views of our world and got them irretrievably committed to such efforts before they began to sense, too late, the costs of cantilevering out into the lonely voids of protoknowledge."

Brown wanted to take on a scientific question for the ages that resonated far beyond the laboratory walls, a question whose significance anyone could understand, a question that spoke to who we are and how we got here. He sat Patterson down one day and announced his plan: they were going to determine the age of the earth.

To do that, they were going to use lead.

By the time Brown enlisted Patterson, the muddy swirl of contentious early theories of determining the earth's age—adding up the ages of everyone in the Bible, for instance, or calculating the time required for the earth's crust to cool from a molten globe—had clarified into one promising technique: radiometric dating. Scientists now knew that uranium reliably decayed into lead, and they believed they could use the process like an elemental egg timer. Because the total number of atoms didn't change, it ought to be possible, at any moment along the way, to measure the amount of uranium remaining, the amount of lead produced, and the rate of decay to create a neat formula for establishing the amount of time that has passed.

In 1946, using a somewhat rudimentary version of the technique on lead ores, a British geologist named Arthur Holmes had estimated that the earth was 3.3 billion years old.

That same year, Clair Patterson arrived at the University of Chicago, where, because of Libby's work on carbon dating, there was already quite a lot of talk about the ages of things. For scientists interested in the ages of rocks or the earth, however, carbon dating is of little use. It is based on the rate of decay of carbon-14, which has a half-life of a little more than five thousand years. It works well for determining the age of ancient bones, but for anything much beyond forty thousand years there won't be enough carbon left to measure.

Uranium-lead clocks, on the other hand, kept accurate time for billions of years. If Harrison Brown had his way, Clair Patterson would be the first to master telling time by them. Brown believed that he and Patterson could do better than Holmes on two fronts. First, they would use not lead ores, which weren't old enough, but meteorites, which Brown and others believed had formed at the same time as the earth and remained chemically unchanged while rocketing around the atmosphere. Second, they would use the mass spectrometers developed during World War II to do the final minute measurements. Patterson would need to perfect techniques for separating and measuring uranium and lead abundances and then for measuring lead's isotopic compositions from meteorites; those measurements would be a thousand times smaller than anything anyone had looked at before—not milligrams, which were a relatively sizable thousandth of a gram each, but micrograms, which were each one-millionth of a gram. No one had yet figured out how to make such measurements, in meteorites or anything else.

"Good, I will do that," Patterson replied.

"You'll be famous," said Brown. "It'll be duck soup."

Patterson wryly wrote later: "It would be an enormous understatement to say that this was not the case."

In fact, it would take seven years of frustrating, painstaking work to accomplish, and then several more decades for that accomplishment to be recognized. But for Patterson, scientific truth was always the goal. When he was done, he would have answered one big question but raised a new one—one that he would devote the rest of his life to addressing.

Even as a child, Clair Patterson was a scientific investigator. "Why is a drop of water round?" he once asked his mother. If he found bones in the woods near his childhood home in Mitchellville, Iowa, he reassembled them to figure out which animal they'd come from. At twelve, he got his first chemistry set, built some shelves and a bench, and set himself up in the basement near a sink. He carried out experiments in qualitative analysis and developed "an intuitive appreciation for the chemical rhythms of the periodic table," as he later put it. When Patterson's father, the town mail carrier, received a package marked hydrogen cyanide, he delivered it to his son without complaint. "My parents allowed me to go off in any wild direction I wanted, provided it had a sound basis," said Patterson. "I was always different from most youth." Patterson had soon taught himself more than his teachers knew and he didn't hesitate to say so. "The science teacher would say something about electricity being a fluid, and I had to explain to them about electrons," he said. But in school, as at home, there was no retribution as long as he was right, "as long as there was quality in what you were doing." It was a principle he would live by all his life.

In 1939, he followed his big brother, Paul, to their mother's alma mater, Grinnell. "He was self-conscious and modest and more interested in chemistry than anything else," says Joe Dykstra, a friend from Mitchellville who also went to Grinnell. Patterson, now known as Pat, loved nothing more than playing around in the laboratory, and he once blew up a corner of the room. His rebellious streak got him suspended for two weeks at the end of his senior year after he threw a beer bottle through a dorm window. But the college made sure he was safely accepted to graduate school before inflicting punishment. (Later in life, he gleefully exaggerated and claimed he'd been expelled.)

At Grinnell, Patterson fell for a fellow chemistry student named

Lorna "Laurie" McCleary. He said, even before asking her out the first time, that he would marry her. She, too, was from Iowa. In fact, her aunt and his mother had been such inseparable friends they'd been known as the Heavenly Twins. But Laurie knew his brother, Paul, better. Pat was just a "character" from her chemistry classes. After their first date, to see *White Christmas,* there was chemistry of another kind. By February of senior year, they were engaged. "He was very intelligent, very interesting, and very determined," Laurie says. "I can't think of anything that didn't interest him."

Laurie's patience and serenity perfectly complemented Patterson's intensity. Socially, she was everything he wasn't: gracious and graceful. And she was smart, which was clearly a large part of the attraction. "We got along very well in science," Patterson said. "She took chemistry and physics with me. I was very good in the laboratory, but she got A's and I got the next grade down. I wouldn't do the homework, so she got better grades than I did."

By 1944, Pat and Laurie were married and he had a master's degree in chemistry from the University of Iowa. World War II was raging. Patterson had tried to enlist but was not accepted for military service on account of his exceedingly poor eyesight. An Iowa professor suggested that Patterson could help the war effort by going to Chicago to work on the Manhattan Project, which had begun in 1942 at the urging of German and Hungarian refugee scientists (including Albert Einstein) who feared a German nuclear weapon. One of the centers of research for the project was the University of Chicago, where the newly created "Metallurgical Laboratories" provided cover for work on the bomb. Both Laurie and Pat took jobs there. But Patterson was unhappy in the city and in his civilian status. "He felt he was the only young man in the city of Chicago," says Laurie. He tried again to enlist but was told that as either a civilian or soldier, he'd be sent back to the Manhattan Project. A sympathetic colonel suggested that the couple might be happier at the nuclear labs in Oak Ridge, Tennessee, where there were more young people.

Oak Ridge was in the hills of East Tennessee and drew on the power of the hydroelectric plants on the Tennessee River. In 1942, twenty-five miles from the Knoxville headquarters of the Tennessee Valley Authority, the Army Corps of Engineers seized sixty thousand acres of farmland and created a city of scientists and engineers dedicated to the Manhattan Project. By the time the Pattersons arrived in 1944, the place was buzzing with more than thirty-five thousand workers.

Pat and Laurie, with their dog, Dibby (short for Dibromomonochloromethane), settled into a small government-issue house that backed up to the Cumberland Mountains. They met up again with Joe Dykstra, Patterson's longtime friend, who was also 4-F, the military classification for those not physically fit for service. Oak Ridge at the time was pulling in young scientists—especially those who were 4-F—as powerfully as the magnets in the mass spectrometers under construction there. "It was much better in Oak Ridge," says Laurie. "We were right on the edge of the mountains and Joe and Pat hunted squirrels and rabbits, like when they were kids." Laurie's job was to determine the chemical purity of the uranium-235 that was being produced. Patterson built and tested new mass spectrometers.

A mass spectrometer works by deflecting particles according to weight. If the same jet of water is shot at both a cannonball and a ping-pong ball, the water will have a bigger effect on the ping-pong ball, deflecting it further from its original path than it does the cannonball. In a mass spectrometer, a magnetic field does the deflecting, and charged atomic particles, or ions, are what's being deflected. Lighter particles are deflected more than heavier ones, and both are collected in separate areas. Today, mass spectrometers have such diverse uses as detecting and identifying steroid use in athletes and locating oil deposits, but they got their start separating uranium for the Manhattan Project. In Oak Ridge, uranium was put into the spectrometer, where it was ionized, or charged, and then accelerated through the magnetic field. When it came out the other end, it had separated into U-238, which was not material for a bomb, and U-235, which was.

Although the Pattersons were happy to be part of the war effort, both of them had misgivings about the bomb. They worried about doing work that might "let the genie out of the bottle much too soon," as Laurie Patterson put it. And they were very unhappy when that proved to be the case. "Oak Ridge was a silent town when they dropped the bomb," remembers Laurie Patterson. "When we left, they gave us lapel buttons that said 'Oak Ridge'; we threw them away." Later in life, Clair Patterson called the atomic bomb a "hideous crime that we were committing."

At Chicago, Patterson was able to put his experience with mass spectrometers to a different use, measuring microscopic amounts of lead. What Brown wanted him to do was measure not just lead abundances, or overall amounts, but isotopic compositions of lead. First identified just as Arthur Holmes was beginning his work on the age of the earth, the understanding and identification of isotopes had progressed considerably.

Isotopes are variations of the same element; like siblings who all have blond hair and grandmother's disposition but different color eyes. The number of protons in an atom defines an element; all forms of lead have eighty-two protons in each atom. But there are variations in the number of neutrons, each of which results in a different isotope. The four main possibilities are lead-204, lead-206, lead-207, and lead-208. (The numbers are the sum of the protons and neutrons.) All lead-204 is primordial lead, lead that was present at the formation of the earth. Lead-206 and -207 are products of radioactive decay of uranium-238 and -235, respectively (they're also known as daughters to uranium's parent). Lead-208 is a decay product of thorium—the rarest of the four. At Earth's formation, each of the three radiogenic leads was present to some degree, and then their relative amounts changed over time according to the varying half-lives of their parents. The lead in the earth today is primarily a mixture of two things: the primordial lead that was there at the beginning and the lead that has been created by uranium decay.

Patterson needed to know exactly how much of each isotope existed from the beginning. Then he needed to work out how much of each radiogenic lead isotope had been created by uranium and thorium decay since. Finally, he had to establish the proportional amounts of all four. He would actually be determining not a uranium-lead age, as Arthur Holmes did, but a lead-lead age that compared amounts of one isotope of lead with another. "If we only knew what the isotopic composition of primordial lead was in the earth at the time it was formed, we could take that number and stick it into this marvelous equation we had," said Patterson. "You could turn the crank and blip, out would come the age of the earth."

Because very few rocks on Earth, if any, are as old as Earth itself, Brown had turned to extraterrestrial rocks. "He had worked out this concept that the lead in iron meteorites was the kind of lead that was in the solar system when it was first formed," said Patterson. "Meteorites may be considered separate little planets, all formed at the same time, all containing the same kind of primordial lead, and all containing varying proportions of radiogenic lead."

So few meteorites have fallen to Earth and been collected that each sample goes by the name of the location where it was found. The resulting list sounds like it belongs in an atlas, not a chemistry lab: Aguila Blanca, Argentina, for example, or Florence, Texas, or Zemaitkiemis, Lithuania. Harrison Brown secured fragments for Patterson from, among others, Forest City, Iowa, Modoc, Kansas, and Canyon Diablo, Arizona (a piece of which was held in a collection at Grinnell).

Brown had recruited, in addition to Patterson, another graduate student: George Tilton, an Illinois native who had some experience with radiogenic materials. "I was the lead man, and Tilton was the uranium man," said Patterson. Duck soup it was not. "We had to get a procedure going that would work," says Tilton. "I was just learning how I was going to do uranium, and Pat was just learning how he was going to do lead." They used mass spectrometers to separate and measure lead isotopes, but they had to continually refine their process for smaller and smaller samples.

Patterson was so absorbed in his work that he couldn't wait to get to the lab every day. Sometimes, as he bicycled to work, he pulled out a book and read while he rode—a practice that occasionally ended badly, with his long frame sprawled across the ground, the book flung some distance away. Sometimes, Laurie brought dinner to the lab, where they picnicked, and then Patterson would go on with his work. He often slept late and then worked much of the night. That changed when their son Cameron was born in 1949. Three more children, Carol (who later changed her name to Claire), Chuck, and Susan, followed in the next three years. With small children at home, Patterson made a point of coming home for dinner, but he often returned to the lab later.

Patterson and Tilton had strikingly different personalities. Patterson was outspoken, Tilton soft-spoken. Patterson was caustic, Tilton mild. Tilton and his wife, Elizabeth, were devout; Patterson regularly took the Lord's name in vain. "George put up with a lot from Pat," says Laurie. But Tilton appreciated Patterson's "warm laugh and devilish grin." Both were very good chemists, and they developed a deep friendship and trust that continued for the rest of their working lives.

Harrison Brown mostly left his two students to themselves. "He was always traveling," says Tilton. "Pat and I used to joke that we were each other's advisors. Harrison was always [out] talking to a lot of people about things that were interesting or puzzling to him. He would come home and bring us into his office and talk to us about it." Brown would stop off periodically at the U.S. Geological Survey in Washington, D.C. There he met a retired Harvard geologist named Esper Larsen, who was working on age determination of rocks. "Larsen knew that zircons had quite a bit of uranium," says Tilton. "He worked out an approximate age thing, where he was estimating uranium from how radioactive a uranium sample would be. Harrison came through and saw that. He didn't have to be a genius to see that Patterson and I could give him exact dates for these things. Our work would tell how much 206 to 207 there was and separate uranium from thorium."

Zircon is a mineral; its richest concentrations are in granite. "We would take ten kilos of rock, grind it up to something the size of minerals," says Tilton. "We might get a few tenths of a gram of zircon and would analyze a tenth of that. We used to have to do a lot of work for every sample we got." Each zircon sample was not much bigger than a large grain of sand. Of that, there were only a few parts per million of uranium and then even smaller amounts of lead.

The zircons served as a trial run for meteorites. If the isotopic composition of the zircons could be accurately established, Patterson and Tilton would know their techniques were solid. But working with zircon introduced a new problem. The two graduate students' results did not match their predictions. In frustration, Patterson pored over the neatly inked columns of numbers he had entered in his lab notebook looking for the reason why.

Uranium provided the critical clue. Because it was a closely controlled substance, Tilton had initially been sent to a high-security government lab to work. "They had been handling uranium all over the place," says Tilton. His measurements were distorted by the old uranium still lingering in the lab. He moved to an unused lab in the geology department—with his own security guard sitting outside—where uranium had never been handled. The problem went away.

So, Patterson reasoned, he needed to find and remove the lead in his laboratory. That, it turned out, wasn't going to be easy. Unlike uranium, which is rarely used in industrial products, lead was literally everywhere: in the reagents, in the containers, in the water, in the air. It was added during collection and during handling. Not one of the university's labs was free of lead. "I tracked back and I found out there was lead coming from here, there was lead coming from there; there was lead in everything I was using that came from industry," said Patterson. "It was contamination of every conceivable source that people had never thought of before."

Following standard chemistry practice, he ran "blanks" to see how much lead his processing was putting into the samples. That meant he ran each experiment exactly as planned with one important difference: he left out the lead sample. A lead experiment with no lead in it should result in no measurable lead. If Patterson had lead in his blanks, he knew it was being added during the process and not coming from the sample. Not only was there lead in the blanks, there was sometimes two hundred times more than they expected.

Painstakingly, Patterson found and eliminated the sources of the lead. "When he got going on something, he just threw himself into it and didn't get distracted," says Tilton. The two made their own distillation device with pure silicate glass and a stem nearly three feet high to triple-distill their own water. They covered work surfaces with plastic Parafilm and wrapped equipment and samples tightly in plastic. Plastic seals were broken only when materials were being transferred, and were immediately resealed. In addition to the standard hoods that both chemists worked under, they made up "cages" of plastic with pumps attached, essentially hoods within hoods, and worked inside the cages, looking vaguely like neonatal doctors caring for babies in incubators. Patterson became an early convert to Teflon, which was first marketed by DuPont in 1945.

They became obsessive about cleaning. They mopped and vacuumed the lab frequently and regularly scrubbed benches and hoods. The glassware—all Pyrex—underwent a five-step cleaning process: it was scrubbed with scouring powder; rinsed with distilled water; immersed for twenty minutes in a 10 percent solution of potassium hydroxide held near the boiling point; then rinsed again with double-distilled water. Platinum-ware was also scrubbed with scouring powder, then a new surface was etched with aqua regia (a mixture of nitric acid and hydrochloric acid) and it, too, was rinsed with double-distilled water. Finally, in the same dusty lab where he had started, Patterson managed blanks that had only about 0.1 microgram of lead—an impressive achievement.

By 1951, although they still didn't know the age of Earth, Patterson and Tilton had developed accurate techniques for measuring samples in microgram amounts, or less—samples that weren't much bigger than the dot on an "i" in fine print. They had established the isotopic composition of the zircons and confirmed the age of the zircons from Esper Larsen's sample as 1.05 billion years. "When we determined how to measure the ages of these zircons," said Patterson, "that blew the whole thing apart."

Patterson recounted his work with lead in his dissertation; Tilton did the same with uranium. They also published their first article together in a scientific journal. As is the way with such work, the technical title—"Isotopic composition of lead and the ages of minerals in a Precambrian granite"—didn't hint at the tribulations they'd encountered. Nor did it signal the significance of the work. The techniques they had developed provided a window into the formation of the continents and the planets. It meant that wherever there was zircon—and it was common—scientists could determine accurate ages. A whole new field of geology known as geochronology opened up. Eventually, hundreds of age determinations based on zircon were made, allowing scientists to slowly build a model for the geochemical evolution of the earth. (Tilton went on to do just that at the Carnegie Institution in Washington, D.C.)

Turning his attention to meteorites, Patterson discovered that all published measurements of lead in meteorites were off dramatically. Instead of about 50 micrograms of lead per gram of meteorite, there was more like 0.05 micrograms—one thousand times less. Clearly, he was on to something, but much work remained to be done. He still hadn't answered the big question. And now he had new questions.

When Patterson looked at his Chicago lab with new eyes, he knew that he was never going to be able to get enough clean samples to determine the age of the earth there. He looked at people differently, too. "You know Pigpen, in Charlie Brown's comic strip, where stuff is coming out all over the place," he said. "That's what people look like with respect to lead. Everyone. Lead's coming from [your hair], your clothing, and everything else." He needed another place to work; a place where he could control the people, the air, and the equipment. But where? Such a place didn't exist.

### Pasadena, California, 1952

After two days of traveling west, the view out Clair Patterson's train window had changed dramatically. He had left Chicago in the grip of a harsh winter. As he arrived in Pasadena, the San Gabriel Mountains rose dry and green behind the city and palm trees stood tall over the red-tiled roof of the train station. For Patterson, a lifelong midwesterner, Southern California held out the promise of a dramatic new environment. Here, in the land of roses, oranges, and, ironically, smog, was the California Institute of Technology, where Patterson might be able to build the pristine laboratory he needed to accurately measure lead.

First, he had to get the job. Waiting for him on the platform was a young man close to Patterson's age. They sized each other up as they shook hands. Leon Silver, Lee to his friends, was a World War II veteran. He was shorter than Patterson with curly hair and an affable air. An Easterner by birth, Silver possessed a love of geology that had brought him west to study in Colorado and New Mexico. After a few seasons of fieldwork for the U.S. Geological Survey, he had come to Caltech to get his Ph.D. As a junior member of the geology department, he got the job of collecting Patterson from the station.

As they drove to the campus, Silver and Patterson found they had much in common: both were trying to build careers in science, both had young families, both were trying to manage on the meager salaries of their chosen profession. In demeanor, however, the two were very different. Silver was sociable and diplomatic, whereas Patterson was a bit of an oddball. "Pat started off very carefully minding his manners, but he was one of those guys who would always break through with some very strong or even outrageous statement," says Silver. "He did it without being ugly, but he was a kook." Despite that tendency, Silver liked Patterson, and that would prove to be important. In the political world of academia, Patterson needed tactful allies to help blunt his rough edges. At Chicago, he had Harrison Brown. In Lee Silver, the first person he met at Caltech, he had found another protector.

It was because of Harrison Brown that Patterson had come to Pasadena. Caltech was looking to reinvent its geology department and sought out Brown for the exciting work he was doing in geochemistry. Brown, in turn, wanted to bring from Chicago three promising young scientists: Charles McKinney, Sam Epstein, and Clair Patterson. Epstein and Patterson were pure chemists; McKinney was a physicist. They weren't an obvious fit in a geology department made up, as one Caltech professor said, of "a bunch of geologists and seismologists who had forgotten most of what they had ever learned of isotopes in elementary chemistry courses."

But Caltech was serious about developing a geochemistry program, and Patterson's work fit into their plans. It made sense for him, too. He had finished his dissertation at Chicago in June of 1951.

Brown had kept him on as a postdoctoral fellow to continue trying to determine the age of the earth. Patterson knew that was a temporary solution, and he thought often about what to do next.

Brown's political skills did more for Patterson than serve as buffer; they got him money. At Chicago, Patterson and Tilton had been paid through a five-year Atomic Energy Commission grant to Brown. As a Ph.D., Patterson was supposed to jump from the nest and support himself. His first effort didn't go well. "Pat couldn't sell anything," says Laurie Patterson. "How to sweet-talk somebody was not in his personality." He labored over a proposal to continue working toward determining the age of the earth. The Atomic Energy Commission wasn't interested. Patterson cried on Brown's shoulder and got a reprieve. "That's all right, I'll rewrite your proposal in my name," said Brown. Patterson knew Brown was better at "explaining things in a nonscientific way—in [a] way that says of what use it is." The commission cared about uranium fuel, and Brown essentially told the commission that Patterson's work would help find it. The proposal was funded immediately. ("Boom!" said Patterson.) Since Brown was going to Caltech, the money would go to Caltech; Patterson would follow the money.

During the February visit, Patterson agreed to become a research fellow in the Division of Geological Sciences. In the 1950s, Caltech was small and focused, as it is today. Then half its current size, with a little more than a thousand students, it was already among the nation's premier research institutions. At various times, it was the academic home of Robert Oppenheimer, Max Delbruck, Richard Feynman, and Linus Pauling, who determined the nature of the chemical bond there in the 1930s. Although Patterson would teach a few introductory courses in geochemistry, he could dedicate most of his time to the laboratory. He and Laurie piled Cam, Carol, and Chuck, then ages three, two, and one, respectively, in the car and moved across the country in April. They settled in La Cañada, a Pasadena suburb in the foothills of the San Gabriel Mountains, and their fourth child, Susan, was born a few months later.

Patterson took his new connection to geology seriously, which meant he needed an education in rocks. Lee Silver appointed himself Pat's tutor, and the summer after Patterson arrived at Caltech, Silver and others took him on a geology field trip in the Sacramento Mountains of southern New Mexico. It was hot, dry country in the summer, and the work was dirty and physically demanding—a new experience for a chemist who'd been shut up in laboratories for years. "I am sunburned, cracked and full of cactus needle holes," Patterson wrote to a colleague. "But I love it! This is for me—it's great stuff—never had a better time."

Patterson's willingness to throw himself into this hard work unrelated to his research—the goal of that trip was to add detail to a contour map—earned him respect and approval from his new colleagues. He hammered the geologists with questions about their thinking and procedures. Soon, field trips became a regular part of his work, and cactus needles would later seem a minor irritation compared to the Arctic temperatures, volcanic gases, and other hazards to which Patterson regularly subjected himself in pursuit of answers. "Pat was not a half-way guy," said Robert Sharp, who became chairman of the Geology Division that year. "He put his heart and soul into every endeavor."

Nowhere was that more true than in his new clean lab. No one had yet undertaken to create the kind of lead-free environment Pat had in mind. He needed to apply everything he'd learned in his years of fighting contamination in Chicago. "Clean, clean, clean," says Lee Silver. "He was only as good as he was clean. Other people didn't understand how many sources [of lead] there were." The geology department was housed in two three-story yellow stucco buildings, called Mudd and Arms, in the southwest corner of campus. The entire basement of Mudd was given over to the fledgling geochemistry program. Several chemical laboratories, including Patterson's, were built out of what used to be storage rooms and geological laboratories. State-of-the-art equipment was installed, including three mass spectrometers and an emission spectrograph.

Throughout the summer of 1952, Patterson was more general contractor than analytical chemist. From his new office in a small courtyard between Mudd and Arms, he fired off lengthy memos specifying how things should be done. Some changes were fairly obvious though no less extensive because of it. In an ordinary laboratory, Patterson wrote later, there were "lead gaskets used in compressed gas fittings and lead oxide putty used to seal windows, plumbing fixtures and patch walls." In his lab, water pipes could not have any lead in them, so the building's plumbing had to be rerun. In 1952, most interior paints still had lead in them; these walls had to be lead-free. The electrical system had to be rewired because most electrical connections contained a solder in which lead was a primary component. Patterson sourced every instrument, container, and reagent himself. His preferred materials were Teflon and stainless steel. The tabletop was made of a single piece of stainless steel—joints would invite contamination. He also figured out how to control the air by creating an elaborate baffle system to pump in purified, pressurized air—when the door opened, air blew out rather than in. "In Chicago, Pat had a little box that he would keep pumped out and clean," says George Tilton. "At Caltech, they built a whole room."

Impatient and impolitic, Patterson pushed his new colleagues hard. "We all learned what a no-compromise, intense, dedicated, demanding, zealous character we had on our hands in the person of Clair C. Patterson," wrote Sharp. "Get the lead out became almost a Geology Division motto. Certainly it was our battle cry. We ultimately claimed with pride that Patterson's lab had the cleanest air in all of southern California."

The result was unlike any other laboratory of the time. "Patterson was the father of clean labs," says Silver. The lab accommodated several researchers at once, including Silver, who had his own bench on one side of the room. There were separate rooms for grinding rocks and for separating minerals, for washing sample containers, purifying water and chemical reagents, preparing samples, and analyzing samples. Water was purified in specially constructed distillation equipment, and samples were handled with specially designed tools. Everyone who entered had to remove shoes and wear lab coats. In later years, Patterson required his colleagues to strip down to their underwear and put on Tyvek suits when they worked in the lab.

Once the lab was built, Patterson had to maintain the uncontaminated state. He developed detailed and laborious lab procedures. Anyone who worked in his lab spent time on hands and knees washing down the floor. One of his early lab assistants, Betty Duffield, kept a notebook of instructions that listed each step of fifteen different procedures from washing equipment made of glass, Teflon, plastic, and polyethylene (each requiring a different process) to distilling water and purifying borax and other reagents. Some of the reagents needed to be twice distilled. Others were acid-washed and distilled before use. The procedure for separating zircons took Duffield three pages to describe. The back of her lab notebook listed specific suppliers for each item needed: lambda pipettes, polyethylene bottles, plastic wrap, tall cylinders for acid washing, and so on.

Here, in this pristine, lead-free environment, Patterson believed he could finally determine Earth's age. His first significant success with a meteorite came from a piece of the Canyon Diablo, Arizona, sample. Patterson prepared the samples in his new labs, but since his Caltech mass spectrometer wasn't ready yet, he had to travel back to Chicago to measure them.

### Argonne National Laboratory, 1953

Twenty-five miles southwest of Chicago, Argonne is owned by the U.S. Department of Energy but managed by the University of Chicago, so it wasn't hard for Patterson to use his connections to gain access and the necessary security clearance. One of the leading researchers at Argonne was Mark Inghram, a University of Chicago physics professor who had furthered Patterson's education on mass spectrometers by demonstrating such fine points as how to change a sample by breaking a glass tube with a wire and then resealing it by blowing the glass. Patterson arrived with his precious samples encased in layers of plastic and protective coverings. He carefully loaded the samples into the machine and began the runs.

It was late when he finished. The lab was quiet. He knew immediately what he had. No one had ever seen lead like this in any terrestrial sample. It had to be from something very, very old. Standing alone in a laboratory in the middle of a midwestern night, Clair Patterson, still only thirty-one years old, put the new numbers he had just produced into the old equation he'd been considering for seven years. He turned the crank and, blip, out popped the age of the earth: 4.5 billion years.

Patterson was so excited he almost fainted. "The discovery electrified my soul," he wrote later. His first thought was of the many scientists who had gone before, helping him to reach this moment. Forgetting the hour, he called Mark Inghram to tell him the news and woke his former professor.

"That's wonderful, Pat," said Inghram sleepily. "Why don't we talk about it tomorrow?"

The next day, as Patterson drove from Argonne to his parents' home in Iowa, his excitement was still so great he thought he was having a heart attack. His mother took him to the hospital, but there was nothing wrong—perhaps just a little too much adrenaline coursing through his body coupled with Patterson's lifelong hypochondria.

He later expanded on his description of the experience: "True scientific discovery renders the brain incapable at such moments of shouting vigorously to the world 'Look what I've done! Now I will reap the benefits of recognition and wealth.' Instead such discovery instinctively forces the brain to thunder 'We did it' in a voice no one else can hear, within its sacred, but lonely chapel of scientific thought."

Patterson knew the significance of what he had accomplished, but he also knew that more work remained to be done—both to confirm the number (he eventually refined it to 4.55 billion years) and to convince others he was right. He announced his results in mid-September 1953 at the Conference on Nuclear Process in Geologic Settings, held in Green Bay, Wisconsin, and sponsored by the National Research Council of the National Science Foundation.

Patterson was not a captivating speaker. "Pat had a habit, both in speech and in writing, to start in the middle and work both forwards and backwards simultaneously," wrote Sharp, who had to translate Patterson's research into lay terms for Caltech's annual reports. Patterson habitually argued for more time in any presentation. Once, when a red light indicated that only a few of his allotted minutes remained, he unscrewed the light bulb and kept talking until he was done.

At the Green Bay conference, however, his remarks were to the point. The paper he delivered, titled "The Isotopic Composition of Meteoric, Basaltic and Oceanic Leads, and the Age of the Earth," gave the values he had found for meteoritic lead and then for terrestrial leads—all of them in lead/lead ratios. He finished with a qualified announcement: "The minimum age of the earth is then about 4.5 billion years and is probably somewhat older."

Reaction was equally qualified. It wasn't until the following February that the *New York Times* mentioned the news of Patterson's discovery in a three-paragraph write-up deep inside the paper. The world was slow to acknowledge the enormity of Patterson's achievement in part because so few others could replicate the work; they hadn't mastered the techniques, and they didn't have the facilities. It was more than ten years before Patterson's value for the age of the earth made it into geology textbooks. Today, he is only occasionally mentioned by name. In 2003, Bill Bryson devoted a chapter to Patterson's achievement in *A Short History of Nearly Everything,* his best-selling look at the history of science, but many books simply cite "radiometric dating" as the technique that ultimately provided the answer. (There were a few who immediately understood the implications of Patterson's work, however, including a Pasadena evangelist who paid Patterson a visit to tell him he would burn in hell.)

Patterson was more interested in other implications. The contamination he had discovered en route to the age of the earth worried him enormously. Now that he understood how to measure such tiny amounts of lead, he understood something else as well. "There were tens of thousands of published numbers of lead concentrations in these common ordinary things," he said. "They were [all] wrong!" Even he didn't see how significant that would be.

CHAPTER TWO

# *The Faces of the Children*

CHILDREN'S HOSPITAL OF PHILADELPHIA, 1957

Herbert Needleman strode through the hospital toward the baby ward. He had to dodge stray oxygen tanks and stretchers housed in the hall for lack of space, but he was accustomed to the obstacle course and navigated it easily. His mind was on the little girl he was about to visit. He'd never treated a case of lead poisoning before, and he was both intrigued and confident.

Needleman was not yet thirty, but he wore his doctor's uniform of short white jacket and duck trousers with a low-key assuredness—some would say cockiness. Six feet tall, he had brown eyes, dark hair, and a broad, amiable face. For a resident, he had quite a bit of experience. He had just returned to the Children's Hospital of Philadelphia after two years in the Army. At Fort Meade in Maryland, he had run a twelve-bed pediatric ward, his only supervision the periodic visits of a senior Johns Hopkins pediatrician. Whatever came along, from diarrhea and cramps to delivering babies, Needleman handled it. He had chafed at the restrictions of Army life, but the on-the-job training sharpened his ability to diagnose a problem and fix it. His medical acuity impressed his colleagues at the Children's Hospital. One day, Needleman noticed a resident bent over and limping a little.

"You've got acute appendicitis," Needleman declared.

"No, I don't," said the young doctor.

"Well, call me if it doesn't get better," said Needleman.

An hour later, Needleman drove his colleague to the Children's Hospital's sister hospital at the University of Pennsylvania for an appendectomy.

The Children's Hospital of Philadelphia, founded in 1855, was the first hospital in America devoted solely to children. Today, it goes by the crisp, contemporary acronym CHOP and occupies a cluster of modern high-rises in West Philadelphia near the University of Pennsylvania, with which it is still affiliated. But in the 1950s, when Needleman arrived, everyone affectionately called it "the Children's," and it was located in a stolid, four-story brick and stone-faced building at Eighteenth and Bainbridge streets in Southeast Philadelphia, in the midst of a predominantly black and very poor neighborhood.

Nonetheless, it was at the forefront of research on the major pediatric problems of the day such as tuberculosis, polio, and rheumatic fever. Its laboratories had produced vaccines for influenza, mumps, and whooping cough. C. Everett Koop, who went on to become U.S. surgeon general, was the hospital's surgeon-in-chief and was busy in the three small operating rooms transforming pediatric surgery from an afterthought to an innovative specialty. The Children's treated both neighborhood children and complicated cases referred from across the country and the world—two patient populations that neatly satisfied Needleman's twin desires to see challenging cases and to help the children most in need. For a pediatrician, few places were better than the Children's, and Needleman was proud to be there.

He even liked its slightly shabby aura. The building was old and crowded. At night, the front door would be locked and the janitor put on a policeman's cap and became a security guard. If a mother turned up, she would ring the bell at the big iron gates on Bainbridge Street and the janitor would let her in across the cobblestone courtyard. The small, close-knit staff was like family. (When they moved to the new campus in West Philadelphia in 1974, employees were in tears. One nurse refused to leave.) For Needleman, the hospital was a haven, full of the right mix of support and intellectual challenge.

• • •

Even though lead poisoning was new to Needleman, he expected the three-year-old's case to be routine. When he found the little girl in her glass-partitioned cubicle, she lay still in one of the forty cribs on the baby ward. Her eyelids drooped, and her mouth was slack. She didn't cry or even whimper; her pulse and breathing had slowed. She didn't respond to any of the standard stimulation tests such as pinching or pushing on the eyes. Soon, Needleman knew, she would fall into a coma. Her mother, a young Hispanic woman who lived near the hospital, had come to the emergency room when the girl's persistent headaches and sleepiness turned to lethargy.

Unlike Needleman, the ER doctor who had seen the little girl had a lot of experience with lead poisoning. Evelyn Bouden had come from New York City; one rotation of her internship had been at Kings County Hospital in Brooklyn, where lead poisoning was rampant. Public outcry over misdiagnosed cases such as that of Celeste Felder, who died in 1951 after five hospitals, including Kings County, misdiagnosed her, had brought lead poisoning sharply to the attention of New York City doctors. Once they knew to look for it, they found it all too easily. In the eight weeks of her internship, Bouden felt at times like she was seeing nothing but lead poisoning and gastrointestinal problems. "I spent so much of my time putting in lines to do [lead poisoning] treatments," she remembers. So she quickly recognized this little girl's problem and sent her to the pediatric ward.

If Needleman didn't get the lead out of the girl's body, it would continue to damage her nervous system and her brain. He didn't know exactly how she had come into contact with the lead, but he could make an educated guess. She had probably been playing with her toys on the floor of her house. Perhaps there were paint chips on the floor near the window, knocked loose when the window was opened or shut. Perhaps paint had peeled off the ceiling and fallen to the floor. Even if her mother had swept up the chips, there would have been paint dust left on the floor until she mopped. Or maybe the girl played in her meager yard, a little patch of dirt into which flakes of the house's exterior paint could have fallen. One way or another, the girl got lead on her hands and, like all children, she eventually put her hands in her mouth. She may have sucked her thumb or discovered that paint chips tasted sweet. If there was enough peeling paint in her house, she might have merely breathed in the dust as she played.

Once it was in her body, the lead was absorbed into the bloodstream. It bullied its way into her red blood cells, where it began a biochemical version of clipping wires and flipping switches, throwing off the efficient machinery of the cell. It interfered with mitochondria, the part of the cell structure responsible for producing energy. It disrupted the tree-like formation of dendrites, which conduct impulses to nerve cells. It disturbed the myelin sheath surrounding nerve fibers. And it interrupted the production of heme, the iron-rich pigment without which hemoglobin can't do its job of carrying oxygen through the body. From the bloodstream, lead was carried to the bones (where it took the place of calcium, to which it is chemically similar) and to the body's soft tissues. There it was stored—hidden but ominous. Unlike some metals, lead has no known health benefits. As lead built up in the body, only harm ensued.

The cumulative effect was greatest in the central nervous system, particularly the brain. Because she was only three, the little girl's nervous system was still developing and more susceptible to damage than an adult's. In her case, the lead had caused encephalopathy, swelling of the brain, which triggered the headaches and stupor. In other children, the effects could be different. Lead poisoning could cause fatigue or sleeplessness, irritability or malaise, loss of appetite or persistent vomiting—abdominal pain was common. It could cause anemia and muscular weakness or paralysis as well as extreme dizziness. It could affect sight and hearing. In the worst cases, it brought on kidney failure, convulsions, comas, and death.

At the University of Pennsylvania Medical School, Needleman heard only one lecture on lead poisoning. In the 1950s, physicians didn't fully know all the ways in which lead was damaging the body, but they had developed a straightforward treatment for children whose lead levels were high enough to bring on clinical symptoms. Needleman would do as he had been taught. Dr. Bouden had already established the amount of lead in the child's blood. It was well over

60 micrograms per deciliter, the level at which a child was considered poisoned in Philadelphia in the 1950s. Next, Needleman had to start chelation, the chemical process of removing the excess lead from the child's body.

Chelation could be done in one of two ways: BAL or EDTA, or both together. BAL, British anti-Lewisite, was first created during World War II as an antidote to nerve gas. Like a magnet sweeping through the body, BAL binds with metals including lead, pulling it out of its unwelcome spot in the cells, to form a less toxic compound the body will excrete in urine. Given as an injection, it led to a quick drop in blood lead levels, though they often rose again within a few days as lead continued to leach out of the bones and tissues into the bloodstream. CaEDTA, calcium ethylenediamine tetraacetic acid, was introduced in the early 1950s. It worked in the same manner as BAL, but could be given orally or injected and was especially effective in treating children. A medical journal in 1953 reported that a child "who was suffering from coma and convulsions when treatment began, was sitting up feeding herself 36 hours [later]...and began to talk in 48 hours." In a separate study, six out of nine treated with EDTA survived. Another journal declared a few years later, "The physician of 1957 has sufficient knowledge to diagnose accurately and treat successfully most children or infants with lead poisoning."

Needleman gave the girl EDTA intravenously, which was less painful than an injection. Over the next few days, she began to rouse pretty much on schedule with the textbook reports. Her eyes brightened, her energy returned. She smiled sweetly at Needleman, and he felt marvelous.

"She's going to be okay," he told her mother, "but you can't take her back to the same house."

The young woman looked plaintively at him. "Where can I go? The houses I can afford are all the same."

Needleman was taken aback. His confidence vanished. What have I really done, he thought. "It wasn't enough to make a diagnosis and prescribe a medication," he said later. "I'd treated her for lead poisoning, but that was not the disease—the disease was much bigger. The real causes of lead poisoning were in the lives of the people. Her disease was where she lived and why she was allowed to live there."

The link between lead poisoning in children and the homes those children lived in had first been made many years earlier far away from Philadelphia. At the turn of the twentieth century in Queensland, Australia, there was a little boy who liked to peer through the railings of his family's porch. At two, he wasn't big enough to see over the top, but according to his father, "he was very fond of standing grasping the verandah railings and placing his face against and his nose through them." Another child, this one a slightly older girl, lived in a house with a narrow passage full of sharp turns leading to a flight of steps to the garden. At each turn, the paint on the walls was rubbed and worn just at the height where children's hands would come into contact with it "when going smartly downstairs." Together, these seemingly unremarkable play habits helped solve one of the medical mysteries of the day. These two children and hundreds of others in Brisbane and the surrounding towns turned up in hospitals complaining of paralysis of arm or leg muscles, colic, vomiting, acute pain in the head and neck, and paralysis of the nerves of the eye, which sometimes resulted in blindness.

Until then, lead poisoning—not only in Australia, but around the world—was considered a disease of adults who worked with lead, such as printers, painters, or potters. One set of gastrointestinal symptoms was known as "painter's colic." In the few instances where children were affected, it was usually because their parents worked with lead. In the mid-nineteenth century, for example, a German pot-glazier's family was virtually wiped out by daily exposure to the lead fumes from his work. According to an account in a medical journal, "the father suffered from the comatose variety of lead encephalopathy. Seven children died in convulsions, four others had frequent cerebral disorders and suffered from peripheral neuritis. Several of the grandchildren died in convulsions."

Horrific as that case was, it was unusual only in its ferocity. Just as humans have been finding uses for lead since at least 3500 BC, they've known it was toxic for almost as long. The compound "white lead," which is actually lead carbonate though it is indeed pure white, has been particularly popular—it mixes well in oil and goes smoothly onto any surface. It has also been particularly potent. In the second century BC, when the Greeks were using lead in their cookware, the poet-physician Nicander called white lead "deadly" and described classic symptoms of lead poisoning including paralysis and hallucinations. Two thousand years later, in 1786, Benjamin Franklin, who saw lead poisoning cause "dangles and gripe" (wrist drop and colic) in printers, commented: "The opinion of this mischievous effect from lead is at least above sixty years old; and you will observe with concern how long a useful truth may be known and exist before it is generally received and practiced on." In the nineteenth century, European countries began to focus on the occupational hazards to lead workers. A comprehensive study of lead's neurotoxic effects was published in France in 1839.

Despite this long and lethal history, doctors did not look for lead poisoning in children. So Australian doctors didn't immediately recognize what they were seeing. A. Jefferis Turner was a resident physician at Brisbane's Children's Hospital at the time of the lead poisoning epidemic. In 1890, he treated a five-year-old boy with paralysis in his arms and legs and persistent vomiting. After considering progressive muscular atrophy, polio, and even alcoholism, Turner hypothetically compared the case to chronic lead poisoning. As he began to see more cases, he referred those with eye troubles to John Lockhart Gibson, the area's only ophthalmic surgeon. Gibson agreed with the tentative diagnosis of lead poisoning. But when the two presented their findings to the rest of the Queensland medical community, the response was skeptical.

Undaunted, Gibson and Turner continued to report cases of lead poisoning and, in noting that other doctors were *not* reporting it, suggested that the mistake lay with their colleagues. As the cases mounted, Turner and Gibson only became more certain of their diagnosis. But for more than ten years, the source of the lead remained a mystery. By 1897, Turner had astutely observed that even children who recovered fully in the hospital got sick again when they returned home. He called childhood lead poisoning a "toxicity of habitation." But what, exactly, was toxic?

By 1904, after considering and rejecting several possibilities including tin foil and water tanks, Gibson had an answer: paint. To prove his theory, Gibson visited the homes of his young patients with a government analyst named Henderson. The two men rubbed squares of calico against the walls, floors, and railings of the houses and measured the lead that came off on the fabric. They determined that there were two conditions in which the paint was particularly dangerous: when it was new and sticky, and when it had dried out in the sun and become powdery. In either case, it came off easily onto the fingers and hands of small children, who, as Gibson pointed out, often put their fingers in their mouths.

The house of the little boy who liked to peek through the porch railings "provided a simple lead trap," said Gibson. "The child is in the habit of putting everything into his mouth, and he may have sucked on the verandah railings. No doubt his hands were often on the floor as well as the rails, and no doubt also he carried them sometimes to his mouth." As for the little girl who grabbed the walls while running down the hall, it turned out she sucked her thumb. She had repeated attacks of lead poisoning.

Gibson made other observations as well. After visiting one house on a particularly hot day, Gibson noticed that the paint came off more easily on his sweaty hands. He reviewed hospital admission dates and found the majority of cases in the summer. He also recognized that lead paint particles became part of household dust, which, he wrote, "of course, is capable of being both swallowed or inhaled." Gibson ended his report with conviction. After years of frustration at not being able to tell parents what was causing their children's illness, he wrote, "I shall henceforth, unless I am offered a better explanation, blame paint." He also believed his findings would put a stop to the epidemic.

That was 1904.

In the United States, where the hazards of weathered verandahs seemed distant and tropical, few took the message seriously. As one pediatrician said, American doctors seemed to think the Australians "primitive or addlepated by the heat." But a few did pay attention.

Kenneth Blackfan and Henry Thomas, two Baltimore doctors, were the first, in 1914, to link the death of a lead-poisoned American child to paint. An orphan at Baltimore's Home of the Friendless, the boy had chewed the white paint off his crib. At the time, infectious diseases like meningitis were by far the largest killers of children and accordingly were the first causes a doctor would suspect. Blackfan and Thomas later realized that many doctors were mistaking lead poisoning for "so-called serious meningitis." It's impossible to know just how many cases were misdiagnosed but probably quite a few. In an analysis of deaths from tuberculosis meningitis at Boston Children's Hospital before 1920, social historian Christian Warren found that in a time period in which *not one* lead poisoning case was reported, fatalities from tuberculosis meningitis among children under three (of which there were ten to twenty a month) peaked dramatically in the summer months. Meningitis, however, shows no seasonal variations; incidence of lead poisoning, as Gibson showed, goes up in June, July, and August.

By the 1950s, when Herb Needleman treated his first case, American pediatricians were still missing plenty of lead poisoning cases. Needleman, who wondered just how many, got his first chance to find out in 1958. By then, he had been named chief resident at the Children's. He enforced a new rule: In the summertime, any child with any possible symptom of lead poisoning—vomiting, anemia, staggering, and so on—would be given a blood lead test. Assume lead poisoning until proven otherwise, he told his staff. Even so, the young doctors sometimes missed the signs.

Charles Reilly, one of Needleman's assistant residents, spent two years in Ohio before coming to Children's Hospital. "We had not seen lead poisoning in Akron, or if we did, we didn't diagnose it," he says. "One day in Philadelphia, we had a child come in with persistent vomiting. That's not a good sign, but a lot of different things can cause it, and the child was reasonably alert."

"Get a lead level on him," Needleman told Reilly. "And get a history on him. See where he lives. Does he eat things he picks up off the ground?"

Reilly did as he was told. "Sure enough, within the next two hours, the child became really lethargic. It was lead poisoning."

None of the symptoms they saw were subtle. "We were more concerned with gross cases, then," remembers Reilly. "There were kids who died, some with massive cerebral edemas. The neurologists couldn't do much. It was a matter of trying to keep those kids alive."

In 1959, following Needleman's instructions and testing for lead, the Children's Hospital admitted twenty cases of lead poisoning compared to twelve the year before; the twenty cases represented only a little less than 40 percent of those reported in Philadelphia between the beginning of July 1959 and the end of June 1960. "That really taught me the amount of lead that was out there," Needleman says.

Struck by the number of cases it was probably still missing, as well as those that weren't caught until the encephalopathy stage—too late—the hospital decided to study the problem more extensively. Beginning in July 1960, in a program run by the hospital's poison control officer, Dr. Walter Eberlein, a new urine test was used to detect lead poisoning earlier. That produced thirty-three cases, or 52 percent of the total citywide. Convinced even that wasn't a true indication of the depth of the problem, the hospital planned a special screening program for August 1961. That month, each new clinic patient over one year of age—no matter the reason for the visit—got a lead test. Of the 829 patients tested that month, 113 had results suggesting possible lead poisoning. Of the eighty that doctors could recall and test further, thirty had blood lead levels above 60 micrograms per deciliter, the official threshold for poisoning at the time.

The implication was staggering. Given that thirty children seen in one month were lead poisoned, the hospital estimated that anywhere from 5 percent to 29 percent of its annual outpatient population of twelve thousand to fourteen thousand could be lead poisoned—at least six hundred children, and perhaps as many as four thousand, were sick from lead. Previously, the same symptoms had been attributed to gastroenteritis or some other malady common to children. Put another way, by paying more attention to lead poisoning, the hospital recorded a 500 percent increase in cases.

Like termites nibbling at the foundations of a house, lead poisoning was doing harm unseen and unheeded. Having now opened the door to the basement and glimpsed a little of the damage, Needleman was haunted by the potential extent of it. Every day, he wondered about it. "I'd take the trolley to the hospital," he remembers. Much of his route from his home in West Philadelphia to the hospital in South Philadelphia ran through poor black neighborhoods with rundown houses. As Needleman looked out the trolley windows, "I'd see little faces sticking out of windows in the houses we passed and wonder how many were lead poisoned."

Needleman had been a child himself when he decided to go into medicine. At the age of ten, he put his hand through a window and needed stitches. It was 1938, and doctors still made house calls. When the family's physician arrived at their Philadelphia home to sew Herb up, the boy was enormously impressed. "He looked sharp in a gray tweed suit which I really envied, and he drove a new Buick," remembers Needleman, whose only male role models until then were the pickle merchants in his mother's Jewish immigrant family and his father, Joseph, a lackluster furniture salesman. "When I said I was going to be a doctor, I became a celebrity. I got a lot of encouragement." Though his initial decision was for superficial reasons, his commitment soon deepened. "I never was interested in anything else."

Smart enough to skip two grades, Needleman was only sixteen when he became the first in his family to go to college. He won a scholarship to Muhlenberg College in Allentown, Pennsylvania, some 30 miles northeast of Philadelphia, where Joe had opened a furniture store and Herb could live at home. He focused on his premedical courses and was president of the Medical Club, but he also found time to work as a reporter, and eventually editor, at the student newspaper. When he wasn't covering sports or writing breezy pieces about where to find girls, he wrote opinionated articles and editorials that regularly told college administrators what they were doing wrong.

From Muhlenberg, Needleman went to medical school at the University of Pennsylvania, again on a scholarship. It was an era when there were few Jews, women, or blacks in medical schools, and to be on a scholarship further tested Needleman's usual confidence. But he rose to the challenge and, despite the heavy workload, was known among his classmates both for his good humor and for the thoroughness and rigor of his work. While at Penn, Needleman married his college girlfriend, Shirley Weinstein. Their son, Sam, was born when Needleman was still only twenty. Like many couples who marry young, they soon found that they wanted different things in life, and the troubles in the relationship were exacerbated by Shirley's poor mental health, for which she was hospitalized in 1955.

Though the early 1950s were trying times for Needleman personally, he was very happy professionally. Immediately after medical school, he and his best friend, Bob Phillips, interned together at Philadelphia General Hospital, a large public hospital that treated mostly poor patients. They often made rounds as a team. As a doctor, says Phillips, Needleman was low-key and reserved. But he was intolerant of injustice and bad behavior. When he learned that other interns were being rude to young black mothers in the obstetrics wing by suggesting indelicate names for their new babies, Needleman went on the warpath. "He didn't have any authority except moral authority," says Phillips, "but he took on a few people over that. He was always one or two flights up the stairs from where I was, looking around to see who was oppressing whom."

After his internship, Needleman did a one-year research fellowship in rheumatic fever at the Children's and then was called up for Army service. When he finished his stint at Fort Meade, the physician-in-charge at the Children's, Joseph Stokes, welcomed him back and made him chief resident the next year. In a recommendation, Stokes wrote of Needleman: "He showed a noteworthy interest in new studies and also demonstrated unusual originality in his approach both to clinical problems and to the obtaining of new scientific data."

Needleman seemed to live at the hospital. "I don't know when he slept. He was there all the time," says Reilly, one of his three assistant chiefs. "You had to be on your toes because he was going to be around checking on you." He did not go easy on those who didn't meet his expectations. "Some people saw Herb as a little gruff," says Reilly. "He was very intense and focused. He knew what he wanted done. He was tireless and thought that everybody should be 100 percent focused on what they were doing because these were serious problems."

He was, however, always teaching. "When he taught you something, you really learned it, and you didn't forget it," says Patrick Pasquariello, who worked with Needleman in the 1960s and is still a pediatrician at Children's Hospital. "He'd just get right down in the trenches with you." When a senior doctor insisted that Pasquariello and other residents observe procedures rather than perform them, Pasquariello was frustrated. "I went to Herb and said, 'This isn't going to work. We have to be able to do the procedures,'" says Pasquariello. "Next thing you know, we were doing the procedures."

At the end of each day, Needleman gathered his residents to review their cases. "That's when he would advise and teach," remembers Reilly. "He had an ability to see to the core of a problem, to make a decision and to set up a treatment program." He also talked to his residents about larger issues. "He was concerned about environmental hazards that caused trauma to kids—kids falling out of windows; seat belts were just emerging. He wanted to counsel parents routinely about keeping medicines out of reach of kids. Aspirin poisoning was big in those days." When lead poisoning cases came up, Needleman didn't hide his growing anger. "Why isn't something being done?" he would demand. "Where are the people raising a fuss about this?"

"He was indignant at the lack of response from the lead industry," says Reilly. "He felt this was a concrete environmental hazard and that lead in paint and gasoline should be banned or at least lowered. In those bull sessions, he'd get off on something like that." In those conversations, Reilly sensed that, happy as he was at the Children's, Needleman was restless. "Something drove him," he says. "He saw it as his responsibility to use his intellect to better the world. I always felt he was looking beyond for something else."

Needleman didn't fully understand it at the time, but he had already seen the effects of lead poisoning firsthand. One summer during medical school, in need of money to support Shirley and Sam, Needleman found work at the DuPont plant in Deepwater, New Jersey, across the Delaware River from Wilmington. The plant made several different chemicals and dynamite.

It was a horrible job by any standard. For $1.65 an hour, Needleman was a day laborer shoveling chemicals in the Sulfonating House, the building where substances were treated with sulfuric acid. "They would bring in the train car, the bottom would come out, and there was a press," he says. "They pumped stuff through cloth filters. I would stick my head in and scrape it all out. It was just brutal. It was so hot and smelly. We were drenched with sweat in twenty minutes. I couldn't eat anything during the day, just drank milk and all the water I could get. The guys I worked with—this was their life. It's hard to consider. I told the section chief, 'I don't think anyone with a nervous system should do this work.'"

He would soon discover how right he was. This was the early 1950s, and most of the men smoked. "Everyone carried a pack of cigarettes in a plastic case—a regular pack would melt from the sweat. We weren't allowed to carry matches in there, so we had smoking breaks in a shack outside. People would pour out and smoke two cigarettes back to back and drink a Coke." On smoking breaks, Needleman noticed a group of older men nearby. He saw them only on these occasions, but they made an impression. "They were gray and mute, staring off into space, not talking to anybody." When he asked a fellow laborer about the men, he was told they had worked in the House of Butterflies.

Decades passed before Needleman learned the whole story of the tragedy that had happened twenty-five years earlier.

It had started with hallucinations. On Thursday, October 23, 1924, a young man named Ernest Oelgert was at work at the Standard Oil Bayway plant near Elizabeth, New Jersey, when he began seeing things and claiming he was being persecuted. The next day he ran around the plant in terror shouting that there were "three coming at me at once." He was taken to a hospital in Elizabeth, where convulsions set in. By Saturday, he was dead, and four other workers from the same plant were hospitalized—one had become so violent he had to be taken from home in a straitjacket. All five worked in what Standard Oil employees nicknamed the "looney gas building"—where the company was developing a lead additive for gasoline, called ethylene or tetraethyl lead. When Oelgert's death and the other illnesses were reported on the front page of the *New York Times* the following Monday, the article noted that employees were well aware of the risks of the gas: "Men who took up work in this building came in for 'undertaker jokes' and serio-comic hand-shakings and farewell greetings when their comrades learned of their actions." Standard Oil's management, however, voiced a different view: "These men probably went insane because they worked too hard," said one executive. By the end of the week, four more had died, and thirty-one others were in the hospital suffering hallucinations, violent episodes of insanity, and convulsions. Only nine of the forty-five workers from the looney gas building were unaffected.

As the Bayway death toll mounted, similar stories emerged from other plants. In Dayton, Ohio, where tetraethyl lead was refined at a General Motors plant, two had died. At the DuPont plant in Deepwater, where Needleman later worked and which was engaged in the same development work on tetraethyl lead as the Standard Oil plant, DuPont's president, Irénée DuPont, admitted that the company had "experienced much trouble with men becoming poisoned, even to the extent of fatalities." The *New York Times* spent several months investigating, and by June of 1925 had uncovered the truth of the "trouble" at Deepwater. The headline read:

> **TETRAETHYL LEAD FATAL TO MAKERS**
> **8 Dead, 300 Ill, in 1 Plant**
> Illness Begins with Hallucinations of Butterflies
> and Terminates in Violent Insanity and Death

The first death at DuPont, of a thirty-seven-year-old dye worker named Frank Durr, had occurred on September 21, 1923, a full year before Ernest Oelgert died in Elizabeth. The deaths continued through March of 1925, and the plant was closed, temporarily, the following month. According to the *Times,* leading neurologists had been baffled by the unusual symptoms. "An early symptom is a hallucination of winged insects. The victim pauses, perhaps while at work or in a rational conversation, gazes intently at space, and swishes at something not there. The employees at Deep Water have ironically dubbed the plant 'The House of the Butterflies.'"

Twenty-five years later, a few of the three hundred lead-poisoned workers who had survived, still at DuPont, still gazing at space and swishing at something not there, attracted Herb Needleman's attention during his smoking break. Something was wrong with these men's brains. It would be another twenty years before he understood what exactly was wrong and why, but always the image—gazing and swishing, gazing and swishing—stayed with him.

## Temple University, 1965

Needleman was accumulating his own lead exposure of a sort: exposure to the effects in other people. The DuPont workers, the three-year-old girl he treated first, the misdiagnosed cases at the Children's, the faces he saw from the trolley—each provoked more questions. Up close, he could only see the cases individually, like a brushstroke on canvas; if he stepped back and broadened his view, a picture emerged. But what did it really represent? One critical piece was missing. He found it in North Philadelphia.

Needleman had spent the years immediately following his residency running a private pediatric practice on City Line Avenue, on the border of Philadelphia and its western suburbs, but he didn't find it as challenging as hospital work. And there was an unexpected aspect; he experienced firsthand the symptoms of women's discontent that Betty Friedan was then crystallizing in *The Feminine Mystique*. "I realized that a lot of mothers were bringing in their children because they, the mothers, were sad and lonely," Needleman says. "We ended up talking about them."

That got him thinking about the importance of mental health. It was the mid-1960s, and the federal government was encouraging doctors to become psychiatrists by paying a reasonable amount of money for practitioners who would take on a residency in psychiatry. Unfulfilled by his pediatric practice and yearning to get back to helping poorer families, Needleman decided to take on this new challenge. In 1965, he took a psychiatric residency position at Temple University in North Philadelphia. The decision surprised many of his colleagues who thought him "medically oriented" and not particularly introspective. But Needleman threw himself into the work, teaching classes and working in the Child Guidance Clinic.

He also had a new family to keep him busy. He and Shirley had finally divorced while he was at the Children's. A few years later, he met Roberta Pizor, who was the girl next door—or across the hall to be exact. When they first met, while taking out the trash, neither thought much of it. "He was a very attractive man, but older with a son," says Roberta. "I wasn't paying a lot of attention." She had just graduated from Bryn Mawr and was living with her parents while she started her career as a social worker. Then one day she had to take a client to the Children's. She and Needleman ran into each other in the lobby. Perhaps it was the new setting or the fact that she was dressed professionally, but Herb saw Roberta in a new light. A few weeks later, they went on their first date, and they were married soon after, in 1963. Their two children, Joshua and Sara, were born in 1965 and 1967.

Although most of the doctors at Temple didn't share Needleman's liberal leanings, he found a soul mate there. In 1966, a few days after the death of comedian and social critic Lenny Bruce, Needleman noticed an old Volvo with "Lenny Bruce Lives" painted on the back. In the cafeteria, he introduced himself to the tall young doctor he'd seen behind the wheel, cardiologist Harold "Hal" Rutenberg. "We were instant friends," says Rutenberg. They bonded over their shared love of jazz and left-wing politics, and they spent much of their time together. Most days, they met up for lunch. When they did, the conversation turned to the same subject: Vietnam. Both were appalled by the war.

Needleman thought of a way they might do something about it. At a dinner party one night, he'd been seated next to a friend's wife. "Do you know of Terre des Hommes?" she asked. It was a Swiss group of doctors trying to get war-injured children out of Vietnam for medical treatment. Then she showed him pictures. "I kept seeing these horrible pictures of kids burned to hell by napalm and white phosphorous," he remembered later. And he thought, Well, we're the ones over there using that stuff. So why shouldn't we be the ones to help them? Needleman discovered that some physicians in Boston had the same idea, and he decided to get involved. He sat down at his desk at Temple and wrote a personal letter to about two hundred doctors in Philadelphia. Rutenberg was immediately on board.

The Committee of Responsibility (its full name was Committee of Responsibility to Save War-Burned and War-Injured Vietnamese Children, but it was called COR for short) was formally incorporated in December 1966. Needleman became chairman, a position he held throughout the life of the organization. The group, consisting of doctors, scientists, clergymen, and concerned citizens who had agonized over American involvement in Vietnam, believed that "to rescue as many children as we could reach would be an act of essential justice that would speak clearly of the importance of life in a time of wholesale killing." It would bring the children to the United States, enlist doctors to donate medical services, and foster families to care for the children. Big-name supporters such as Dr. Benjamin Spock, Julie Andrews, and Coretta Scott King helped bring in publicity.

Needleman spent the next few years living a kind of double life: part of the time, he was a psychiatrist helping troubled families in one of Philadelphia's poorest neighborhoods; the rest of the time, he was the head of a high-profile, controversial organization making his case on the *Today Show* and in national newspapers. Reporters who visited his office were thrown off by the modest surroundings, and some spent hours just trying to find him. COR's endeavor was extremely difficult, both because of bureaucratic complications and because of the political tensions in the United States. The first children arrived in the United States in October 1967, and within the first year sixty were in American hospitals. But in the next five years, the group brought only a fraction of that number to the United States—the total over the life of the organization was seventy-seven.

"Herb was always absolutely patient," says John Balaban, who worked for COR in Vietnam. "That was his great asset as chair of the board. There were times when COR was fraught with argument, even among like-minded people. The one abiding argument was how far could we go to speak out about the war and still be allowed to function." The battle threatened to split the organization, but those in favor of not pulling punches, a group that included Needleman, won in the end. In 1969, COR took out a full-page ad in the *New York Times* opposing the war.

It soon became apparent that Needleman was constitutionally incapable of not saying what he thought. In his view, the evidence was incontrovertible. "You can't live with that kind of horror and not speak out about it," he told a reporter at the time. When the rest of the country got tired of the war or engaged in what Needleman considered "incredible self-denial," he remained a tireless and outspoken critic of the war. He was unapologetically emotional about the issue, as he always had been about anything he considered important. "Anger, joy, sorrow, you got the whole package, he never hid his emotional candle under a bushel," says Bob Phillips, who ran a North Carolina chapter of COR.

Emotion was meant to be COR's strongest weapon. "The very presence of these injured children...would be so upsetting to Americans that a grass-roots antiwar effort would spring up in the cities where these children were to be treated," wrote Balaban in *Remembering Heaven's Face,* his book about Vietnam. "Naive as this now sounds, the plan reflected an implicit faith in the goodness of Americans."

The faith that Americans want to do the right thing also informed Needleman's early thinking about lead poisoning. Throughout the years working with COR, Needleman didn't forget about lead. Day in, day out at Temple, he worked with troubled children and dysfunctional families who suffered all of the indignities of life in poor and sometimes dangerous neighborhoods. From teachers and principals, he heard continually about children with limited mental capacity, children with behavioral disorders, and children with learning disabilities.

He had come across a study done in the 1940s that had disturbing implications. Randolph Byers was a pediatric neurologist and Elizabeth Lord a psychologist at Boston Children's Hospital. Struck by the fact that some of the school-age children referred to them for learning and behavioral problems had histories of lead poisoning, the two decided to investigate the possibility that lead poisoning was a common cause of developmental problems. In hospital records, they found 128 lead-poisoning cases, and they tracked down twenty of the children involved. They performed periodic psychological evaluations of the children and followed their progress. Only one of the twenty was doing well in school. There was evidence of learning disabilities, attention deficits, and erratic behavior. Published in November 1943, the study was the first to suggest that children might not have been "cured" of lead poisoning after all. How many cases of school failure, Byers asked, were really cases of undiagnosed lead toxicity?

The study caught the attention of both the media and the lead industry. Ironically, the media focused on abnormal behavior in the children, such as paint eating, whereas the industry understood the implications for public health if the study was accurate. The secretary of the Lead Industries Association, Felix Wormser, said: "If what this article describes is correct, then we have indeed a most serious public health hazard." Except that he didn't believe it. He wrote to other industry officials of the need to highlight the study's flaws before "other doctors . . . accept as authoritative this paper . . . and probably build upon it still more fantastic assertions."

Wormser and other industry representatives went to Boston to see Byers (Lord had died just before publication) and took him to lunch at the Ritz. Byers said later that the industry representatives threatened to sue him for $1 million, but the conversation ended with a deal for industry to fund Byers's work for the next eight years. In fact, Wormser was correct in recognizing the flaws in Byers's study. By today's standards for epidemiological research, the study was too small and too simplistic. But Byers and Lord were the first to put the idea on record that lead's effects could last longer than anyone had previously admitted. For that, Herb Needleman considered Randy Byers a hero.

Part of Needleman's job at Temple was to work with local organizations. One evening he talked to a group of teenagers—mostly boys—at a black church. In the clutch of people waiting by the lectern after he finished, he noticed a young man. In his late teens perhaps, and earnest, the boy wanted to talk to the visiting doctor about his ambitions for the future. "[He] was a very nice kid, but he was obviously brain damaged. He had trouble with words, with propositions and ideas." Was it possible, Needleman wondered, that this boy could be suffering from lead poisoning? How many of these kids who were coming to the clinic were in fact missed cases of lead poisoning?

The prevailing wisdom on lead poisoning said that at certain high levels you were poisoned, but below those levels you were not. To Needleman, this logic didn't sit right. Although little biochemical research had yet been done, it didn't make sense that a substance that could cause so much harm wasn't having any effect along the way. It was like looking at a raging forest fire in the treetops and assuming that no ground cover had been harmed. To care about the ferns and the seedlings, the less dramatic damage, and ask what it meant for the future of the forest was a new way of thinking. Until then, most doctors were focused on infectious disease and acute damage, according to public health historians Gerald Markowitz and David Rosner. To ask about the implications of what was going on inside the body, unseen, was to open up new ideas of what constituted a problem. "Needleman redefined disease," says Rosner.

The windows of Needleman's office looked out at the playground of the Kenderton School, a public elementary school. Behind its four-story brick building, Kenderton's macadam playground was surrounded by high chain-link fence. Needleman watched the kids playing basketball and hopscotch during recess and after school. On the far side of the playground, through the fence, he could see rows of dilapidated old houses typical of the area, exactly the kind of houses most likely to contain exposed lead paint.

The Kenderton children brought to mind the faces Needleman used to see when he rode the trolley through poor black neighborhoods on his way to the Children's. When he thought of the adults with mental illness and behavioral problems in his psychiatric work, he wondered if the two were related. The last piece of his picture fell into place. What if there really was a lot more lead poisoning out there than anyone knew, and what if it was having effects far beyond what anyone had ever imagined? If a lot of lead makes a person retarded, he thought, does a little lead make a person dumb? How many of those kids were lead poisoned? How could he know? How could he prove it?

Needleman knew he wouldn't get answers using the old methods. Blood tests, for instance—the standard way of measuring the amount of lead in the body—told only part of the story; they reflected lead levels at the time, measuring current exposure, but they didn't tell of a person's lifelong lead exposure. Needleman knew that the body stores lead in bone. How to get at it? He considered and rejected several possibilities. Bone biopsies would be painful and unethical. Fingernails were too dirty and contaminated by external sources. Hair, too, was contaminated by external sources. "You can't tell how much is deposited from the outside and how much reflects what's in the blood and brain."

One day while he looked out at those kids playing in the schoolyard, he got an idea. All kids lose their teeth, and teeth, like bones, are made of calcium. Lead would be stored in the teeth just as it was in the bones. Perhaps he could collect children's baby teeth as they fell out and measure the amount of lead in each tooth. That amount might be the most accurate reflection yet of a child's total exposure to lead. When he looked into the idea, he discovered that one study in the 1960s had found increased lead levels in the teeth of children who had died of lead poisoning.

Just as he thought that pictures of napalmed children would end the Vietnam War, Needleman hoped that evidence of the effects of lead on children would put an end to the problem of childhood lead poisoning. "The government will wake up if I can show the effect lead is having," he remembers thinking. "They'll take lead out of gasoline. They'll fix all the houses, spend a lot of money, but the disease will disappear."

That was 1970.

CHAPTER THREE

# *That Nut at Caltech*

WOODS HOLE OCEANOGRAPHIC INSTITUTION,
MASSACHUSETTS, 1963

Even the experienced marine scientists who wandered past the workshop on the dock wondered what Clair Patterson was doing. They could see he was wrestling with a Bodman bottle, the standard 1960s water sampler for trace metal chemistry. But why? Shaped like a torpedo, a Bodman bottle was bigger than a filing cabinet and not easy to maneuver. It was also traditionally painted yellow, and that paint contained lead. Therein lay the problem. Patterson had commandeered a dentist's drill and was removing the paint inch by inch.

He had set his sights on the ocean. At first, this was intended to further his work in geochronology. Once he determined the age of the earth, Patterson and his colleagues realized that lead isotope techniques were a valuable new resource that could answer many more geologic questions. Patterson could use lead as a tracer to follow the course of chemical processes over time and shed new light on the separation of Earth's crust from its mantle and on the formation of the continents. To start, he wanted to find a single source that could represent all the lead on present-day Earth. "The ocean was one place to look," explains Lee Silver, because rock erodes into sediment, which eventually washes into the ocean. "It touches so much of the solid earth, it's possible that the lead in it is a mixture of all the lead in the earth."

Patterson began by collecting samples of sediments from the ocean floor. To analyze the sediments, he got help from Tsaihwa J. Chow, the first of a string of doctoral students and postdoctoral fellows Patterson would train in his lab. Chow, known as Jimmy, was a Shanghai native who'd done his graduate work at the University of Washington. He joined Patterson's lab in 1955 and quickly became a trusted colleague. Although Patterson wasn't a great classroom teacher, he was a powerful communicator one on one. "Patterson could take strangers into his lab and charm the hell out of them," says Silver. "He'd convince them that what he was working on was the most important thing there was and get them working on it. When they were through with their work with Pat, they swore by him even though he could fly into a rage in a moment. They loved him more than any other disciples I've seen. For Pat, they took off their shirts and pants and got to their underwear to clean things."

With Chow, Patterson developed a picture of the concentration and isotopic composition of lead in the ocean floor, both in the present day and in the ancient past. Then, Patterson and Mitsunobu Tatsumoto, another postdoctoral fellow, began to measure lead in seawater. But traditional methods of water sampling—dropping a metal bottle on a metal cable from a metal ship—wouldn't work for Patterson; it would take him years to perfect his anticontamination measures. There were other challenges: Patterson got terribly seasick ("sicker than a dog," in his words)—a regrettable problem for a man developing an interest in marine chemistry. But he persevered. Using his own decontaminated equipment (like the paint-free Bodman bottle), his team collected "profiles," a series of vertical water samples that provided snapshots of lead concentrations at different depths.

To pay for the work, Patterson needed more money. "Heck, the oil companies ought to be interested in this," Harrison Brown told him. Again, Brown did the writing, with Patterson listed as project director, and submitted a proposal to the American Petroleum Institute. He argued that Patterson's work would allow the API to use the isotopic composition of lead as a tracer to help identify the stage, or the age, of sediment, which could help locate and identify oil deposits. In Patterson's view, he was doing basic research that had "nothing whatsoever to do with oil in any way, shape, or form." But he needed the money. Called Project 53 and titled Age Dating of Rocks, Patterson received between $20,000 and $30,000 per year from API beginning in 1955. It paid the salaries of Chow and other lab technicians and bought equipment. But then, Patterson said, "A very bad thing happened." His work turned out to have something to do with oil after all—in a way that the petroleum industry was not going to like.

Patterson was astonished by the results. "Something is wrong here," he thought. First, he and Chow established that more lead—a hundred times more—was entering the ocean than was leaving it every year relative to the ancient past. Then he and Tatsumoto found that the water in the younger, upper layers of the ocean contained far more lead than the older, deeper layers ("they don't mix that rapidly"). Patterson tried to explain this by calculating how much lead was entering the oceans from rivers, using lead concentrations in river waters reported by other investigators. But those numbers didn't gibe with his data and he suspected other investigators had unrecognized contamination in their labs.

Where else could the lead be coming from? He looked at data on the production of leaded gasoline. "If you took those [seawater] profiles and extrapolated from that over all the world's oceans, it could easily be accounted for by the amount of lead that was put into gasoline and burned and put into the atmosphere." He and Tatsumoto said so in a paper published in 1963. Patterson knew he had a problem. "The oil companies were financing my work," he said. "We [were] in serious trouble."

The first teaspoonful of lead was poured into a gallon of gasoline on December 9, 1921. For the staff of the General Motors research division, it was a glorious moment. They had spent years searching for an additive that would solve one of the most frustrating problems of the young automotive business: engine knock, an annoying pinging and bucking that damaged engines and caused cars to lose power.

Charles Kettering, the head of GM's research effort, took engine knock personally. Kettering, who would one day grace the cover of *Time* magazine as an industrial pioneer and would co-found Memorial Sloan-Kettering Cancer Center, had invented a self-starting battery ignition to replace the heavy iron hand crank required to start a car. Many a man had his arm broken by the crank, and most women couldn't use it, so when Kettering's system was first showcased in General Motors' 1912 Cadillac, it was a great improvement. But competitors seized on the new starter as the cause of engine knock. To prove the naysayers wrong, Kettering had to stop the knock. He assembled his small staff in the converted tobacco warehouse that housed his young company, then called Dayton Engineering Laboratories Company or Delco (GM bought Delco in 1920), and set them a challenge: discover the real cause of knock, find a way to stop it, and find a way to manufacture the antiknock solution.

Sitting in the laboratory that day was a twenty-seven-year-old man who had just arrived at Delco. Like Kettering, Thomas Midgley Jr. had an engineering degree and was a natural inventor. (In high school he had been the first to rub a baseball with slippery-elm juice instead of spit, thereby increasing the accuracy of his curveball.) Midgley rose to "Boss Ket's" challenge.

The first part was relatively easy. Midgley built a high-speed camera out of a tomato can and rubber bands and photographed what was happening inside the engine: some of the fuel was exploding prematurely. Finding a way to stop the knock was harder despite some accidental success early on. On the theory that an oil-soluble dye might help, Midgley found a bottle of dark-colored iodine in the stockroom. He added it to fuel, and the knock disappeared entirely. Midgley promptly bought samples of every oil-soluble dye he could find and tried them all: none worked. But something had stopped the knock. He went back to iodine and tried a colorless version. Success. Iodine, not dye, stopped engine knock. But iodine could not be mass-produced: it was prohibitively expensive, smelled horrible, and corroded engines.

For years, with time out to work on airplane fuels and robot bombs for World War I, Midgley tested thousands of chemical compounds. Two more successful antiknock additives, selenium and tellurium, smelled as bad as iodine—this time of garlic and onions. The stench clung to anyone who worked with the compounds and led Midgley's wife to insist that he sleep in the basement for the seven months he experimented with them.

In addition to his engineering prowess, Midgley was an amateur chemist and later became president of the American Chemical Society. (In what Bill Bryson called "an uncanny knack for the unfortunate," he went on to invent chlorofluorocarbons, aka CFCs.) At a chemical society meeting, Midgley learned about a rearranged version of the periodic table. This one ordered elements not by their atomic number but by the number of electrons and vacant spaces in their outermost shells, information that related to their ability to combine with other elements. Looking at the elements in this way, Midgley quickly recognized a useful fact. All of the successful antiknock agents he had so far discovered—iodine, tellurium, and selenium—were grouped in the lower right-hand corner of the table. His hit-or-miss days were over; now, he could continue the hunt on a rational scientific basis. Midgley pinned his hopes on lead, the heaviest element; more specifically, he thought the compound tetraethyl lead would do the job best.

Tetraethyl lead (TEL) was invented in the 1850s by a German chemist. It was lethal—a splash on the skin could kill a person—but it was also soluble in oil. When Thomas Boyd, one of Midgley's staff, mixed a teaspoonful of TEL into a gallon of gasoline on that December day and put it into the Delco-Light test engine in the laboratory, the effect was immediate. The engine stopped knocking and started purring. Experimenting with smaller amounts, they got the same effect with one-twentieth of one percent TEL to gasoline. Engines using tetraethyl lead ran smoothly and more powerfully. Gasoline burned more efficiently and increased fuel economy. The knock was gone. There was a hiccup, though; over time TEL built up and clogged spark plugs and corroded other engine parts. It took Midgley two more years to find a solution to that problem: he added bromine, in the form of ethyl bromide, which scrubbed the lead away.

The first gallon of leaded gasoline was sold at a gas station at Sixth and Main streets in Dayton on February 1, 1923, under the brand name Ethyl. Kettering chose the name to avoid the word lead. He had also pushed to begin selling the product before the bromine solution had been worked out. "He explained that despite its limitations many people wanted the new mixture and that its deficiencies would be remedied more quickly if it were on the market and customer reactions were observed," wrote Joseph Robert in a commissioned history of Ethyl Corporation, the joint venture created in 1924 by GM and Standard Oil to sell TEL. If a customer asked for Ethyl, a few drops were added to their gasoline purchase. Advertisements listed gas stations that sold the product. Drivers immediately noticed the difference, and the new additive got valuable publicity the following May when the top three finishers in the Indy 500 used leaded gasoline in their cars.

Of course, there was another potential problem. Burning tetraethyl lead meant putting a known toxin into the air. In 1922, Midgley consulted public health experts, including Yale's Yandell Henderson, a leading toxicologist, and discussed conducting experiments on possible health hazards, but Midgley didn't follow through. Boyd, who had put the first teaspoonful of TEL into gasoline, said years later, "The first opinions of doctors who were consulted were full of such frightening phrases as 'grave fears,' 'distinct risk,' 'widespread lead poisoning,' and the like." Health experts worried about both lead dust in engine exhaust and about workers coming into contact with tetraethyl lead. The latter danger was soon horrifyingly confirmed.

Ernest Oelgert, William McSweeney, Walter Dymock, William Kresge, and Herbert Fuson—these were the men who died making tetraethyl lead in the Standard Oil plant in New Jersey in the fall of 1924. As the deaths and stories of violently insane workers at Bayway and Deepwater mounted, the public grew increasingly alarmed. Now, advertisements for other fuels prominently featured the fact that their product did *not* contain Ethyl. New York City, New Jersey, and Philadelphia banned Ethyl altogether. Public health advocates launched a campaign to ban the additive everywhere.

Buried in the dramatic stories coming out of New Jersey was the fact that two had died in Dayton, Ohio, back in the spring of 1924. These were men Midgley knew. Another sixty "became seriously ill with frightening symptoms of mania." One of the Dayton victims "saw the wallpaper converted into swarms of moving flies and thought pictures of his family on the walls were alive and moving about." Midgley himself, who had worked closely with the compound for years, had a bad case of lead poisoning and spent six weeks recuperating in Florida in the winter of 1923. "I contain a pair of lead-lined lungs," he wrote to a colleague just before he left. His assistant, Carroll Hochwalt, also got sick. The lead poisoning cases in Dayton were kept quiet until the New Jersey news broke, but the deaths of his friends upset Midgley, who then considered abandoning TEL. Kettering doesn't seem to have had such qualms. He was reportedly upset that Standard Oil hadn't done a better job keeping its troubles out of the newspapers.

Five days after Ernest Oelgert died, Thomas Midgley participated in a press conference at Standard Oil's New York headquarters on behalf of Ethyl Corporation (of which Midgley had been named a vice president). If he still had misgivings, he hid them well. To demonstrate the safety of the additive, he poured some directly onto his hands in front of reporters. "I'm not taking any chance whatever," he claimed to reporters. "Nor would I take any chance doing that every day." But he did not, in fact, do that every day; he had long before taken to wearing gloves in the laboratory because he knew TEL was particularly dangerous when absorbed through the skin.

Although he hadn't engaged academic experts, Midgley did arrange to pay for an investigation by the U.S. Bureau of Mines. (The federal Public Health Service did not have the money to investigate the matter itself.) Preliminary results were released at the height of the hysteria over the deaths at tetraethyl lead plants. Based on their studies of guinea pigs, rabbits, and dogs exposed to exhaust from leaded gasoline, the investigators gave Ethyl a clean bill of health because they saw no overt signs of lead poisoning in the animals.

(When they increased the concentrations of tetraethyl lead or applied it to the animals' skin, the animals died.) But the fact that industry paid for the study and that the company had control over the final report didn't convince skeptics who worried about long-term accumulation and effects.

To resolve the question, the U.S. surgeon general called a hearing at the end of May 1925. As the meeting opened, the Public Health Service made clear it had no power to regulate ethyl gasoline. Ethyl Corporation and its affiliates had voluntarily suspended production of TEL earlier in the month, but they now mounted a strong campaign for tetraethyl lead that occupied the whole morning. Charles Kettering began with the history of the search for a successful antiknock additive. Then a succession of industry representatives and medical experts outlined the research done so far—all of it done on behalf of the industry. In addition to the animals studied by the Bureau of Mines, there were reports on lead levels in garage workers, drivers, and others likely to come in contact with ethyl gasoline. Though all had lead in their bodies, none showed clinical signs of lead poisoning. Where there were problems, speakers blamed careless workers.

For industry, the critical point was technical progress. Tetraethyl lead, declared Ethyl Corporation's vice president Frank Howard, is "an apparent gift from God." "Our continued development of motor fuels is essential in our civilization," Howard said. "What is our duty under the circumstances? Should we say, 'No, we will not use a material [that is] a certain means of saving petroleum?' Because some animals die and some do not in some experiments, shall we give this thing up entirely?"

Public health advocates got their turn in the afternoon, but without independent evidence they could only react to points made by industry's researchers and emphasize the cumulative nature of lead poisoning. They wanted conclusive proof that there was no harm, but they knew that science might not be up to that task. Yandell Henderson, who had cautioned Midgley in 1922, summed up the basic conflict. "We have in this room two diametrically opposed conceptions. The men engaged in industry, chemists, and engineers, take it as a matter of course that a little thing like industrial poisoning should not be allowed to stand in the way of a great industrial advance," he argued. "On the other hand, the sanitary experts take it as a matter of course that the first consideration is the health of the people." Henderson knew which side was likely to win. "It seems probable on the basis of the evidence that we have heard this morning" that lead will soon be back, he said, and take its place as "the commonest industrial poison."

He was right. As a result of the conference, the surgeon general called a committee of seven to gather hard evidence on leaded gasoline. The panel spent seven months studying the blood and stool of garage workers and drivers. All such workers—whether they worked with leaded gasoline or not—were found to have lead in their bodies. Those who worked with ethyl gasoline had slightly higher levels, but none had clinical lead poisoning. The committee took those results to mean "there are at present no good grounds for prohibiting the use of ethyl gasoline." It did note that "longer experience" might show a different result, such as "chronic degenerative disease of a less obvious character." But neither the science of the day nor the American embrace of progress allowed for such fears to win out.

It was a turning point. Confronted with an early choice between corporate interests demanding absolute proof of harm and health ex-perts insisting on absolute proof of safety, America chose business. Tetraethyl lead went back on the market. The costs of that decision couldn't fully be calculated for another fifty years. Millions of tons of lead were put into the environment between 1925 and 1986, when it was finally taken out of gasoline. By 1960, almost 90 percent of all gasoline sold contained tetraethyl lead. Ironically, some fifty years after the 1925 surgeon general's hearing, when Americans next grappled with the same basic choice, all that accumulated lead gave health experts and environmentalists a lot more ammunition. Until then, it was industry that learned the biggest lesson from the lead scare of the 1920s: control the science.

The next person to seriously question the use of lead in gasoline was Clair Patterson. When he created his clean lab, he understood better than anyone just how many sources of lead contamination there were. And he knew without a doubt that the lead from gasoline exhaust had indeed accumulated in the environment, just as Henderson and his public health colleagues had feared. When Patterson measured lead in the oceans, he got the first indications of just how far and wide the blanket of lead accumulation extended and he knew what it meant. Handing a colleague his seawater paper, he said in his straightforward way: "Read it, it's important."

He also found out quickly how high the stakes were. In 1963, within months of publication of his article theorizing that excess lead in the ocean was due to exhaust from leaded gasoline, the lead industry mounted a campaign to change his mind. It began gently enough. Don Fowler of the Lead Industries Association wrote to say he had "read with great interest" an item on Patterson's work in the *New York Herald*. Fowler suggested that Patterson should have a look at an industry-sponsored study being conducted at Stanford.

Then some petroleum industry executives visited Patterson at Caltech. There was plenty of research money available, they said, if he would change the direction of his research and the tenor of his comments about it. "They tried to buy me off," Patterson said later. He didn't just say no. He treated his visitors to a long lecture, complete with what he called "conclusive illustrations." One can only imagine the effect of Patterson's manic lecture style on this particular group of visitors. He energetically scrawled charts and tables across the chalkboard, whirled around to fix his audience with a stare, stalked the room and waved his arms for emphasis, then returned to his charts and tables. True, he didn't have enough data yet; it was mostly theoretical. But he tried to convince the oil executives of the degree to which leaded gasoline had "probably" covered land and water, and had contaminated animals and humans. Contamination is on a "world scale," he told them. "Lead-poisoned environments exist everywhere." It spelled the end of the lead industry to Patterson. His final message to them was stark: Do something about it, or I'll put you out of business.

Instead, they tried to put him out of business. His grant from the American Petroleum Institute was terminated. Industry had given him more than $200,000 since 1955, but it would support him no more. J. Haworth Jonte was a chemist who represented Texaco on the advisory committee that oversaw Patterson's work for API. According to Jonte, the project was coming to a natural end. "The committee felt that he had completed his job of establishing whether lead isotopes in sediments would help us find oil," says Jonte. Though Patterson had made major contributions to basic science, he had not actually done much about finding oil. The research, in Jonte's words, was always about "how to help geologists do a better job of predicting where to dig a hole." The timing spoke volumes, however. Patterson never questioned the real reason behind the end of his funding: the petroleum companies did not like his results.

But they couldn't stop him from publishing. Just like the lead spewing from automobile exhaust, once Patterson's theory was out in the world, it would never entirely go away. Industry was going to have to deal with it. And so, for that matter, was Patterson. Like many scientists, he preferred the purity and objectivity of science to the messy, emotional world of politics. Science came naturally to him; activism did not. "There's a bewitching attraction to pure science," he said. "It remains an abstract, beautiful refuge . . . disconnected from the dirty world." To some extent, he thought his research could speak for itself, possibly more eloquently than he could.

Once he realized how much lead was in the oceans, however, his vision of widespread lead pollution—and its implications—snapped into sharp and painful focus as if he had put on a new pair of glasses. The clarity of it propelled him out of his own reluctance. And the inability of others to see the situation as clearly as he did frustrated him and made him more determined to prove his case. "My science got entangled with social problems," he said. "It threatened the beauty of my refuge. But there was no way out." Something else drove him, too: guilt over his role in the development of the atomic bomb, which he later said combined with his outrage over lead pollution to spur him into action.

Though his opponents would increasingly try to write him off as "that nut at Caltech"—this was a man who wore a gas mask around campus on smoggy days—not everyone thought Patterson was crazy.

A handful of other researchers had similar ideas. At Harvard in the late 1940s for example, toxicologist Mary Amdur developed a pump to measure micrograms of lead in the air. It was meant to demonstrate that lead particles from gasoline accumulate, but her work was largely ignored. Still, concern over air pollution had been growing in California through the 1950s and spread to the rest of the country in the 1960s. In 1962, the year before Patterson's paper on lead in the ocean was published, Rachel Carson published *Silent Spring,* the best-selling indictment of pesticide use that helped create America's environmental movement. That nascent movement was fertile ground for Patterson's ideas, and the lead and petroleum industries knew it. They had to discredit him. For that, they turned to the man who had been their staunch defender for forty years: Robert A. Kehoe.

Robert Kehoe arrived at Ethyl in May 1924 soon after the first cases of lead poisoning occurred in Dayton. The story wasn't in the press yet, but Charles Kettering realized quickly that he was facing what a company memo called "a deadly threat"—not to his workers but to "the survival of the industry." He needed a medical expert both to care for the men and to more fully investigate the dangers of tetraethyl lead. Kehoe was then an assistant professor of physiology at the University of Cincinnati who was studying the effects of lead and other toxic materials on proteins. His résumé didn't match the doctors that Midgley had consulted at Harvard and Yale. He was only thirty and just four years out of medical school, but, like Kettering, he was from Ohio and had attended Ohio State University, and his boss was a friend of Kettering's. Kehoe began by looking at safety for workers in the Dayton plant and then turned to studying the toxicity of tetraethyl lead. By early 1925, Kettering had named Kehoe medical director of the Ethyl Gasoline Corporation.

Despite his relative youth and inexperience, Kehoe assumed his new responsibilities with authority. He was a small man who carried himself with assurance. His emphatic black eyebrows behind rimless glasses and the serious line of his mouth gave him a formal air. He was presentable, articulate, and a true believer. One year into the job, he defended the company at the surgeon general's hearing in May 1925. In the company's view, that conference, "in which highly emotional, sometimes lurid, and wholly unsubstantiated statements were tempered by the observations and facts made available" by Kehoe's studies, did more than put tetraethyl lead back on the market; it established Kehoe (and by extension, the lead industry) as the nation's expert on lead.

Kehoe spent the next forty years building on that foundation. He was Ethyl's medical director for thirty-three years. In addition, he was director of the Kettering Laboratory at the University of Cincinnati, which was created in 1930 with money from Ethyl and DuPont, for whom Kehoe was a consultant. After establishing "strict controls and procedures" for the manufacture and distribution of tetraethyl lead, Kehoe headed a series of "balance studies." Young male volunteers were hired and exposed to lead both by eating lead salts and by sitting in rooms filled with leaded exhaust. Then Kehoe measured the lead in their feces, urine, and blood. He conducted further experiments on garage mechanics, gas station attendants, and the like. And he traveled to a remote village in Mexico to measure the lead intake and output of its residents.

From all of this work, Kehoe arrived at four defining principles: that lead levels in the environment and in humans had remained relatively consistent "for a long time" and could be considered "normal"; that human bodies excreted nearly as much lead as they took in from food, beverages, and air, maintaining an "essential balance"; that lead was "harmless" below a threshold of 80 micrograms per 100 grams of blood (for both children and adults); and, finally, that the amount of lead taken in by the general population was so far below the threshold that it was not a concern. He also believed that in the absence of clinical symptoms such as encephalopathy or convulsions even levels above 80 didn't necessarily mean a person was poisoned.

"When Dr. Kehoe speaks, he will voice many of our opinions," said a DuPont executive at a 1960 meeting with the Public Health Service. And so it was. From 1925 through the 1960s, Kehoe spoke for the lead industries on health issues. He worked most closely for Ethyl Corporation and DuPont, but he also conferred with Standard

Oil, National Lead, and trade associations such as the American Petroleum Institute, the Lead Industries Association, and the International Lead Zinc Research Organization. Far from considering this a conflict of interest, Kehoe believed strongly that it was industry's responsibility to pay for research on lead. He was passionate about the need to build up the field of industrial medicine and believed a close relationship with the industries he served was necessary and appropriate. From the companies' point of view, Kehoe was indispensable. "The president of the company did not make decisions about what was going on in our plants; Dr. Kehoe did," says Gary Ter Haar, who worked in Ethyl Corporation's health department for decades.

The pinnacle of Kehoe's career was the invitation to deliver the 1960 Harben Lectures, a distinguished series of talks by eminent researchers given at the Royal Institute of Public Health and Hygiene in London. In his three lectures, he summed up the "high points" of his decades of work on lead—essentially laying out the research behind his views—and was so pleased with the results that he had one thousand blue-cloth hardcover copies printed and distributed to colleagues. Recipients sent congratulatory notes saying, "the last word has been said on lead" and "you are God in the field." Kehoe seemed to agree, equating his monopoly on lead research with a monopoly on knowledge. At one conference, meant to be a forum for a variety of researchers, Kehoe held the floor for the duration—eight hours a day for five days.

Then along came Clair Patterson.

### Massachusetts Institute of Technology, 1963

After losing his API funding, Patterson found himself with little research money and lots of questions. It was a good moment for a change. He had been at Caltech for ten years, and when he was asked to spend a year as a visiting professor at the Massachusetts Institute of Technology, he quickly said yes. He and Laurie moved the children, by then twelve, thirteen, fourteen, and fifteen, to the Northeast, where they reveled in snow and found Boston "ancient" compared to California. Patterson gave a series of small, non-credit talks at MIT and other nearby institutions. "This gives me the opportunity to spread the gospel," he wrote to Caltech colleagues.

It also freed him to talk about what he really cared about. He had been brought east to educate his colleagues about the age of the earth and lead isotopes, on which he was now considered the leading authority. But that was old news for Patterson. He wanted to talk about what lead was doing to the human environment. "He was very opinionated and animated," says Bob Duce, who was then finishing up his graduate work in marine chemistry at MIT. "I remember being really impressed by meeting one of the first top-notch scientists who was interested in the impact this had on the environment and humans."

Given that there was far more lead in the oceans than in the ancient past, Patterson wondered if the same pattern could be true for people. During his year at MIT, he spent hours in the Harvard Medical School library studying how the body worked. One day in the library, he had what he described as a "flash" of insight. He had been considering how the body processes beneficial metals such as calcium, potassium, copper, and zinc. Looking at the periodic table, he saw that those four metals were all on the same horizontal row, which he sometimes referred to as "the nutritive ridgepole of the periodic table." One row below were metals that were relatively neutral—rubidium, strontium, silver, and so on ("relative" is the critical term because this line includes metals that are toxic). Down one more row, the metals turned distinctly nasty. Barium, for instance, was two below calcium and mercury was two below zinc. Some "triples" fit the theory better than others, but a general pattern of increasing toxicity held.

Patterson then considered the source of calcium in the body. "You track it back—you look at the food that we eat, the organisms that made that food, and you keep going down the food chain until you come to plants . . . to the earth, to the ground, the soil . . . to the rocks that the soil came from," he explained. Throughout that chain, calcium is absorbed and pulled in at each level. But barium, though chemically similar to calcium, is treated in the opposite way; it is repeatedly pushed out like an unpopular child on a playground. The result is a continual change in the ratio of calcium to barium—as one gets higher, the other gets lower.

"Pat got the idea that as a biological system evolved, it developed mechanisms to take the good metals that it needs for nutrition to incorporate into its system and discriminate and reject similar related poisonous metals," explains Todd Hinkley, who helped Patterson study the idea. To test his theory, Patterson looked at data from atomic bomb tests, which measured radioactive strontium and barium in food and then in the bodies of humans who ate it. The exclusion mechanism worked just as he predicted; the barium ratio went down by a factor of 100.

Logic said that the same reduction Patterson observed with barium should occur with lead, which sat to the right of barium and mercury on the same row of the table. "Lead comes in with calcium, and it's distributed in the body much like calcium . . . it's in our bones," he said. "I knew what the lead/calcium ratio is in average people. So I had the ratio going from rocks to food to people. And do you know, the ratio of lead to calcium in people was about the same as that in rocks?"

Again Patterson had the now familiar thought: "This has got to be wrong." Instead of dropping as it moved through the food chain the way barium did, lead inched upward relative to calcium. Patterson thought he knew why. Like a bathtub drain overwhelmed by a running faucet, the natural rejection of lead couldn't keep up with the amount coming in. If no one turned off the tap, too much lead in our bodies was as certain as a flood on the bathroom floor. In his lectures, Patterson laid out his new theory, which he called "biopurification." "I said, 'Look, lead and barium is wrong. The barium ratio shows that lead should be 100 times less than it actually is in us today. We are being poisoned by lead. And guess where it's coming from? Look at the ocean. You see this curve with all this lead up here? That's coming from tetraethyl lead. Why do you think it took me all these years to measure meteorite lead properly in the laboratory? We are as contaminated as the laboratory.'"

Hardly anyone believed him. "They thought it was a pile of crap!" said Patterson. But he struck a chord with at least one listener; she, in turn, struck a chord with him. Nearly twenty years older than Patterson, Harriet Hardy was formidable in her own right. By 1963, when she knocked on the door of Patterson's MIT office, Hardy, a medical doctor, was known around the country for her intellect and for her determination to do right by America's workers. As head of MIT's occupational medical service, she watched over the many hazardous projects on campus. (She later became the second female physician appointed full professor at Harvard Medical School.) Hardy was someone who went looking for trouble—in the best sense. She didn't wait for problems to make their way to her office. Instead, she regularly dropped in on laboratories around campus looking for anything "that demanded her attention." If she found a problem, she was tenacious in rectifying the situation.

In lead, Hardy found something that demanded her attention. After she encountered the problem of lead through hazards to workers, she quickly recognized that there were larger dangers. She believed children were at far greater risk than was generally believed. When she heard about Patterson's work, she decided to attend one of his talks and then paid him a visit. Sitting in his office, she didn't mince words: "You have to help me save the children of Boston."

Hardy was someone to whom it was difficult to say no. In effect, she pushed Patterson out of his lab and into the political world. She wanted him to talk about what lead might be doing to our bodies. Patterson wrote back to Bob Sharp at Caltech what would turn out to be a considerable understatement: "I have become involved to some extent with the health aspects of leaded gasoline and may have to devote some time to that."

A fitting opportunity was at hand. Just before leaving Pasadena for Boston, Patterson had received an intriguing letter. It was from Katherine Boucot, a medical doctor and the editor of *Archives of Environmental Health*, a journal of the American Medical Association concerned with occupational health issues. Boucot's son, Arthur, was a paleontologist at Caltech. When she visited him in Pasadena for Christmas in 1963, the smog prompted Arthur to tell his mother about Patterson's work on lead in the oceans. Within days of returning home, Boucot wrote to Patterson requesting an editorial "on the increased concentration of lead in the sea, with some reference to the implications of this as a measure of air pollution." This was a chance, Patterson knew, to present his ideas to a larger audience and an important one. Many of the readers of the *Archives* were industrial toxicologists. Preeminent among them was Robert Kehoe, whose studies appeared regularly in the journal. His power and prestige were such that a few years later, in 1966, an entire issue was packaged as a tribute to him.

After his flash of insight at the library, Patterson decided that all previous work had asked the wrong question. Patterson didn't want to know how much lead was in people's bodies today; he didn't much disagree with Kehoe's assessment of that. He wanted to know how much lead should have been there in the first place. He was unimpressed by Kehoe's contention that lead levels had remained relatively consistent "for a long time." By using lead tracers, he had been able to make reasonable determinations of the level of lead in the ancient oceans. Now he wanted to calculate how much lead was in ancient people. But it took him time to work out his ideas. As usual, he was incapable of concision. The editorial that Boucot requested grew into a first draft of eighty pages that took most of his year at MIT to write. Hardy helped to edit it on hot August days sitting in the shade of the apple trees in her garden. She persuaded him to get rid of some of his "wild rhetorical questions." But there was no hiding the emotion and urgency that Patterson felt.

Americans are being subjected to "a severe chronic lead insult," he wrote. Everything hinged on the word "natural," which Patterson argued should be restricted to descriptions of lead levels that existed before industrial production of the metal. What Kehoe called "natural," Patterson labeled "typical." Then his argument worked its way down and across the periodic table to discuss the differences between calcium and barium and lead. Based on the fact that relative amounts of metals are similar in Earth's crust and in the body, he arrived at an estimated natural body burden of lead—that of prehistoric humans—of 2 milligrams per 70 kilograms of bodyweight (about 150 pounds) or 0.0025 parts per million. After reviewing the many sources of lead—fallout from gasoline exhaust, paint, water pipes, solder in cans, ceramics, lead arsenate insecticides, and so on—Patterson calculated that "typical" lead levels, or those of contemporary humans, were 200 milligrams per 70 kilograms of bodyweight or 0.25 parts per million. That meant the average American in 1965 had one hundred times more lead in his body than did his ancient ancestors.

Patterson did not hesitate to lay the blame on the lead industry: "It is virtually certain that all toxicologically significant amounts of lead in the air originate from industry because the difference between existing concentrations and inferred natural concentrations of lead in the air is extreme and contributions from natural sources are relatively well-known." (By natural sources, he meant volcanoes, sea salts, and the like.) After addressing the existing threshold for classical lead poisoning of 0.8 parts per million, the equivalent of Kehoe's 80 micrograms per 100 grams of blood, he attacked Kehoe's "threshold of damage concept" as fundamentally unsound and unsafe by an order of magnitude. "Why is there so narrow a margin of safety and the body so poorly defended?" He questioned the logic of the belief that "a worker must be either perfectly healthy or classically intoxicated with lead but cannot be neither."

What should be done? Public health had to come before economic interests, Patterson concluded. And the public couldn't wait for the science to catch up. "It would be tragic if, many decades from now, it were recognized from accumulated evidence that large segments of populations in our and other nations had suffered needless disability and torment because early warning signs like those recognized in this report went unheeded."

The peer review process for the article, in which recognized experts assessed its quality for the journal editor, was heated. "[The paper] seems to be very unfortunate in its aggressive tone, somewhat sophomoric in organization, extraordinarily verbose, and generally bedded in very poor English," said one. "Assumptions and presumptions are substituted for rigor and objectivity." Another called the piece a "polemic" and noted that it "impugns the life work of Bob Kehoe." However, one eminent reviewer, later revealed to be Arie Haagen-Smit, a colleague of Patterson's at Caltech and an expert on air pollution, said that Patterson was "probably right or close to right."

Patterson sent drafts to other scientists and to government health departments (including California's) for comment. Many were bewildered or simply didn't buy his theory at all. A well-known researcher at Massachusetts General Hospital objected to Patterson's complete dismissal of "the beautiful mechanisms of the body, which protect it from serious exposure." Others angrily wrote to Boucot. One accused Patterson of "rabble-rousing" and asked: "Is Patterson trying to be a second Rachel Carson?"

Kehoe, who could be as long-winded as Patterson and was one of the peer reviewers, wrote: "It has some exceedingly bad spots in it . . . The inferences as to the natural human body burden of lead, are, I think, remarkably naive, and at the same time, from the geochemical viewpoint, very interesting. It is an example of how wrong one can be in his biological postulates and conclusions, when he steps into this field, of which he is so woefully ignorant and so lacking in any concept of the depth of his ignorance, that he is not even cautious in drawing sweeping conclusions. This bespeaks the brash young man, or perhaps the not so young, passionate supporter of a cause. In either case hardly the mark of the critical investigator." Kehoe expressed disappointment with Patterson's supposedly poor understanding of the significance of the Kettering Laboratory work—this despite the fact that he had sent a copy of the Harben Lectures to Caltech, which Patterson refused to acknowledge. ("I'm told he has no intention of knowing me," Kehoe wrote to a colleague.)

Despite his criticisms, Kehoe told Boucot that she should publish the article for strategic reasons. "The issue which he has raised, in this article and by word of mouth elsewhere, cannot be 'swept under the rug.' It must be faced and demolished, and therefore, I welcome its 'public' appearance. It creates a stage on which the need for full information on many of the metals can be demonstrated practically."

The article—trimmed to seventeen pages—appeared in the September 1965 issue of *Archives of Environmental Health,* with an editorial by Boucot saying that although Patterson may have misunderstood some physiology, his article presented cogent reasons "to take a new look at the long-term influence of such toxic materials as lead."

Patterson had fired a cannon into conventional wisdom; predictably, there was an explosion. Kehoe was patronizing and indignant in his own four-page response, published two months later. "Dr. Patterson has ventured, without caution, humility, or appropriate critique, into what is clearly, for him, an alien area of biology," he said. After reviewing the evidence of his own work at length, he called Patterson's dismissal of the threshold concept "astonishingly dogmatic (and absurd)" and reiterated that there was "no evidence of any current threat to the health of representative populations in the United States." The American Petroleum Institute, Patterson's erstwhile supporter, released a statement declaring it "impossible to interpret geological findings in biological terms." All "accepted medical evidence," it went on, "proves conclusively that lead in the environment presents no threat to public health."

Internally, industry scrambled to decide how to react. An Ethyl Corporation memo analyzed the article and, apparently mistaking geochemist Patterson for a geologist, concluded: "He is playing fast and loose with both physiology and chemistry and since he is an expert in neither, should be vulnerable in both." Ter Haar joined Ethyl as a research scientist in 1964. "Did this greatly concern the company? Of course it did," he says. "Patterson was a man of considerable reputation, though not an expert in the health area. Our view was let's get in there and do research. Did we buy into the idea that concentrations of lead in the environment must be one hundred to five hundred times lower? No, we didn't agree with that. I still don't agree with that."

While industry scrambled to mount a counterattack, Patterson found himself in the pages of the *New York Times,* which reported his findings under the headline "Warning Is Issued on Lead Poisoning." "Worldwide contamination of the environment by lead from motor gasoline was reported yesterday to have reached 'alarming' proportions," the article began. "The level of the poisonous metal in the blood of the average American was said to have risen to almost half that which produces obvious symptoms of poisoning."

Patterson's few allies rallied around. "I am writing to congratulate you on bursting into print," said Harriet Hardy. "I would have been glad to stand up and be counted with you." Boucot wrote a long defense of the decision to publish, and Patterson wrote a rebuttal to Kehoe which finished: "It behooves industrial toxicologists and physicians in occupational health not to respond to this challenge as though their heritage was being stolen, but to reflect whether they have renounced it."

Although he complained bitterly of the exhausting battle to publish the piece, once it was finished, Patterson made sure that it got to the right people. He sent copies to the health ministries of ten countries. He also began corresponding with politicians such as California's governor, Edmund Brown (He kept those letters in a file titled "Educating the Gov. of Calif." When there were signs of progress, he added a gleeful note: "Gov. Brown Knuckles Under"). When he felt the governor was ignoring him, he enlisted Harrison Brown's wife, who worked for the state, to write to Governor Brown's secretary. "Clair Patterson is not a nut," she told him.

Patterson also wrote to Senator Edmund Muskie, who headed the subcommittee on air and water pollution. The eight-page letter urged Muskie to consider the importance of the geochemical point of view and accused Kehoe of attempting "to cloak any quantitative knowledge of natural lead contributions in an aura of impenetrable mystery." Muskie proved an eager listener and was ready to give Patterson an even wider audience.

But first Patterson wanted to accumulate more proof. He planned to find it in the ice and snow of Greenland and Antarctica.

### Antarctic Ice Sheet, January 1966

Patterson was the first one up in the morning. From his one-man tent pitched near the train of sleds, he made his way to the Sno-Cat, which resembled a huge tractor with snowmobile tires and held a kitchen with a stove, table, and chairs. His several layers of clothes had dried overnight in the warmth of the tractor. He dressed quickly and woke the other men. As the others dressed and ate breakfast, Patterson climbed forward in the tractor and settled into the observer's seat near the engine. He took out his paper and pencils and began to draw. Every day, he produced one or two cartoons depicting the group's adventures on the ice. The drawings featured frozen breakfasts and sarcastic penguins. After the morning's cartoon drew chuckles (or "sour grunts or yawning mumbles"), the crew left the relative coziness of the Sno-Cat and buckled down to work. By hand, using picks and shovels, they were digging a tunnel in the ice—a hundred feet long on an incline—to collect samples of snow.

Patterson was continuing his battle the only way he knew how: with rigorous science. When he returned to Caltech from MIT in 1964, Patterson was determined to show the true level of lead in the atmosphere, biosphere, and oceans. More critically, he would show that the level had changed over time. But how? His friend and colleague Ed Goldberg, a geochemist at the Scripps Institution of Oceanography in San Diego, had recently developed a method of using a lead isotope to assign ages to ice layers in glaciers in the Swiss Alps. Look for snow that doesn't melt, Goldberg told Patterson. In the polar regions, snow and ice had been preserved for thousands of years. "It comes out of the air, which has lead in it," explained Patterson. "Lead is in the snowflakes. It goes down, and you have a layer there. Next year you have another one. Each layer is an intact record of what was in the air when the snow came down. They just accumulate like pages in a book."

By combining age determination techniques with his ability to measure minute amounts of lead, Patterson would be able to read those layers to assemble a record of the lead in the atmosphere. (Scientists have since done the same to determine how $CO_2$ changes relate to global warming.) Of course it wouldn't be easy. He had to apply everything he'd learned in his seven-year search for the age of Earth and all his subsequent work on lead in sediments and seawater, then transfer the equipment and techniques to the harsh and hostile environment of Greenland and Antarctica. He needed to visit both poles because he wanted to assess both the Northern and Southern hemispheres. He would have to extract his samples using ultraclean techniques and then keep those samples pristine on the long trip home. Happily, the National Science Foundation was willing to foot the bill.

Preparation was laborious. Patterson developed his own tools from stainless steel and Teflon. Each piece of equipment—tools, bottles, ten-gallon plastic drums—went through three stages of cleaning before being sealed in plastic. "The summer before we went to Greenland, we spent evenings on the roof of Mudd making sample boxes and washing bottles," says Patterson's son Cam, who was fifteen the year he accompanied his father. "We were washing with nitric acid and filling bottles with argon gas." Because the lead concentrations in the snow would be so minute, Patterson needed to collect one hundred gallons of snow to do an analysis.

In July 1965, Patterson and Cam arrived at the military base at Thule, Greenland, where five thousand soldiers monitored Russian Cold War activities. At both poles, the military provided transport in and out and support for researchers on the ground. Most work in Greenland was done at Camp Century, a center for U.S. arctic research 140 miles east of Thule. Clair and Cam traveled there by helicopter and found a warren of deep snow tunnels with metal Quonset hut roofs. As at Thule, there were shops, laboratories, barracks, and mess halls under the snow. Originally part of the U.S. Nuclear Power Demonstration Project, Camp Century was heated and powered by an atomic reactor until it was shut down and the camp switched to oil. "The main thing we saw was big piles of oil barrels all over the ice," says Cam Patterson. "Everything [else] was under the ice. There were ten to twenty feet of ice over the tops of the roofs by the time we got there."

The Pattersons worked in an existing thousand-foot-long tunnel that had been dug three hundred feet down into the ice at a 20-degree angle. Steps were carved out of the ice down one side, and sleds were pulled up the other side to bring ice samples back to the surface. "We worked when everyone else was asleep so there was no contamination from people going by," says Cam. Dressed in acid-washed plastic suits, they used Patterson's homemade saws to cut two-foot cubes of ice from the sidewall. They hauled the blocks up the sleds to a trailer (also acid-washed and covered in plastic sheeting) on the surface, where Patterson melted the snow and ice into his pre-cleaned ten-gallon containers for transport back to Pasadena. They dated the snow on the spot, with samples dating back to the eighteenth century and even one from 800 BC.

Camp Century was too contaminated by human activity to provide samples less than fifteen years old. Accordingly, in August, Patterson and about a dozen soldiers from the U.S. Army Research Support Group set out from the camp to find virgin snow; by then Cam had returned to start school. In three fifty-ton Caterpillar snow tractors, each pulling a train of supplies and research and communication equipment, they traveled hundreds of miles upwind through a terrible storm. "When the storms obscured the sun, we held our course by sighting back along flag-markers that we set out as we went," said Patterson. "At a desolate, virgin site, [we] dug a trench fifty feet deep and three hundred feet long to collect samples."

The Greenland samples were flown to the lab, but Patterson didn't have time to start analyzing them yet. Within months, he set out for Antarctica to do the same thing all over again. It was November now, summer in the Southern Hemisphere. Because there is much less land mass in the Southern Hemisphere, it is less polluted generally than the Northern. But would lead still turn up in the ice at the bottom of the planet?

This time Patterson took three Caltech students, who could manage to get away at that time of year, plus four young men from the University of Canterbury in New Zealand who were on summer break. (He sought out young, strong men for the punishing work.) They flew on an Air Force C-130 from New Zealand to McMurdo Sound in Antarctica and then on to Byrd Station, halfway between the South Pole and the edge of the Antarctic ice sheet. Conditions in Antarctica were more difficult than in Greenland. Even midsummer, the temperature falls well below zero. The winds are among the strongest on Earth. As in Greenland, everyone lived and worked in Quonset huts dug down into snow tunnels. "It was warm, stuffy, and smelly, like gym socks, because there wasn't much ventilation and there wasn't a whole lot of washing going on," says Sam Savin, one of the students who accompanied Patterson.

In Antarctica, there were no existing incline tunnels. Using electric chain saws and an electric winch, the team had to dig two tunnels by hand. The first, where they collected the oldest samples, was close to Byrd. It was 300 feet long, 140 feet deep, and took four weeks to dig, with the men working ten to twelve hours per day. As in Greenland, the second tunnel, for more recent samples, required a virgin site, uncontaminated by even the few workers at Byrd. Four of them went many miles upwind of Byrd on the mile-high Antarctic plateau with a single Sno-Cat pulling a freight sled. There, after admiring Patterson's daily cartoons, they excavated another hundred-foot-long shaft.

The men worked completely encased in clear plastic suits, which they pulled on over their cold weather clothes. They had soft plastic helmets and plastic gloves. External temperatures rarely got past 10 above zero (though one day it got warmer, maybe 12 or 13 degrees, and Hugh Kieffer, the biggest and toughest of the group in Savin's estimation, said, "I'm going to take a sunbath" and did, wearing nothing at all). Samples were taken from ten different time-levels in each deep shaft, from five different time-levels in each virgin site trench, and from several different levels at each glacier edge site. The ice blocks gathered from each site were melted in the surface laboratories and transferred to large, chemically clean plastic drums for transport to California. Patterson thought of everything. "It drove Pat nuts that everybody's nose dripped, as it does in the cold," says Savin. "The worry was an unnoticed drip would fall on a block. If your nose did drip, we would take tools and chip a few inches around the spot where it fell."

Patterson liked to call the paper he published on the work his "snow job," but the results were no joke. Patterson showed that in the Northern Hemisphere between 1750, the start of the Industrial Revolution, and 1930, the level of lead in the atmosphere had risen 400 percent. From 1930 through to 1965, with leaded gasoline in use, the lead concentrations had risen an additional 350 percent. In the

Southern Hemisphere, however, where air currents provided a natural barrier, the highest concentration in a sample equaled the *lowest* in the Northern Hemisphere, which came from an exposed vertical ice sheet in Greenland and dated from 800 BC. To Patterson, this was irrefutable proof that the level of lead in the environment was far from natural.

### WASHINGTON, D.C., 1965

While Patterson was in Antarctica, the battle was joined at home. In large part because of his work, the Public Health Service held a symposium on lead pollution in December 1965. Patterson was frustrated at not being able to be there and was suspicious of the timing, but he made sure his voice would be heard. Arie Haagen-Smit, the colleague who had defended Patterson's *Archives* paper, would be there. So would Harriet Hardy. Patterson wrote to Jimmy Chow, who had moved to Scripps. "Would you be willing to go to Washington to fight Kehoe, Goldwater, the American Petroleum Institute, Lead Industries Inc., etc.?" Chow was willing and was invited as an observer.

The meeting was held in a large Washington conference room. "It was no 'shirt-sleeve' session," wrote Hardy, "for there were two tables of press and more than 100 senior officials of the lead industry. The few of us who were invited to talk took little space in the front row of seats." Chow took his "observer" status perhaps more literally than the organizers ever imagined and served as Patterson's eyes and ears. He annotated his program with specifics on the remarks (or lack thereof) and bias of each participant. Industry touted the results of the Tri-City Study, on which they had cooperated with the Public Health Service to analyze lead in the air of three American cities. The results had been released in the spring of 1965 and failed to show an increase in air lead concentrations. The anti-lead forces were unimpressed with the study. It "keeps your blood pressure up," Haagen-Smit had told Patterson when it came out.

Like Chow, Hardy reported to Patterson on the meeting: "We

fought your side, you may be sure." In her autobiography, she described it further: "The discussion was noisy, angry, and sometimes incoherent because of emotion. After lunch there were more talks by government staff trying to make the atmosphere less tense, and the meeting broke up. A few of us were asked to stay for the press conference, a very cold-blooded affair. I almost felt sorry for one of my industrially hooked, very senior colleagues. The press asked him what his salary was and who paid it and what money supported his laboratory. Unhappily, all his funds came from one large industry. This meeting was, I think, a small-stage warning of the restrictions to come." That colleague was Robert Kehoe, who was reduced to tears by the drubbing he took. "I seem to be under the gun," he said.

Chow was triumphant and unsympathetic. He wrote to Patterson's assistant: "Kehoe & Co. could not degrade Pat's paper. The table was turned around that Kehoe was on the defense—his work, the Kettering Lab and his motivation.... Kehoe has met his Waterloo. Hardy and Haagen-Smit are the Wellingtons."

Patterson got his own chance the following June when Senator Muskie invited him to testify in Washington. Muskie's subcommittee was considering amendments to the mostly symbolic 1963 Clean Air Act and grappling specifically with the question of lead pollution. Kehoe was among the first to speak, arguing exhaustively that there was no health risk from leaded gasoline. At one point, he defended his view on the grounds that "it so happens that I have had more experience in this field than anybody else alive." Representatives from the Lead Industries Association and the American Petroleum Institute also spoke, as did Harriet Hardy.

Patterson took the stand on Wednesday, June 15. After laying out his geochemical theories, he made his case that environmental lead had accumulated dramatically, that the health threat from lead pollution was real, and that it must be thoroughly investigated by independent researchers. Science is ever changing, he said. Kehoe and his colleagues willfully refused to admit what they didn't yet know, which was considerable when it came to what lead was doing inside the body. "No one can show, because they don't have the knowledge, what does happen," Patterson said. "We can't describe the biochemistry involved." Kehoe was so stuck in his ways, Patterson said, that he spoke of the outdated measurement of micrograms per whole grams of blood instead of parts per million, which had become the standard term to describe dilute concentrations of substances.

All through Kehoe's testimony, Muskie had appeared frustrated and pushed for better answers. With Patterson, on the other hand, he was like a prosecutor enjoying the performance of a well-prepped witness.

MUSKIE: On the value of establishing the natural level of lead if we can, it is my understanding that that would serve as a very useful benchmark.... What has happened is an increase in the concentration of lead in the human being, as a result of exposure to environment. Is that right?
PATTERSON: That is correct.
MUSKIE: Now in identifying the typical lead levels, as you have termed it, you use actual observations?
PATTERSON: Yes.
MUSKIE: Are these observations different from those that we have been hearing about during [this hearing]?
PATTERSON: They are the same observations.
MUSKIE: So they are the same observations leading to different conclusions?
PATTERSON: Yes.
MUSKIE: You know, this is something we expect from lawyers and senators but not from scientists.
PATTERSON: No; I would not agree with that.
MUSKIE: I am reassured to hear that. I thought somewhere in this world there must be certainty. At least that was the impression I got in the last two days of hearings that there is a great deal of certainty in the world...I think it is true that that distinction [between natural and typical lead levels] has not been made. Now

why has it not been attempted by these organizations or by others than yourself in studying this problem? It seems such a logical approach to a lawyer.
PATTERSON: Not if your purpose is to sell lead.

The scientist had come out of the lab fighting.

## CHAPTER FOUR

# *Proof of Principle*

TEMPLE UNIVERSITY, NORTHEAST PHILADELPHIA, 1970

Herb Needleman placed his tray on the table across from Hal Rutenberg and sat down. They were in the hospital cafeteria, their usual lunch spot.

"I've been looking at the kids in the schoolyard," Needleman said to his friend. "Something is wrong. Some are strong and wild. Others are not keeping up. I think maybe it's lead."

Then he described how he wanted to use teeth to see if he was right.

To Rutenberg, the idea seemed to strike out of the blue. But it became clear that Needleman had been thinking about lead poisoning for some time. Now he was ready to do something about it. He had an innovative new idea for how to tackle the problem and was tantalized by the possibilities.

Lead would also be an antidote to Needleman's growing frustration with his work at Temple. As his friends had predicted, he quickly became disenchanted with psychiatry and its lack of "a scientific basis." In his work at the Child Guidance Clinic, he often suggested taking a blood lead measurement for kids with cognitive or behavioral problems. "They'd say, 'Are you crazy? We don't do that,'" says Needleman.

After completing his psychiatry residency, he escaped by going out into the neighborhood, where he felt the work was important. He took a position at Temple's Community Mental Health Center as director of outreach and education. But community work had its own complications. The center was part of an idealistic plan to bring psychiatry to poor residents of the inner city. It hired neighborhood women to serve as the first level of counselor. Doctors oversaw the program and worked with local organizations. "We were going to solve the world's problems," says Needleman. In his view, they didn't succeed. "There was no systematic recruiting, evaluation, or training. The real problem was that these people were poor, and you can't counsel people out of poverty. I began to feel very frustrated. I felt like it was all rhetoric. We were just sitting around and talking, but not doing anything." If you want to do something for these people, Needleman told himself, look at lead.

Research would be another kind of refuge. "Few things compete with having a problem that people have been bothered by," he says. "Set it up, specify it, and solve it. There's great tedium at times, but also lots of fun. When you figure out a way of answering it and it turns out it is right, it's exciting. To decrease the amount of uncertainty in the world, I really get a kick out of that." He began to plan his first lead study.

Bruce Dobkin was in his first year of medical school when he answered Needleman's ad for a researcher. In Needleman, Dobkin found a kindred spirit. By 1970, at forty-two, Needleman was "a bit of a hippie." He had grown his sideburns and hair out a few inches, wore corduroy, and smoked a pipe. And he was against the Vietnam War. That made him an exception to the young person's rule that you can't trust a person older than thirty. Temple students loved him—he was as antiestablishment as they were. "For me, he was like a blood brother," says Dobkin, who had gone to medical school to stay out of Vietnam and showed up at Temple wearing clogs and a pin celebrating the fiftieth anniversary of the Soviet Union. "He was fun, and we talked politics a lot. The other students in my class tended to find him as a person to chat with. It was hard to find someone who was smart and with some experience, who saw the world the way we did." Dobkin was quickly converted to Needleman's passion about lead poisoning. "I hated medical school my first year," he says, though he went on to a successful career in neurology. "Herb's project was one of the things that kept me sane."

Needleman found an expert in teeth at the University of Pennsylvania. One evening he gave a talk about lead poisoning to a group there. In the audience was a young assistant professor from the dental school named Irving Shapiro, a thoughtful Englishman who specialized in the biochemistry of teeth and bone. He was intrigued by Needleman's suggestion that teeth might provide a useful window on the problem. Shapiro could tell right away that Needleman needed an education on teeth—he had no idea how complex a structure each tooth is. But Shapiro also knew that Needleman had hit on something. "It was a really bright idea," he says. "I saw the tooth as a resource that could be probed for more information." And he liked Needleman. "I thought Herb was a great character. He was very bright, very political, and had an amazingly charismatic personality."

Together they started the Philadelphia Tooth Fairy Project. With his first $500 grant, Needleman got a supply of silver dollars from his father-in-law, who was a bank president. He enlisted dentists to pass these along to each kid, $1 per tooth (after all, he or she was giving up on the other tooth fairy by giving Needleman the teeth). It didn't work quite as planned. Needleman met a child who had given teeth and asked what he thought of his silver dollars. The child looked at him oddly. "I got two quarters," he said. Apparently some of the dentists liked the silver dollars too much to give them away. "My first experience of the corrupting power of cash in science," Needleman likes to say. That wasn't the only problem. When word got out that researchers were buying teeth, some wanted to create a market. "One day thugs came to my lab with a handful of broken teeth asking for $50," says Shapiro. "All I could assume was that they had knocked the teeth out of children. I paid them, but I didn't use the teeth."

Needleman and Shapiro collected sixty-nine teeth from dental clinics in the "lead belt" of urban Philadelphia, the area with the most reported cases of lead poisoning, and forty teeth from suburban dentists in areas where very few lead poisoning cases had appeared. Needleman also sent Dobkin to St. Christopher's Hospital for Children to search the records for patients who had been diagnosed with lead poisoning and discharged. He was able to find three who were at the right age to be losing teeth.

From the start, Needleman wanted the study to include a neuropsychological evaluation to assess what the cognitive impairments from lead might be. His first efforts were rudimentary. Bruce Dobkin had the job of administering tests. With a few pencil-and-paper tests such as Portius mazes and a standard test of word knowledge in hand, he visited the families who'd given teeth. He was not always well received. "I was in North and West Philadelphia. It was summer, and the people were sitting on the steps of the row houses. I'd drive up in my Corvair, and they'd say to me, 'What are you doing here?'" It wasn't easy to walk into someone's living room and say you wanted to know if his or her child was affected. "I would always couch it as lead could have some small effects on people that were negative," says Dobkin. It quickly became obvious that this was a sensitive and complicated subject. Needleman needed a more sophisticated way of studying the problem.

Work with the teeth was more successful. Shapiro ground them into a powder, then extracted lead from the powder and measured it. He found distinct differences in tooth lead levels between the two groups. For the suburban children, the mean tooth lead was less than 15 parts per million. For children from the inner city, the mean tooth lead was between 51.1 and 109 parts per million. The three teeth from children with a documented history of lead poisoning were in the high end of the range: 110, 92, and 62. Clearly, teeth could be used as an "indicator of lead intake." Needleman and Shapiro published those results, leaving out the cognitive question for the time being, in a short article in *Nature* in January 1972.

Later that year, Needleman was invited to a symposium on Environmental Health Aspects of Lead. Held in Amsterdam and sponsored by the brand-new U.S. Environmental Protection Agency, the symposium was full of industry representatives. It was an eye-opening experience for Needleman. "You could tell who was who," he says. "Industry was well-dressed, clustered together, and very well prepared. The others were not." The cavernous room and simultaneous translation into three languages reminded him of the United Nations; and the questions he received were as hostile as Khrushchev disrupting the General Assembly. For ten minutes, he described his study and another small study in which children with a history of lead poisoning were found to have lead concentrations in their teeth seven times higher than suburban American children and eighteen times higher than children in Iceland. He argued two main points: that mild neuropsychological damage should be considered a possible effect of lead exposure, and that lead in teeth was a marker that could be used to identify that exposure.

"Implausible," said one questioner.

"Meaningless," said another.

"I am sorry that the questioner does not see the relevance of the data I presented," replied Needleman formally but assuredly. "We think that the analysis of dentine levels of lead presents a window into the past exposure of children when other, more transitory indices such as blood lead... have returned to normal." He explained that if he and his colleagues were right, they could identify children who had high exposures, and then design a controlled epidemiological study to measure their neuropsychological performance. That would allow them to "test the hypothesis that children with elevated body lead burdens who have not come to medical attention, are paying neurologic, cognitive, or behavioral costs."

He began to understand what he was up against. "That's when I realized this was a contentious issue," says Needleman. "I woke up to the fact that it wasn't just that the truth will out." But he was sure of his data and thought he was right. Perhaps as important, he was not afraid of a fight; in fact, he sometimes relished the challenge. "He's the toughest person I've ever met," says his son Joshua Needleman, now a pediatric pulmonologist in California. "He seems fearless and unstinting and uncompromising in what he thinks is right." Whether the issue was big or small, Needleman's children learned early that their father saw right and wrong in stark terms. One Saturday, the family went into the city, and Needleman drove into a garage. "The sign said $2," remembers Josh, "and the guy said, 'On weekends it's $3. I keep telling them to change the sign.'" But Needleman said, "When it says $3, I'll pay $3." Then he parked half a mile away and walked. Needleman regards acting on principle as an obligation. "If you see things are going on the wrong track, you have to say so," he says.

In Needleman's view, the paint industry had been going on the wrong track for a very long time. From colonial times, Americans put lead in their paint. The resulting product was celebrated for its ease of application and its staying power. Although there were alternatives, the lead industry framed the debate as one of quality and purity versus cheap adulterated paints and urged high-end painters to call themselves "white leaders." There were energetic arguments over whether or not paint manufacturers should have to include lists of their ingredients on labels. But the concern was fraud, not health: pure lead was good; "adulterants" were bad. House painters, homeowners, and others, the argument went, had the right to know whether the paint they were using was top quality or a cheap imitation.

By the twentieth century, the largest player was the National Lead Company, which produced more than twice the lead manufactured by the other nine American lead companies combined. (National Lead later became NL Industries.) In 1906, National Lead created the Dutch Boy painter—the name derived from part of the manufacturing of lead known as the "Dutch" process—and used him to market lead paint as part of a clean, healthy life for children. In 1929, for example, the Dutch Boy showed up in a "Children's Paint Booklet." In a series of cartoons, a boy and girl were shown bored and listless because their room was dull and gray. In came the Dutch Boy, who brightened up toys and furniture with a gleaming coat of lead paint. On top of each panel was a note to children: "Give Coupon to Father or Mother." The Dutch Boy campaign won marketing awards for National Lead. Between 1910 and 1977, Americans put an estimated three million tons of lead on walls, toys, and furniture.

In other countries, however, lead paint was viewed differently. Concern had been building since 1904, when the Australians Gibson and Turner first linked lead paint with childhood lead poisoning. By the 1920s, when National Lead was marketing directly to American children, twelve countries banned lead from interior paint: France, Austria, Belgium, Spain, Sweden, the United Kingdom, Greece, Poland, Czechoslovakia, Tunisia, Cuba, and parts of Australia.

When American lead, paint, and gasoline companies founded the Lead Industries Association (LIA) in 1928, one of its mandates was to combat negative press. The organization worked just as tirelessly to avoid regulation. Generally, industry blamed the victim, not the toxin: workers failed to follow instructions, and children had incompetent parents. The association's Manfred Bowditch once complained to Robert Kehoe: "Until we can find means to (a) get rid of our slums, and (b) educate the relatively ineducable parent, the problem will continue to plague us." Finally, in 1954, as they were beginning to develop alternative pigments like titanium dioxide, paint manufacturers voluntarily established a limit on lead in interior paint: it should contain less than 1 percent by weight when dry. But they continued to blame parents. In his 1960 Harben Lectures, Kehoe described some poor minority children as unsupervised, "unwanted, and unloved."

It was the individual stories of what happened to some of those poor children, told by the parents who loved them, that ultimately galvanized communities into action. At a Chicago block association meeting, after a young mother described how both of her young children were suffering convulsions because of lead, the group decided to found the Chicago Coalition to End Lead Poisoning, a community organization that was instrumental in raising awareness in that city.

In New York, the *Village Voice* put reporter Jack Newfield's story of twenty-three-month-old Janet Scurry on its front page in 1969. "Plaster from the walls started falling all over the place," her mother, Brenda Scurry, told Newfield. "I asked the landlord a couple of times to do something about it, but he never did. Then in April one morning my daughter wouldn't eat anything. She started trembling and couldn't breathe. I got scared and she started to change color." A neighbor helped Scurry get her daughter to Morrisania Hospital, near their Bronx home. But doctors, although they knew Janet had eaten paint chips, said the girl would be fine and sent her home.

At home, Janet did not get better. After five days, doctors gave her a blood test for lead poisoning. Before the results came back, she was dead. "The day after she died, the blood test came back positive," said Brenda Scurry. "Later they sent me a death certificate that said Janet died of natural causes. The doctors did an autopsy, but I still haven't gotten the results.... The hospital doesn't want to say it was lead, I guess." Scurry had to use her rent money to pay for the funeral and, when she talked to Newfield, was trying to avoid being evicted from the apartment that had killed her daughter because she had nowhere else to go.

"How do you show a process, how do you show indifference, how do you show invisible, institutionalized injustice, in two minutes on Huntley-Brinkley?" Newfield wrote in the *Voice*. "How do you induce the news department of a television network to get outraged about nameless black babies eating tenement paint when the public health profession, schoolteachers, housing experts, scientists, the NAACP, and the politicians haven't given a damn?"

Putting names and faces to the victims helped. So did the changing politics of the time. By the next year, when Needleman was starting his first lead study, Americans were starting to give a damn. What had once proven a barrier to action—that lead poisoning predominantly affected poor blacks living in rundown urban housing, keeping it out of sight and relatively out of mind for the rest of America—was now a call to arms. After the War on Poverty and the Civil Rights Movement took hold, "lead became a focus," wrote historian Christian Warren: "a symbol for all that was wrong with housing and medical care in America's largest cities."

A groundswell of awareness spread across the country as one city after another—Chicago, Rochester, New York—established "case-finding" programs and made a concerted effort to identify childhood lead poisoning and not mistake it for something else. And, as Needleman's experience at the Children's demonstrated, once you started looking for childhood lead poisoning, you found it. Of the hundreds of thousands who were tested, a quarter had lead levels exceeding 40 micrograms per deciliter, awfully close to the threshold for classical poisoning.

In 1970, the U.S. surgeon general called for more mass screenings and an emphasis on prevention. Much of the surgeon general's statement was taken from the work of Jane Lin-Fu, a pediatrician working at the Children's Bureau of the Department of Health, Education, and Welfare (HEW). Back in 1967, Lin-Fu had been assigned to write the federal government's first real information pamphlet on lead poisoning. Since then, she'd become something of a one-woman army fighting against lead poisoning within HEW.

In 1971, New York Congressman William Fitts Ryan and Senator Edward Kennedy, spurred to action by Jack Newfield, sponsored and passed the first Lead-Based Paint Poisoning Prevention Act. The bill charged government agencies—the Departments of Health, Education, and Welfare and Housing and Urban Development—with helping to set up screening and treatment programs and with defining the problem more clearly. And, for the first time, it banned the use of lead paint in federally funded housing.

As the case numbers rose, so did recognition that lower levels of exposure might also be a real threat to children's health. The official threshold for lead poisoning—the point at which pediatricians took action—had ranged from 50 to 80 micrograms per deciliter from city to city. As part of his call for screening, the surgeon general created a committee to create guidelines for doctors. It declared anything over 70 micrograms per deciliter to be an "unequivocal" case of lead poisoning requiring chelation, and recommended monitoring children whose levels were above 50. Over much objection on the grounds that it would generate too many cases, Jane Lin-Fu battled for and got a third category called "undue lead absorption." It covered children from 40 micrograms per deciliter to 60 micrograms per deciliter and recognized that they might be suffering health effects that had been ignored or unrecognized.

In 1972, Lin-Fu followed her earlier informational pamphlet with a review article in the *New England Journal of Medicine* subtitled "A New Look at an Old Problem." Armed with statistics from the screening programs of the last few years, Lin-Fu argued forcefully that the country was faced with an undeniable and substantial problem. "Lead poisoning mimics a hundred different things. If you turn your head and say it doesn't exist, it doesn't exist," Lin-Fu said in an interview. "I really hammered it into the heads of everyone—you can't say we don't have it because you don't see it."

Industry did not accept the new activism quietly. It continued to insist that an absence of clear clinical symptoms equaled an absence of illness. If there were neurological effects, how could you convincingly link the effects to lead when there could be so many other causes? It found support for this view among some of the first generation of pediatricians who had treated lead-poisoned children, such as Julian Chisholm, a pioneer in chelation treatment at Johns Hopkins, and Henrietta Sachs, who oversaw a large lead-poisoning clinic in Chicago from 1966 through 1972.

At the Amsterdam conference in 1972, the same year Lin-Fu declared the problem undeniable and substantial, one of the questions thrown at Needleman by an industry representative was a seven-part argument for all the other possible reasons for neuropsychiatric problems in children, including "domestic environment" and "the very real and frequent occurrence of child abuse." To counter such arguments effectively, someone had to prove the principle that low levels of lead were capable of causing harm.

### Philadelphia, 1972

When he returned from Amsterdam, Needleman's next, expanded study was already under way. He and Shapiro had quickly realized what they needed to do differently. They needed more children, more teeth, and a better collection process. They decided to go through the school system. Needleman enlisted the help of his old friend Ed Sewell, who had been a pediatrician at the Children's with him and was now in charge of medical care in the Philadelphia Public School System. Shapiro also had a new idea about how to analyze the teeth more precisely, by using not the whole tooth but a specific part of it: secondary dentine. Secondary (or circumpulpal) dentine surrounds the "pulp" where the nerve is, and continues to form as we age. As new dentine is created, lead is incorporated into the tooth structure. "Teeth are a sink for lead," says Shapiro. A history of the child's exposure to lead could be read in the layers of dentine, "like tree rings."

This time, Needleman and Shapiro collected teeth from 761 Philadelphia children in two different school districts. The black children from District 5, who lived in housing that was in "a severe state of deterioration," had four times more lead in their teeth than did the white children from District 8 who lived in newer homes. Twenty percent of the black children had levels high enough to be considered clinically toxic. Needleman and Shapiro had designed a double blind study, so that Shapiro and his staff didn't know whose teeth they were working on as they did the chemical analysis—they identified each tooth by a number. But it didn't matter what precautions they took. "It was always stunningly obvious," says Shapiro. Needleman held the codes pairing teeth with children. "[Irving] would send me the tooth lead level and I'd guess on that basis if it was a black kid," says Needleman. "Nature doesn't usually sort itself out so crisply."

But then something odd happened. A series of high lead levels came in, all from children with Irish and Italian names who lived on three blocks in East Kensington, in the eastern half of District 5. All the children went to the same Catholic school, St. Ann's—a school that Needleman had added to the sample only because Ed Sewell asked him to include parochial schools.

Needleman and Shapiro investigated in person. When they visited St. Ann's, the nuns invited them to stay for lunch in the cafeteria. "Before lunch, a nun appeared with a brush and pan and brushed down the table," says Shapiro. Being Jewish, he wondered if this was some unfamiliar Catholic ritual. "She said no, look up. Paint was peeling off the ceiling and they had to sweep it off every day." Lead was not just in the cafeteria. Looming above the school, Needleman and Shapiro saw smokestacks. What did the factory manufacture? Lead paint. "St. Ann's was right next to the National Lead Company. These kids were living in the shadow of the NL stacks," said Needleman later. Armed with small pots and paintbrushes, Needleman and Shapiro roamed the neighborhood collecting dust from gutters and streets to take back to the lab for analysis. While they were working, men came out of the factory and approached them.

"What are you doing here?" they said menacingly.

"I'm from the city," said Needleman. "Just collecting some samples."

"Get the hell out of here."

They got out, but not without their samples. Analysis showed the street dirt and the dust in the area was heavily contaminated with lead. The two researchers urged teachers and parents to ask for the school to be repainted. The city set up a lead screening study in the area; 15 percent of the children tested had blood lead levels above 40 micrograms per deciliter. (In 1987, people from the area, with Needleman as a witness, sued National Lead and Anzon Inc., which had bought the plant, for damages attributable to lead poisoning. A jury found against the individual plaintiffs but required Anzon to spend $2 million on cleanup.)

The results of the study of the two school districts were published in the *New England Journal of Medicine* in 1974. The article established that inner-city children clearly had higher levels of lead than did other children and that teeth were a good marker of past exposure.

A handful of other researchers were looking at the same problem, and they became allies with Needleman. "Herb was beginning to think out loud about the possibility of subclinical damage," says Philip Landrigan, then a young doctor with the Centers for Disease Control (CDC). "There were so few of us, we sought each other out." Landrigan came to the issue by chance. When he finished his pediatric training in 1970, the Vietnam War was raging. Rather than wait to be drafted, he joined the CDC as an alternative to military service. His assignment was measles, but when a call came from Texas about a possible lead-poisoning problem, Landrigan was sent to investigate.

El Paso health officials were disturbed by the discovery that a lead smelter had, between 1969 and 1971, released more than a thousand metric tons of lead as well as zinc, copper, cadmium, and arsenic into the surrounding area. In 1972, Landrigan and his CDC colleagues found extensive contamination of the air, soil, and dust around the smelter. When they tested families, nearly 60 percent of children under age ten living closest to the plant, in a neighborhood called Smeltertown, had lead levels exceeding 40 micrograms per deciliter (the national average was less than 10 percent). Farther away, 27 percent of the children between ages one and four, those most at risk, had elevated blood lead levels.

In 1973, Landrigan went back to El Paso to try to determine if the children had suffered cognitive impairment from lead exposure. His team performed evaluations on a group of children who lived within four miles of the smelter. The evaluations found no difference between lead-exposed children and controls on most of the measures, but statistically significant variations emerged in two areas: performance IQ and a test of fine-motor skills. The study was small and was done under field conditions that were less than ideal, but at the very least it made clear that more work had to be done.

The next year Landrigan was sent to Kellogg, Idaho, to investigate the area around another smelter after two children (siblings ages two and three) were hospitalized with chronic unexplained abdominal pain, blood lead levels of 68 and 89 micrograms per deciliter, and "lead lines" in their bones. Lead was big business in Idaho. The state was home to four of the five biggest lead mines in the country and, through 1980, accounted for one third of the U.S. production of lead. (Missouri, Alaska, and Montana are the three other largest producers.) The smelter in Kellogg had released approximately ten metric tons of lead per month for almost twenty years. In September 1973, that amount tripled after a fire in the filtration unit.

A twenty-four-year-old researcher named Ian von Lindern joined Landrigan as part of a state team looking at the environmental issues. They found a clear relationship between the level of lead in the environment and blood lead levels in area children. "Within a mile of the smelter, 99 percent of the children were lead poisoned," says von Lindern. Five miles out the number was 75 percent. But most were asymptomatic. (According to von Lindern, a follow-up study did find long-term health effects in those children such as hypertension and reproductive and kidney problems.)

When the results of the lead testing were released, the *Los Angeles Times* called Kellogg "the dirtiest town in America." "It caused a real controversy here in the state," says von Lindern. "People didn't believe it was a problem because they had lived with it for fifty years." Landrigan and the CDC staff were "kicked out of the state," says von Lindern. But the results stood, and what they demonstrated, both in El Paso and Idaho, was a strong association between the level of lead in the air and the level of lead in children's blood. That would prove critical in the coming battle over leaded gasoline.

Others were looking further into what such lead levels might be doing in the body. In 1972, a young woman named Ellen Silbergeld had just begun post-doctoral work in the environmental health department at Johns Hopkins. Thanks to Baltimore's high lead levels and some enlightened early public health officials, Johns Hopkins was one of the few places in the country with a historic and consistent focus on lead. It was home to one of the early American experts on lead poisoning, pediatrician Julian Chisholm.

As Silbergeld was casting around for a research project, she realized that little was known about lead except that it was dangerous at high levels. Silbergeld, a toxicologist, wanted to use animal research to develop a clearer picture of lead's toxic effects. She set herself the problem of understanding one of the known occupational symptoms of lead known as "painter's wrist." "Nobody really knew why painters acquired this wrist drop," she says. Along the way to explaining the reasons for a known symptom of lead poisoning, she stumbled onto a significant lead effect that had barely been looked at: hyperactivity.

For her study, Silbergeld raised rats and fed them lead. "I happened to observe that when I'd go in, they were really crazy," she says. "When I'd take the cover off, they'd jump about and try to get out of the cage. That's unusual for rats during the day—they're nocturnal. I thought they were hyper. I measured their activity. Quantitatively, they were in fact hyper." Then she experimented with Ritalin, a drug used to calm hyperactive children, and saw exactly the same effects that pediatricians saw in children. "My control animals with Ritalin became hyper, the hyper animals calmed down immediately," she says. "It was quite striking." That result was particularly important given the tenor of much political discussion of lead. "There were always arguments that related to poor parenting or other kinds of confounders and observations of neurodisease," says Silbergeld. "I could say my rats have perfectly lovely mothers and excellent nutrition, the only difference is that they're getting lead."

At the urging of her academic advisor, who thought her results significant, Silbergeld presented her paper in October 1973 at a conference in North Carolina on low-level lead toxicity held by the EPA and the National Institute of Occupational Health and Safety. "It's amazing how naive I was," she says. "I gave my talk and had no real notion of what to expect since I was just starting out in science. Somebody got up in the audience and launched right into me with a huge attack as if my science was suspect. I realized I was in a different world. Scientists might ask questions, but they don't attack you as if you're doing something obviously evil. I thought, 'What in God's name is going on here? I don't think I like it.'" Shaken, Silbergeld went outside to take a break. Up walked Herb Needleman and Phil Landrigan. Silbergeld remembers the conversation vividly. "They said, 'You might have wondered what was going on here. You probably don't know what's at stake.' Then Herb said, 'You're going to have to make up your mind which side you're on. Do you want to be part of the debate or not?'"

It took one more experience to persuade Silbergeld to put herself in the line of fire. One day in the lab, she got a call from an industry representative who said her paper was really important and people were paying attention. "That impressed me because I was a post-doc." But there was more. "Some people are overinterpreting your work," said the caller. "You have to be careful that people don't go farther than you know." Then he talked about his organization's sponsorship of lead research. The next international meeting it was hosting would be in Paris. "I thought that sounded nice," says Silbergeld. "But then they went too far, even for me in my naive state."

The caller suggested that Silbergeld might want to write to *Science* explaining what her paper was really about. "We've drafted a letter for you," the caller told her.

"The scales fell from my eyes," says Silbergeld. "I was converted. I could have called up Herb and Phil and said, 'Sign me up.'"

### Washington, D.C., 1972

Concern about effects from lead at lower levels gave new urgency to the question of where the lead was coming from. Paint was the largest source of lead poisoning in children and almost always the only source concentrated enough to bring on convulsions, coma, and death. But there was lead in food cans, ceramic dishes, and water pipes. And, of course, there was lead in gasoline; it accounted for 90 percent of airborne lead. (The rest came primarily from stationary sources like smelters.) By the time an engine burned two hundred gallons of gasoline, a pound of lead had gone through it. As Clair Patterson had shown, lead from gasoline exhaust had settled everywhere in the environment, from the oceans to the icecaps, and, closer to home, on the dirt where children played and on the crops that ended up on the dinner table. "It's not [just] what people breathe in," says Idaho's Ian von Lindern, "it's what falls in the dust and what young kids eat in the dust. That's the key route."

The lower the level of concern, the more likely it was that these other sources, alone or together, could bring a child into the danger zone. Medically, not much could be done for such children. Chelation is painful and relatively ineffective at lower levels. Improving nutrition by increasing calcium and iron intake helped the body's natural detoxification process somewhat. Nothing, however, was as effective as getting the lead out of the child's environment.

With so many sources, that would be a monumental undertaking. The most pitched battle was over gasoline. Ethyl Corporation, which was still primarily in the business of making and marketing tetraethyl lead, had a lot at stake. So did other lead industries. The 1970 Clean Air Act, a result of Senator Muskie's committee work, put the job of regulating lead in the hands of the EPA. The agency was required to make a list of harmful pollutants within thirty days, set ceilings for those pollutants, and then impose controls on emissions of those pollutants to keep them below the ceilings. In other words, the EPA was empowered to declare what and how much could go into the air, and then to police the polluters.

One of the EPA's first acts was to endorse the catalytic converter. The device lowered emissions of carbon monoxide and nitrogen oxides, but its platinum catalyst was incompatible with lead. Any car with a catalytic converter would have to run on unleaded gasoline. The EPA decreed that catalytic converters would be installed in all 1975 model cars and that at least one grade of unleaded gasoline must be available by that time. But not everyone drove new cars. What about the roughly 100 million old cars still running on leaded gas? Left to the catalytic converter, the natural phase-out of leaded gasoline would take many years. And what if technology changed from catalytic converters to something that could run on leaded gasoline? Any benefits would be erased. To justify a separate phase-down of leaded gasoline, the EPA had to make the case that health considerations warranted such a step. An EPA doctor named Kenneth Bridbord got that job.

Bridbord, a pediatrician by training, thought that the available literature, though undeniably sparse, allowed him to make a strong enough argument—one that centered on children. A 1966 study, for example, followed more than four hundred lead-poisoned children and found that nearly 40 percent had neurological problems. Bridbord put together a methodical review focused on making the connection between airborne lead levels and blood lead levels. Landrigan's El Paso work was very helpful, as was Needleman and Shapiro's first study and Silbergeld's work on hyperactivity. Bridbord also used Jane Lin-Fu's papers. The closer children lived to busy streets, he noted, the higher their lead levels. Children absorb up to five times more of the lead they ingest than do adults, he wrote, and clinical symptoms appear in children at levels lower than in adults. He used the word "epidemic." He talked about being "prudent" and "conservative" in establishing margins of safety.

What he left out, apart from one relatively minor reference in the first draft, was Clair Patterson. "I had the highest regard for Patterson, and I thought that the man was probably right, more than right about what was happening to people," says Bridbord. He also knew how controversial Patterson was. "In developing the initial health rationale, it's important to try to base the scientific discussion on a broad range of evidence so it's not so easy to pick out one piece and knock it down. My instinct was that if I tried to build a case around [Patterson's work], it would have been attacked." Bridbord did solicit Patterson's opinion on his paper. Patterson's reply was that his own finding that lead levels were one hundred times higher than natural levels should be enough: "The only way to reduce the hazard of atmospheric lead is to eliminate the lead entirely from gasoline." But Bridbord was having a hard enough time declaring 40 micrograms per deciliter to be the upper acceptable limit. "From [Patterson's] point of view," says Bridbord, "you should go to zero."

Bridbord first presented his argument at the same Amsterdam conference where Needleman described his first tooth studies, and the two compared notes over dinner. Not surprisingly, Bridbord's paper wasn't any more popular than Needleman's. Industry vehemently contested the idea that blood lead levels could be affected by leaded gasoline. In their view, tetraethyl lead was "an inconsequential addition" to toxicants in the air. "There is absolutely no health justification for such a regulation," said Lawrence Blanchard, who was in charge of Ethyl's campaign against the EPA. He accused the agency of acting as both "adversary and judge." The EPA staff said later there was more "heat" on this issue than any other they faced at the time. Just as in the 1920s, when tetraethyl lead was introduced, all involved were splashing around in an ocean of uncertainty between the solid ground of absolute proof of harm and absolute proof of safety. But the tide was pulling strongly in one direction: lead was causing harm.

A lawsuit finally forced the issue. Not many years out of Yale Law School, David Schoenbrod had become a staff attorney at the Natural Resources Defense Council, a nonprofit environmental organization, after working for Bedford-Stuyvesant Restoration Corporation, a community development organization. In Bedford-Stuyvesant,smack in the middle of Brooklyn's lead belt, Schoenbrod was among those who began to see environmental problems as social justice issues. He believed in using the law to call the country to account, and at the Natural Resources Defense Council he could do that.

Like many other environmentalists, he had initially welcomed the creation of the EPA and the 1970 Clean Air Act, which "seemed almost too good to be true." But he was frustrated over EPA's foot-dragging, and he was in a position to do something about it. Beyond its instructions on pollutants, the Clean Air Act empowered the public to sue if the EPA's administrator failed to follow through on the job. In 1972, Schoenbrod charged the EPA with "unreasonable delay" on lead. The Court of Appeals agreed and gave the administrator thirty days to issue regulations to phase-down lead in gasoline. "Truthfully, I was happy," says Ken Bridbord.

Even so, the EPA had to fight internally for the regulations right down to the wire. The Nixon White House staff demanded that the agency make last-minute changes to reduce the economic effects on industry. The EPA relaxed the first-year requirements and extended the phase-down from four years to five, with a final limit of 0.5 gram per gallon. Then industry mounted a legal challenge, which the EPA finally won on appeal. Ethyl's Blanchard was furious. "The whole proceeding against an industry that has made invaluable contributions to the American economy for more than fifty years is the worst example of fanaticism since the New England witch hunts in the Seventeenth Century," he said. In his view, "no person has ever been found having an identifiable toxic effect from the amount of lead in the atmosphere today." Nonetheless, in April 1976, the phase-down of lead in gasoline finally began.

### Children's Hospital, Boston, 1971

From the Philadelphia studies, one big question remained: Did the lead make a difference? Did it affect a child's performance? Industry's answer was a resounding "no." Needleman thought otherwise. He sought to prove it in a new place. In the midst of his work with Shapiro, he had left Temple. He was more than ready to go.

Like so many other cities, Philadelphia had not escaped the racial tensions of the late 1960s. With the black power movement in ascendance, a white psychiatrist was not always welcome in minority neighborhoods. Black activists decided that the Community Mental Health Center where Needleman worked should be run by the community and staged a sit-in. After Needleman fired a black instructor for insulting the women staff at the center, his name and address appeared on flyers tacked to telephone poles and left on windshields. Shortly thereafter, the phone rang during the day at Needleman's home in suburban Wynnewood, where Roberta was taking care of their two small children. The man on the phone asked for Needleman. Told he wasn't home, the caller said: "Tell him we're coming to get him." After that, Needleman could feel Roberta's body stiffen every time they heard a car drive down their quiet street at night. "It was time to get out of there," says Needleman.

He was offered a job as an assistant professor of psychiatry at Harvard Medical School in 1971. He would see patients at Children's Hospital (in addition to lead poisoning, anorexia was an interest) and could conduct his research in a lab upstairs. While he managed the second Philadelphia study from a distance, Needleman got settled at Harvard and was already planning the complex, epidemiologically sound review that he hoped would settle the question once and for all.

At Harvard, he didn't have to look far for the expert help he needed. Across the hall was "a crackerjack" named Alan Leviton, who was both a neurologist and an epidemiologist. The two lived in the same suburb, Newton, and occasionally rode the trolley in to work together. "Herb told me about his dreams and his vision," says Leviton. "He had an idea, but he recognized that he was not an epidemiologist and he wanted guidance about how he could answer the question he most wanted to answer."

Epidemiology, in the simplest terms, is the study of the occurrence of disease. In reality, it's like doing a jigsaw puzzle backwards. Investigators begin with the big picture—hundreds of interlinked facts about who gets a disease, when, where, and how. Then they remove individual pieces, through statistical controls, to free the central image from the distraction of extraneous background. The critical connections that remain, called "associations," help us better understand how disease works and how to prevent it.

What such associations cannot do is prove cause and effect. In some regards, it's easier to study rats or roses. Faced with two rosebushes—one lush and full of vibrant blooms, the other spindly and forlorn—a researcher can work methodically through the factors that could account for the difference: sunlight, water, the skill of the gardener, the quality of the soil, and so on. If necessary, roses can be studied in the controlled environment of a greenhouse, just as rats can be studied in the controlled environment of the laboratory. People are another story. It's difficult, and almost always unethical, to subject human beings to such controls or to purposely make them sick even if the goal is to make others better. Instead, epidemiologists use statistical techniques to weed through the thicket of genetic and environmental factors at work in each of us.

In the 1970s, those statistical techniques were not as sophisticated as they are today. But Needleman and Leviton aimed high. For one, they would have a large sample. "That gives you power in the statistical sense," says Leviton. For another, they would address the flaws in previous studies. Some used inadequate markers of exposure such as blood lead levels, which were too fleeting. Others drew their study subjects from families already at clinics, who did not represent the general population. And finally, there were inadequate identification and handling of confounding variables, those interlinking facts that might confuse the picture.

They needed to get at exactly the questions raised by critics: How can one be sure that lead, and not something else, was the cause of the problem? To do so, the study had to exclude children in whom other problems existed that might affect the results, for example, a past diagnosis of lead poisoning, low birth weight, head injury, and so on. For each variable, they had to design a way to tease out the truth while avoiding parental subjectivity. To rule out problems caused by low birth weight, for example, Leviton told Needleman, "The question to ask is, Did the baby go home with the mother?"

They designed a cross-sectional study—a look at a moment in time—of thousands of children that would measure tooth lead levels against performance on a variety of neuropsychiatric evaluations. The evaluations would be done in two ways. Each child who submitted a tooth would be rated on classroom behavior by his or her teacher. Those at the highest and lowest ends of the lead level spectrum would be brought to the lab for neurological and psychological testing. (It was too expensive and time-consuming to test every child in this way.) The evaluation began with the Wechsler Intelligence Scale for Children (an IQ test) and included sentence repetition tests, reaction-time tests, and measures of the ability to express ideas orally.

Getting funding was a battle. Obviously, industry wouldn't support Needleman, and he wouldn't have taken its money anyway. He first applied to the National Institutes of Health in 1972, but knew that the odds were long. Only about a quarter of applications get funded; and most have to be submitted several times. Radically new ideas are particularly difficult to fund. On the third try, with endorsements from luminaries such as Robert Reed, chairman of the biostatistics department at Harvard's School of Public Health ("the grand old man of statisticians," says Leviton), NIH approved the grant in 1976. Needleman's daughter, Sara, remembers that someone on her father's staff adapted a popular T-shirt for the occasion. It had a frog on a lily pad croaking "Rib-it"; the would-be fashion designer had substituted "Funded" for "Rib-it."

Needleman had carefully chosen the communities he would work in. "Boston was undergoing racial desegregation and was in turmoil," he says. "I didn't want to send staff there." Instead he chose Chelsea and Somerville, two primarily white, industrial, working-class cities on the northern edge of Boston. By studying mostly white children, Needleman effectively took race out of the equation. Needleman also liked the fact that the Tobin Bridge connected Chelsea to Boston and that houses sat below the bridge. "Early on, we had the idea that the two main exposures were paint and automobile exhaust," says Leviton.

In both cities, Needleman visited the superintendents of schools. "They immediately saw this could be important," he says. They convened a meeting after school of teachers of the first and second grades. Most were young women. "The teachers were so sharp and highly motivated," says Needleman. "I told them what I wanted to do. They asked questions and were enthusiastic and very helpful." Patricia Hallion was a first-grade teacher at Lincoln Park School in Somerville at the time. "I had a young child myself," she says. "I knew about lead paint and the dangers of it in the home." When a child lost a tooth, the teacher would put it in a coded envelope and mark on a diagram where there was a space in the child's mouth. "When my chemist would open the envelope," says Needleman, "he would look at the type of tooth and the space and see if they were consistent."

After the experience in Philadelphia, instead of paying for teeth, they launched a publicity campaign. A commercial artist drew a tooth with a face, a gapped smile, and the line, "I gave." The image graced posters and badges that were given, with toothpaste and a toothbrush, to participating children. For more than a year, they collected teeth—plus some dogs' teeth and some adult molars and even some white stones; in the end, they had more than three thousand teeth from twenty-five hundred children. "The kids thought it was cool. They were delighted to show you which tooth was loose," remembers Hallion. "But there were tooth fairy issues." Namely, how could the children explain to the tooth fairy that their missing tooth couldn't be left under the pillow? "They had to cover at home, and we said it was okay to leave a note."

As the teeth arrived at Needleman's office, they were analyzed in a lab he had created especially for the study. A series of chemists did the work over the years of the study. In Needleman's view, two were particularly important. Peter Barrett, a doctoral student who ultimately went to the business side selling chemistry equipment, started with "an empty room" and had to develop the technique they would use. Cornelius "Neil" Maher, a Ph.D. who later became a neurologist for the U.S. Army, perfected that technique. Each tooth was placed in a block and sliced very thinly. The tooth slice, a U-shaped specimen from the middle of the tooth, was then broken in half to create two mirror images that could be analyzed and checked against each other. The slices were dissolved in acid, and the lead content was separated and measured.

Initially, the halves didn't always match, and Maher spent a lot of time "looking at both sides of teeth and trying to make sure our analytical techniques were correct and proper." The lack of concordance complicated the process of establishing the high and low cutoffs. They settled on a requirement that two of three measurements in each tooth had to match. "We had no idea what a normal tooth lead level was or what the range was. We had to develop a rolling standard," explained Needleman in a later interview. "As we did a hundred teeth, we'd see what the mean was and then establish the upper ninetieth percentile and the lowest tenth percentile. But then we would do another hundred, and the mean would move around a little bit."

Needleman wasn't a chemist, but he liked to visit the lab. "Herb was a tinkerer. He liked to wander in and see what was happening," says Barrett. "He was always interested in the analytical stuff we were doing and in how we could get better at this." Both Barrett and Maher soon were convinced of the importance of the work. "He was contagious," says Barrett. "His enthusiasm for this, his care for this was inspiring. This was a mission for him."

They initially identified 270 children at the highest and lowest end of the distribution, but the number was reduced to 158 when they excluded those who didn't speak English as a first language, whose parents wouldn't or couldn't participate, who might have a history of lead poisoning, or whose tooth lead analyses weren't concordant. The subjects were brought into Boston Children's Hospital by taxi. "I would interview the mother, give her an IQ test and a medical questionnaire," says Needleman. "The kid had a four-hour examination."

The questionnaires filled out by teachers for every child were relatively straightforward. "Is the child distractible? Yes or no. Disorganized? Yes or no. Can the child follow simple directions, complex directions, et cetera. There were eleven questions like that," said Needleman. "We had 2,146 good datasets, that is, a good tooth analysis and a good questionnaire. Then we arranged the subjects in six groups of forty-two ascending tooth levels. Class 1 was the lowest, Class 2, and up to six. We just counted the negative reports by teachers for each of the six groups." The teacher reports couldn't be subjected to the same level of control for confounders as the high and low groups, but they addressed a fundamental premise of toxicology: the dose-response relationship. By including all the children at every level of lead exposure, the investigators hoped to be able to tell if effects from lead got steadily worse as exposure increased.

Needleman admitted that he was not neutral on the issue. "I wasn't a dispassionate observer," he says. "I didn't allow that to sway my method." Scientists are generally uncomfortable with that approach, however, because it leaves the investigator open to critiques of bias. "Herb was positive we'd find something," says Leviton. "I had a healthy skepticism. Let's see what the data show."

One day in 1976, while the Boston study was under way, Needleman got a call from David Schoenbrod. Despite the success of his first lawsuit, Schoenbrod was not satisfied. The EPA had begun the regulation of lead in gasoline, but the agency had yet to list lead as "a criteria pollutant," the designation reserved for the most widespread air pollutants. Putting a pollutant on the list set a stricter regulatory process in motion and allowed the EPA to control not just the amount of lead in gasoline but the amount of lead in the air. "I wanted to close the loophole," says Schoenbrod. He sued again and won again. But the creation of ambient air-quality standards—an airborne lead limit—required a technical "criteria document" explaining the grounds for determining those standards. The EPA's first draft set the ambient air standard at 5 micrograms per cubic meter of air. Schoenbrod was convinced such a level would have no effect. Lead industries wouldn't have to change a thing. "The first draft was really an apologia for lead," Schoenbrod says. "I thought it was a scientific travesty and an outrage. But I'm a lawyer, and I'd be going against EPA expertise. I knew I needed help."

Expecting not much more than letters of support, Schoenbrod wrote to some sixty scientists and doctors to test the waters. One was Sergio Piomelli, a pediatric hematologist at New York University Medical Center and later at Columbia. In 1973, after years of treating children with blood disorders, Piomelli had developed a new method of screening for lead poisoning that was cheaper, faster, and less painful than standard blood tests. With just a finger prick instead of a blood draw, Piomelli could measure a rise in the concentration of erythrocyte protoporphyrin or EP (an important substance in red blood cells), which proved to be a marker for high levels of lead. When Schoenbrod asked him to look at the draft criteria document, Piomelli took it home to read over the weekend. "It was outrageous," says Piomelli, a fiery Italian who did some of his medical studies in the United States and settled here in 1963. "I couldn't believe my eyes. It made my blood boil." He found the chapter that claimed lead had an essential role in the body particularly egregious. "Industry was denying that lead was bad," says Piomelli. "These people would deny the sun." He called Schoenbrod: "I can come and testify."

Piomelli also passed along another name to Schoenbrod: Herb Needleman.

"I need you to come to Virginia and tell them this is a scientific travesty," Schoenbrod said to Needleman when he reached him in Boston.

"Of course I'll come," Needleman replied.

He and Maher reviewed the draft document before they went to the meeting in Virginia. They agreed with Piomelli. "It was a shabby piece of work," says Needleman. "Five micrograms was like Los Angeles on a summer's day." Says Maher: "We found its survey of the studies of lead's impact on children badly out of date and biased. To us it read as if written by an industry scientist."

When the group—Schoenbrod, Piomelli, and Needleman, who brought Maher along—got to EPA's Science Advisory Board meeting in January 1977 to consider the document, they lined up on one side of the conference room table like soldiers ready to do battle for a cause they believed in wholly. "It was a couple of days of severe fighting," says Needleman. "The good guys in one corner, industry in the other," remembers Piomelli. "We fought on the document page by page, word by word."

Piomelli marshaled his work on erythrocyte protoporphyrin to show cell damage in children at average urban lead levels. His stories of sick children were powerful. Needleman didn't have the results of his Boston study yet, but he knew intimately every study that had been done to date on the neurotoxicology and neuropsychology of lead. They were helped by the fact that the Science Advisory Board included some scientists, such as Samuel S. Epstein (unrelated to Patterson's Caltech colleague of the same name), a prominent pathologist who became a leading expert on environmental causes of cancer, who were equally appalled by the document. "Herb and Sergio spoke to the committee," Schoenbrod reported back to his colleagues at the Natural Resources Defense Council. "The effect was electric. The chairman went around the room. One by one, they agreed with Drs. Needleman and Piomelli." The resolution was to scrap the draft document and start over.

"The agency took a black eye," says Lester Grant, who was then part of a group conducting lead research at the University of North Carolina, a dozen miles away from the EPA's offices in Research Triangle Park. When the Science Advisory Board told the EPA to get expert help in writing a new document, the agency turned to Grant, a neurobiologist, and his colleagues, pathologist Marty Krigman, and analytical chemist Paul Mushak. The North Carolina team scrambled to rewrite the document.

"This was the beginning, not the end, of a scientific war," said Schoenbrod. Almost monthly meetings followed. Piomelli and Needleman went to most of them. The two put together a full report on the health effects of low level lead exposure, and the Natural Resources Defense Council distributed it. Phil Landrigan and Ellen Silbergeld weighed in. So did the other side. The EPA met with Jerome Cole of the Lead Industries Association and other industry representatives. And it conferred with Paul Hammond and Julian Chisholm, who were senior advisors to the Science Advisory Board and tended to believe that Needleman and Piomelli were "overinterpreting" the data. When everyone was in the same room, the discussions were intense. "There were verbal fistfights," says Grant. "I was astounded at the way these people behaved. People had passionate feelings about it, clearly."

As they worked through new drafts of the document—there were three—the question of whether Piomelli's documented rise in EP represented an "adverse health effect" became critical. Industry, in the form of representatives from DuPont, the Lead Industries Association, and several doctors who testified on their behalf, said it wasn't. Piomelli, Needleman, and Schoenbrod said it was.

Needleman likened the change in EP levels to an early warning sign that doctors ignored at their peril: "The history of medicine is replete with examples in which the optimal practice has shifted from recognition of extreme cases of disease, to lesser forms and finally to the identification and management of biochemical changes," he argued, citing elevated bilirubin levels in newborns and antituberculosis therapy on the basis of positive skin tests as examples. "If practitioners were to await the appearance of a gross physical change as an indication of adverse health effects, they would, in many cases be guilty of practicing inferior medicine, if not out-and-out malpractice."

Their arguments carried the day. In September of 1978, based on the new criteria document, the EPA announced an ambient air standard for lead of 1.5 micrograms per cubic meter. The predicted cost to the smelting industries was $650 million. The companies didn't take it quietly. Even though their position had been soundly defeated in the criteria hearings, industry spokesman Jerome Cole said the standard was "based on a faulty interpretation of the scientific facts" and was "totally unnecessary from a health point of view and ruinous for the industry."

The Natural Resources Defense Council celebrated by surprising Needleman and Piomelli with an award at a ceremony in New York. In his letter of thanks, Needleman described the work as "one of the most satisfying and gratifying experiences in my career.... To change the state of affairs required people who knew how to deal with the intractable vested interests who put lead in the air and were working like the devil to keep it there. That's when Sergio Piomelli and I found NRDC and Dave Schoenbrod or vice versa. I was energized by the quality of David's mind and his capacity for hard work.... You do us considerable honor."

• • •

It was a season of celebrating. Needleman found further validation in the results of the study back in Boston. The data had been entered onto Hollerith cards, punch cards that were fed into a huge computer at the Harvard School of Public Health (it was the 1970s). "We had big stacks of these things," says Needleman. "They're read pretty fast. When we printed it out from the computer, it was just stunning. As it came out I could see we had something important."

Those in the highest group had mean tooth lead levels greater than 20 parts per million, whereas those in the lowest had mean levels less than 10. Needleman and his group found that children with high lead levels performed significantly less well on the IQ test, particularly verbal items. They were less competent in areas of verbal performance and auditory processing. Their ability to sustain attention was "clearly impaired." And classroom behavior suffered; they did significantly poorer on nine out of eleven items on the teacher evaluations. "It was extraordinary. The teachers, who didn't know [the kids'] lead levels, could identify all these nonadaptive behaviors [that were] in direct relationship to the level of lead in the teeth," says Needleman. "I anticipated we were going to find a positive result but it was so robust that it really did surprise me." Leviton, too, was impressed. "The data speak for themselves," he says. "There's no question that children who had the highest lead levels in their teeth did less well."

To be sure, they re-ran the data. "In data analysis, you have a plan, but if you're really thorough, you'll see if you can do anything more," says Leviton. He rearranged the subjects according to the mothers' education levels and IQ tests in all manner of ways. "No matter how we grouped the mothers and said within each group, 'Is there a lead effect?' we saw it in each group. We talk about getting a feel for the data, and we got a feel for this. No matter what we did, it was there." They had developed damning evidence: steady low-level lead exposure was harming children's brains.

The results were published prominently in the *New England Journal of Medicine* in March 1979. In addition to Needleman and Leviton, the other named authors were Charles Gunnoe, a psychologist who oversaw the testing, Barrett, Maher, Reed, and Henry Peresie, another chemist. In the same issue, there was an editorial by Jane Lin-Fu. She mentioned Patterson's work in Greenland and wrote of Needleman's work: "The finding that none of these children had overt lead poisoning is particularly ominous. The far-reaching implications of the Needleman study are obvious and disturbing. It's time to reassess the problem of lead exposure in children. What was viewed as undue lead absorption yesterday may have to be considered lead poisoning today." She also argued that concerns over economic consequences should not cause us to lose sight of the value of intact human life. "How does one assign a dollar value to human life and health?"

It was a watershed moment in the fight against childhood lead poisoning. The study made news across the country. But Needleman didn't get to rest on his laurels for long. He had already developed a healthy distrust of the lead industry that amused his friends a little, but even he was surprised by how controversial his study would prove to be. As Alan Leviton said years later: "Just because you're paranoid doesn't mean they're not really after you."

**CHAPTER FIVE**

# *A Majority of One*

YOSEMITE NATIONAL PARK, 1970

Clair Patterson put his backpack down and looked out over the canyon. It had taken the better part of the day to get to this remote spot ten thousand feet up in the Sierra Nevada. On the long walk in with two donkeys, a graduate student, and his daughter Susan, who was studying chemistry and biology, Patterson had quizzed his young companions on scientific method. Now he would put his own method to work.

Tourists did not come to this corner of Yosemite. The people and the cars were on the west side of the park. Here on the east side, there was no traffic of any kind, no fishing or hunting, no mining or logging. More than half the canyon was barren granite. The few trees were mountain hemlock, lodgepole, or whitebark pine. No streams entered the canyon, though a small one drained out at the bottom. It was pretty but unwelcoming. "The altitude is so high and the canyon walls are so steep that it is an unpleasantly exhausting region to traverse in the summer and a thoroughly dangerous place in which to work in the winter," Patterson wrote. In other words, it was perfect. "We chose the top of a mountain," he said, "because that's the last place man has gone to pollute."

In the five square miles of Thompson Canyon, Patterson was

going to create yet another laboratory—a natural one. He needed a closed ecosystem where he could account for everything that came in and everything that went out. After consulting with Caltech's Bob Sharp, he had chosen this forbidding place. In it, he planned to show that he was right about lead pollution and its implications.

He wanted to test his theory of biopurification—the idea that lead was accumulating, when it should have been diminishing, at every level of the food chain. To prove it, he would measure the amount of lead and other metals in each link in the chain: air, rain, snow, rock, soil, groundwater, stream water, plants (sedge), and two kinds of animals—herbivores (meadow mice) and carnivores (pine martens). The martens, at the top of this particular food chain, ate the mice, who ate sedge and so on. How much lead came into the canyon and how? Where did it go while there? How much was in the sedge, mice, and martens? How much left the canyon and how?

In geochemical terms, Patterson was studying the pathways by which lead moved through the environment; he was trying to determine its "fate." Along the way, he wanted to distinguish between natural and industrial lead. Natural lead eroded from rocks into the soil, was taken up by plants and then eaten by animals. Industrial lead could be added at any point if it was deposited on the plants or the animals' fur. "These little particles that zoom around in the air are not brought down to earth just by snow and rain," explained Patterson. "They also bounce around and finally hit the surface of a tree leaf or a blade of grass, where they stick and don't come off."

Perhaps most critically, Patterson wanted to answer his persistent question: What was the natural level of lead? In the 1965 paper that had launched him into the thick of the political battle over lead, he had written that people carry a hundred times more lead in their bodies than did their preindustrial ancestors. But that was just an estimate. Patterson needed evidence.

In Yosemite, the terrain was as demanding as he was. His crew needed samples for every season: summer, fall, winter, spring. From July to September, they could travel in on foot with pack animals—a five- to eight-hour trip from the trailhead in Bridgeport, California. In winter, they could ski or snowshoe in—"from eight hours to two days to impossible," says Todd Hinkley, who worked in Thompson Canyon with Patterson as a doctoral student. Once, in a year of unusually heavy snowfall, Hinkley and Yoshi Hirao, a small, wiry Japanese postdoctoral fellow, skied in and couldn't find the snow shovel they had left tied to the top of the tallest tree in the canyon. They realized it must be buried and dug down six feet, using the tips of their skis, to uncover the shovel. Even in summer, the place was inhospitable. Sometimes the local Indian guides they hired to help with the pack animals abandoned them halfway there. "They said it was too hard for the horses," says Hinkley, who went on to a long career with the U.S. Geological Survey. Stagnant pools in the meadow created the thickest swarms of mosquitoes Hinkley had ever seen. Patterson, in his fifties at this point, began to find it hard going. He made a few visits but left most of the hard physical work of getting to and from the site and collecting samples to his young assistants.

As always, the risk of contamination required constant vigilance. The team made camp outside of the canyon so as not to disturb it with their presence. In a grant report, Patterson noted just how much of an effect humans could have. "The exhaust from 80 gallons of snowmobile fuel spews as much lead onto snow as is discharged naturally during an entire year by the 5,000,000,000 gallons of stream waters leaving the upper region of Thompson Canyon, while one mercury flashlight cell left there in a stream by a camper could contribute more mercury than that discharged naturally from the entire Canyon in 10 to 20 years."

Measurements of lead in the air, to take one example, could be ruined many times along the route from the canyon laboratory to the Caltech laboratory. The samples were collected on dry deposition filters left out in the open on flat rocks. The filters were handled with Teflon holders and connected to a vacuum pump. When lead had collected on the filter, the researcher stopped the vacuum pump and, wearing acid-washed plastic gloves, took hold of only the Teflon filter holder and put it in a clean bag. That bag was carried back to the trailhead either by backpack or horseback. At Caltech, a researcher dressed in protective clothing opened the bag in the lab and removed the filter holder with acid-cleaned tweezers. "It's really bad if you lift up the filter with tweezers and drop it onto the counter or anywhere," says Cliff Davidson, who made several trips to Thompson Canyon for Patterson. "That means the two weeks you spent camping in Yosemite were wasted at least for that sample. You get very paranoid."

But the effort was not wasted. In this mountain canyon 150 miles from San Francisco and 300 miles from Los Angeles, the accumulating lead was unmistakable. Each year, seventy thousand grams of lead from gasoline exhausts in those two cities traveled the wind and was deposited in the five square miles of the canyon, mostly through snowfall; only 250 grams of lead washed out in streams each year. The amount leaving was less than 1 percent of the amount coming in. By using isotopic measurements to distinguish between natural and industrial lead, Patterson's crew could tell that 95 percent of the lead entering the canyon came from auto exhausts. "The entire canyon in this remote area is heavily polluted by industrial lead—and this lead comes from gasoline exhausts originating in Los Angeles and San Francisco," said Patterson.

He had also proved his biopurification theory. Natural lead and barium in rocks—the poisonous metals—diminished at each level of the food chain, but industrial lead, which the team measured relative to calcium, accumulated at every step. With an electron microscope, they took striking photographs of lead particles on blades of grass. "There was substantial deposition of lead on the plants," says Rob Elias, a trained botanist whom Patterson hired to work as a biogeochemist (someone who studies trace metals in plants) for purposes of the study. "It was a tremendous picture to show at national meetings."

A full 83 percent of the lead ingested by the meadow mice came from industrial lead deposited on the surface of the sedge rather than from natural lead the plant took up from the soil. Patterson concluded that the preindustrial ancestors of those mice, those living in the same canyon three hundred years earlier, had at most one-sixth the amount of lead as the mice they studied. Just as mice were getting extra lead from the surface of their food, pine martens were ingesting lead from the surface of their coats every time they preened themselves. "They would end up getting big blasts of lead they weren't evolved to handle," says Hinkley. "It's a curveball being thrown at you by the modern polluted environment."

That same curveball was, of course, ripping toward humans as well. Using his data from Thompson Canyon, Patterson concluded (though this was still an estimate) that humans had lead levels four hundred times higher than natural levels—four times higher than his 1965 estimate. The buildup of lead directly interfered with human biochemistry, given the changing ratio of lead to calcium. "When you're trying to determine what the impact might be, the question was always what is calcium doing in the body," says Elias. Nerve signals, for example, pass along a bed of calcium. When lead gets taken into tissues instead of calcium, it blocks the way. One atom of lead for every ten thousand atoms of calcium does not seriously interfere. But if there are ten, twenty, or one hundred times that amount of lead there, the nerve signal is going to have more trouble getting through. The Thompson Canyon work made it clear that there was far more lead than there should have been.

Patterson thought the link to public health was obvious and the consequences were dire. "It seems probable that persons polluted with amounts of lead that are at least 400 times higher than natural levels, and are nearly one-third to one-half that required to induce easily recognizable poisoning, are now suffering enough partial brain dysfunction, that their lives are being adversely affected by loss of mental acuity and irrationality," he wrote. "This would apply to most people in the United States." He wasn't just talking about mental retardation, but about all the lost geniuses who might have gone on to find a cure for AIDS or cancer.

But Patterson had a hard time getting anyone to listen. Even at Caltech, the administration was hesitant. A few years into his Thompson Canyon study, in 1974, he wanted the university to report his findings and conclusions in a press release. Nearly ten years had passed since he had first confronted the lead industries, but Patterson was as controversial as ever. He had proved that lead was accumulating, but guessed at what it meant. Caltech administrators worried about jeopardizing research funding, and they wanted to wait until Patterson's work had been peer-reviewed. Patterson was furious. In a memo demanding support from the new chairman of his division, Barclay Kamb, Patterson wrote: "The integrity of this Institute requires that no distinction be made between 'safe and innocuous' and 'controversial' subjects in the process of informing the public about the significance of work carried out at the Institute.... In my particular case it is likely that we will gain more than we will lose if the Administration will back me instead of playing it 'safe.'" Caltech tried to appease Patterson by featuring the Thompson Canyon study early the next year in its magazine *Engineering and Science,* which counted government leaders and media among its readers, but Patterson's most extreme statements had been edited out.

### Caltech, 1974

Like the chemicals in his lab, Patterson's emotions had been distilled to a powerful purity, but they could be explosive upon contact. "Caltech is full of odd people. It's very small, and a lot of these people don't get along well in normal society," says Cliff Davidson. "Pat was even odd in that environment." He was unconventional on almost every level. To keep in shape, Patterson exercised obsessively. On the running track, where he could be found most days, he ran in the wrong direction. He often restricted himself to diets consisting of, say, lettuce and raw hamburger, and nothing else.

His relationships with some colleagues consisted of uneasy lulls punctuated by hot flare-ups. Even his job title was controversial. When Patterson arrived at Caltech he was a research fellow and for many years was listed simply as "geochemist"—possibly the only person with such a title in American academia. He would have it no other way. He didn't believe in departmental hierarchy or politics, and when Caltech offered to make him a professor, he refused the title and the salary and benefits that went with it—a decision that caused some hardship to his family.

Although he demanded respect, he loudly rejected the traditional trappings of scientific prestige. Tenure, he said, was antithetical to good science. "It is a debilitating factor...and degrades both the quality of [faculty] activities and the excellence of their science," he wrote. The thing to strive for, he said, was a moment of scientific discovery such as he had experienced at Argonne, when he determined the age of the earth.

That discovery should have earned him election to the National Academy of Science, the highest honor in American science. But Patterson told one young colleague that he'd like to be asked just so he could tell them he would never belong "to such a chicken-shit organization." Perhaps the organization sensed his feelings as, for a long time, he wasn't asked. Had his work fallen squarely within physics or chemistry, says Lee Silver, Patterson might have been awarded a Nobel Prize for determining the age of the earth. As there is no Nobel Prize in geology, there's no way to know if he would have accepted it.

His antiestablishment view won Patterson few friends; by its very nature, his position insulted and indicted those who did accept tenure and awards. That made peer reviews and funding committees, never easy to navigate, both more treacherous and more critical for Patterson. "There were lots of times he didn't know where he would get the money to go on," says Silver.

Yet Caltech also nurtured and supported Patterson. With the indulgent protection and intellectual stimulation of colleagues like Harrison Brown, Bob Sharp, Lee Silver, and Sam Epstein, who had arrived with Patterson from Chicago, he was able to do one important study after another and earned a place in the institute's history. In the 1960s, when Patterson first angered the petroleum industry, a Caltech trustee who was an executive in a gasoline company that added tetraethyl lead to its product called Caltech President Lee DuBridge to complain about Patterson. Get rid of him or shut him up, the trustee said. Without tenure, Patterson was vulnerable. But DuBridge resisted. "[He] properly declined to do anything about toning down Patterson's attack on problems of lead pollution," wrote Bob Sharp, who added that he believed the trustee "was under strong pressures from executives higher up in his company to do something about 'that nut at Caltech.'"

At times, Caltech went to surprising lengths to accommodate Patterson—or perhaps to put a stop to his habitually cranky memos. He "was instrumental" in converting the campus mail trucks to electric motors because he didn't like the noise they made. To block the other distractions of the world, Patterson prevailed upon the institute to build him an office within an office. It had double walls, double windows, and double doors. He locked himself in and wouldn't answer when anyone knocked. The only other person with a key was his analytical chemist, Dorothy Settle, who joined him in 1968 and became his closest colleague until he retired. When others were granted entry, they were amused to find that this hermetically sealed office had papers, books, and junk cascading from every surface. "I see you've been burgled again," joked one regular East Coast visitor.

In the late 1960s, with money from NASA, Caltech also built a new, improved clean lab on the third floor of Mudd down the hall from Patterson's office. This one had an anteroom for changing clothes and a more extensive air filtration system. "It was like an operating room," says Settle, who ran the lab for Patterson for twenty-five years. It was in this lab that Lee Silver and others (though not Patterson) examined the rocks brought back from the moon by the astronauts of Apollo 11.

When he was in the lab, Patterson was quick to criticize, often with four-letter words. "As a mere graduate student, I had to take whatever he dished out," says Cliff Davidson. "He was very exacting. Laying down tweezers in the wrong place—you just didn't do things like that." As Todd Hinkley put it: "He was a hell of a difficult guy." But for Davidson, Hinkley, and many others, the depth of Patterson's integrity and vision transcended his bad behavior. "It was pretty trying, but on the other hand I was converted to his way of thought," says Davidson. "He basically preached that it was the rest of the world that was crazy. He had a remarkable power to convince people that all this was true. The most important [thing about him] was that he was right."

And there was another side to Patterson. Anyone who earned his scientific respect also earned his devotion. He went to unusual lengths to support junior colleagues, often making them senior authors on scientific papers—an almost unheard-of courtesy. One year when Laurie went to Iowa for the summer, Patterson moved out of his house so that a young colleague's family could live there. "He would do anything to further the research, and I was continuing the research," says that colleague, Russ Flegal, whose children loved swimming in the Pattersons' pool. John Rosen, a pediatrician who established the first lead poisoning clinic in New York City in 1972, found in Patterson a mentor and guide. "He touched me in a way very few others have," says Rosen. Whenever they met, which was usually to discuss Rosen's clinical research on lead in bone, Patterson, who was eager for health researchers to make the link to his work, provided encouragement and support. He regularly told Rosen, "You're really on the right track."

And his support wasn't limited to scientists. When the fellow who washed his lab's equipment fell seriously ill, Patterson went to the hospital and sat with him. "He was someone who needed attention and got it," says Settle. For a cranky old scientist, Patterson also had a surprisingly warm way with children. He saw them all as budding scientists and talked to them about the names of plants and other scientific secrets. "At two, my daughter could say the age of the earth was 4.55 billion years," says Flegal.

Despite his efforts to seal himself off from others (literally!), Patterson was now willing to enter the political fray. But the truth was, not everyone wanted him. To the lead industry, of course, he was enemy number one. When data were released that showed the dangers of lead, industry representatives worried about reports "that may provide the Pattersons of this world with a lot of ammunition." They applied their considerable political muscle to keeping him out of government deliberations on lead. But even like-minded scientists and activists found that his uncompromising views made him an uncomfortable ally.

As a result, he was excluded from some major developments. When the Public Health Service launched an expanded version of its Tri-City Study, which had failed to show increasing lead levels in 1965, and which Patterson roundly criticized, he learned about it only by accident. He immediately wrote to the secretary of the HEW, Robert Finch, to find out why he was being excluded. Unsubtle as ever, he in the first paragraph accused the Public Health Service of publishing, with the earlier study, "the undisguised propaganda of the Ethyl Corporation." Then he got to the heart of the matter: "If it is true that a new and more elaborate investigation is under way, there can be no question but that my work triggered it.... It is both puzzling and disquieting to find out now that these actions have been taken without my knowledge, participation, or assumption of a position of evaluative responsibility." He also wrote to Lee DuBridge, who'd left Caltech to serve as a presidential science advisor, to ask him to verify his competence—again, he needed his friends to attest that "Patterson is not a nut." His effort was to no avail. Secretary Finch replied some months later: "Well qualified and competent research scientists from the Federal Government, the National Academy of Sciences, and industry are jointly planning and coordinating the lead research program." Patterson's "recognized expertise" had not been "overlooked," French said. Rather, he would be asked to serve as an expert reviewer for the forthcoming lead criteria document. (The HEW never created that document; the EPA completed the job nearly ten years later.)

The next year, when the newly formed Environmental Protection Agency asked the National Academy of Sciences to form a committee to provide an up-to-the-minute report on lead for use in determining regulations, Patterson was again left out. He wrote angrily to his old mentor Harrison Brown, who had been an officer for the National Academy. "Lawyers are not scientists and neither are government bureaucrats—and when the bureaucrats are elected by people, the majority of whom believe in astrology and do not believe in evolution, then this sort of thing can be expected. My government still does not understand what the lead exposure situation is. They are still concerned with shaded areas, and still believe in thresholds." But Brown couldn't or wouldn't prevail upon the National Academy to add Patterson to its committee.

That academy's report, released in 1971, was interpreted by the press as giving lead a clean bill of health, and "industry executives were openly jubilant," said *New York Times* science writer Philip Boffey in his 1975 book on the National Academy. The report was called "Airborne Lead in Perspective," but the panel included not one scientist who specialized in airborne lead, apparently on the grounds that such specialists didn't have knowledge of biological effects. Nor did it include anyone who had expressed concern over atmospheric lead. In short, the panel had failed to include not just Patterson but various other prominent researchers who were knowledgeable about lead and critical of the lead industry: Patterson's former student T. J. ("Jimmy") Chow; Dartmouth's Henry Schroeder; Paul Craig, a physicist who headed the Environmental Defense Fund's lead committee; and John Goldsmith, head of the California Health Department's epidemiology unit, who was making life difficult for the petroleum companies in California.

Several of the six men who were on the committee, such as its chairman, Paul Hammond, and pediatrician Julian Chisholm, had strong industry ties or had publicly endorsed industry's view of the situation. Both the section of the report on adult epidemiology and that on the role of lead from gasoline exhaust in air pollution were written by a DuPont scientist, Gordon Stopps, who wasn't actually part of the committee. Harriet Hardy served as a reviewer and battled over Stopps's work, which she felt relied on old studies that exonerated lead and downplayed more recent work that suggested otherwise.

Alone in his soundproof office, Patterson was left gnashing his teeth. Desperate, he dreamed up a plan to infiltrate the enemy camp in Washington. He knew he was no politician himself, but he ran into the office of his friend and colleague Bruce Murray, a professor of planetary science and geology, and announced: "Bruce, you've got to run for Congress!" It was the only way to effect wholesale change in science and technology policy, he thought. But Murray demurred, and Patterson returned to his lair to fire off more angry missives.

He did testify at hearings in California to set a state air standard for lead, and there he had the home field advantage. Patterson's colleague and supporter Arie Haagen-Smit chaired the meetings. Patterson's testimony on air lead levels measured by T. J. Chow was greeted with respect. Robert Kehoe's statement, on the other hand, which argued that an air lead level of 10 or even 20 micrograms per cubic meter would be just fine, was less well received. Ethyl Corporation had long viewed California as the sharpest thorn in its side, and those hearings were no different. Several years ahead of the Environmental Protection Agency, Haagen-Smit's California Air Resources Board set a thirty-day average ambient air standard of 1.5 micrograms of lead per cubic meter.

Even as Patterson's despair over industry grew, he retained a dry sense of humor. After Harriet Hardy sent him a news clipping on the lead industry, he wrote back: "This must be evidence of a diabolical plot on the part of the oil companies to discredit us by using the old association techniques. What nefarious and dastardly scheme will they think of next? Oh, how can we ever escape these rascals?"

Patterson couldn't escape industry representatives, but he could continue to show just how wrong they were. And it wasn't just industry scientists. Patterson had utter disregard for most laboratories' ability to get things right. It all came down to one critical principle: accurate measurement. "Pat understood something that nobody else did at that time," says Davidson. "He understood how difficult it is to make accurate measurements at parts per billion. Contamination was so ubiquitous, lead was so ubiquitous—there was so doggone much of it spewed out from autos."

As Patterson said, the few capable laboratories were "like fortress sanctuaries, where we carry out experiments protected against the overwhelming presence and interference of industrial lead pollution." Furthermore, one had to know the natural background levels to make a relevant comparison. Without that, the rest of the scientific world was like a fleet of sixteenth-century explorers traveling the ocean without longitude—they were lost at sea. Unable to quantify how far they'd come, they had no way to tell how far they had to go or what really lay over the horizon.

Patterson, on the other hand, was able to apply his techniques to almost any substance. In the early 1970s, he sidetracked into anthropology and began a series of analyses on the bones of two-thousand-year-old Peruvians. After correcting for all kinds of contamination, Patterson discovered that yet again, the situation was even worse than he'd feared. Americans of the 1970s had three thousand times more lead in their bodies than prehistoric Peruvians had.

In 1972, as part of the International Decade of Ocean Exploration, a UN-sponsored research effort, the Department of Energy held a workshop at its Brookhaven Laboratory on Long Island. The conference's goal was to create a much-needed reference standard, a longitude measurement that would calibrate values of trace metals and marine organisms in the oceans of the world. Various laboratories had been assigned different metals and organisms and provided the values they had found. Patterson arrived on the second day, straight from the Grinnell graduation of one of his children and carrying only an umbrella. "He looked bemused and wasn't saying very much," says Bill Fitzgerald, a marine scientist at the University of Connecticut.

The group listened attentively as the leader ran through the new standard values for different metals. "The leader would give off the value, and people would make their notes of what it was," says Fitzgerald. "He came down to lead. The guy who was leading it, you could see his face change. Pat could just stop everything. He wanted to know who made the measurements." It turned out to be one of the few scientists Patterson respected. "That's fine," Patterson said and sat back in his chair. The relief in the room was palpable. By meeting's end, however, Patterson had persuaded the group to let him conduct an interlaboratory calibration in which participating groups would test themselves against him.

### Southern California Bight, 1976

In time, Patterson had come to realize that even his own data on seawater didn't meet his standards. His earliest measurements, taken with Chow and Tatsumoto, had been instrumental in his understanding of lead pollution. But he had not properly accounted for contamination from the ship. So in 1976 he returned to the sea.

He now had a German graduate student named Bernhard Schaule to help him. Schaule was a doctoral student in nuclear physics who had studied lead in seawater for his master's thesis and had come up against contamination problems. He came to work with Patterson to learn how to do it right. "I was a perfectionist, too, so we got along," Schaule says.

Working from a sketch Patterson had drawn, Schaule labored in Caltech's machine shop to develop a contamination-free deepwater sampler. It consisted of a cylinder that formed a protective shell for acid-cleaned sample bags that held ten liters of water; all of it inside a frame that could be hung from a track or set on legs so that it never touched the ship or lab floor directly. It hung from the end of a hydrowire and had a protective cup on a mechanical arm that covered the intake piston and wasn't removed until the sampler was moving downward deep in uncontaminated waters.

Patterson and Schaule joined forces with Ken Bruland, who was then a new assistant professor at the University of California, Santa Cruz. Bruland had done his graduate work with Patterson's friend Ed Goldberg at Scripps and was working on methods for collecting clean samples of zinc, iron, cadmium, copper, nickel, and manganese. Even better, he had a "clean van," a mobile laboratory that met Patterson's stringent standards. In February 1976, Bruland got a few days of ship time off of Los Angeles on the research vessel *Cayeuse* and invited Patterson and Schaule to join him.

The two drove to the dock from Caltech with their precious sampler. It would be the device's first real test and would provide Patterson with his first absolutely accurate measurement of lead in the seawater. (Bruland had deep respect for Patterson and shared his determination to make proper measurements, but for his own purposes, he worked with manufacturing companies to develop plastic bottles and hydrowire that he felt got the same result. "Pat didn't think any company could do it as well as he could," says Bruland, whose bottles are the routine equipment today.)

The *Cayeuse,* an Indian word for wild mustang, was aptly named. "The winds were blowing pretty good, up to forty-five knots," says Bruland. "It got really rough in a hurry. It was one of those times when I was ready to swear off oceanography to become a limnologist [and study lakes and ponds]." Patterson got so violently seasick that he took to his bunk. Schaule wasn't much better off. "I had this brand-new clean van, and Bernhard was throwing up all over," says Bruland. Then Bruland was called to Patterson's bunk, where he found the senior scientist seriously ill. "It got so bad that Pat was down there shaking. I brought the captain to see him, and the captain said we should go back. Pat heard that and grabbed my wrist with his fingers. He said: 'Ken, you've got to promise me that we're going to get this sample. This sample is more important than my life.'" Reluctantly, Bruland followed Pat's wishes. They got the sample.

Bruland and Schaule also commanded a rubber raft to collect surface samples. That operation required one man to row against the current upwind of the ship and the other to lean over the bow and push sample bottles under the surface of the ocean. As soon as possible, they turned back for shore. An ambulance was waiting, summoned by the captain, but Patterson furiously refused medical attention. "He grabbed Bernhard and the sampler and wanted to take it back to Caltech right away," says Bruland.

That particular measurement shows up as "Station 42" in a 1981 paper that Patterson and Schaule published documenting their new values for lead in the ocean. With the new sampler, they got lead concentrations that were a hundredfold lower than the values Patterson had established with Chow and Tatsumoto. But the pattern they had observed earlier held: upper water layers held large excesses of lead; deeper waters had extremely low concentrations. As they examined the new values, Pat told Schaule: "OK, on the scale of this plot of our new data, Tatsumoto's and my earlier values are indeed located out the door of this room and part way down the hall. But remember and be prepared. In earlier years, on this same plot scale, older values for lead in seawater found by all previous investigators are located out of this building and then way across to the other side of the campus! Those guys are the type who will be evaluating our findings, and few, if any, will believe them worthy, because earlier they found it difficult to accept even the down-the-hall data!"

But in that one respect Patterson was wrong. The rest of the oceanographic world did heed his findings. Before 1975, the field of trace element chemistry in the oceans was "a hodgepodge that didn't make any sense," says Bruland. Measurements were all over the place. "People didn't realize that they had to take such precautions and that the concentrations were so low. They didn't realize the importance of collecting uncontaminated samples." Simultaneously, there was a revolution in sensitive analytical methods that made measurements of such low concentrations possible. "Patterson was a key contributor to the revolution," says Bruland. "We went from none of the data being any good to all of a sudden a beautiful picture of getting oceanographically consistent distribution or profiles. Everything made sense."

Once they had that picture, Patterson's early vision of the implications of his early lead measurements in the ocean was borne out. The new measurements showed the highest levels of lead in the North Atlantic, which received the brunt of the contamination from the United States and Europe. There was also contamination in the North Pacific. "The oceans gave us a great picture of how we had contaminated our globe, our Earth," says Bruland. "Oceans cover 70 percent of our Earth and here we had contamination to that degree."

What of the marine organisms, the other focus of the baseline project? Using an albacore tuna caught off the coast of Southern California in 1971, Patterson set up a test. He and Dorothy Settle prepared samples from the same fish and sent them to several other labs for analysis. For reference, they also sent a piece of leaf and a sample of cow's liver. The results were not encouraging. Everyone got the same value for the leaf: 44 parts per million. For the cow's liver, half got it right at 0.3 parts per million, while the rest said the value was below their ability to measure. For the tuna, about half said it was below their ability to measure, and the others gave values that were an order of magnitude too high.

Patterson's own results showed just what a difference accurate measurement made. He and Settle found there was far less lead in tuna than previous labs had shown. On the skin, they measured about 2 parts per million. When they measured the tuna muscle, the edible inside of the fish, it had a lead concentration of only 0.0003 parts per million. This vanishingly small amount of lead was significant primarily for what it then revealed about contamination. Once it had been through the processing plant, the tuna contained four hundred times more lead than when it was caught; after it was canned, it had a thousand times more lead. Other labs were measuring not natural lead in the tuna, but contamination.

When Settle and Patterson followed up with more studies on albacore a few years later, they went further. They now estimated that canned tuna sold in America in the 1970s contained ten thousand times the lead of its noncanned preindustrial ancestors. Furthermore, Patterson lambasted the Food and Drug Administration's technical abilities. Because the FDA laboratory had erroneously reported average lead concentrations in fresh tuna, it underestimated the level of contamination in canned tuna. Clearly, the agency believed the distance between "average" and "contaminated" wasn't so great.

When their work was published in *Science,* Patterson and Settle made national news with the results. So many inquiries flooded in they finally drew up a sheet of instructions on how to tell a lead-soldered can from a welded can. But Patterson still didn't know how to deliver a sound bite. CBS's science reporter wanted to interview him. "I was walking into his office, and he was yelling profanities into the phone," says Russ Flegal, who was a new researcher in Patterson's lab at the time. "He wanted an hour, not five minutes."

Long or short, his message got through. One of Patterson's major contributions to science was to train others to do the job as well as he did. "He spread the skills," says Bernhard Schaule. And he created a band of worshipful acolytes who followed in his acid-cleaned, plastic-slippered footsteps. "I spent a long time in Pat's lab on hands and knees cleaning up every speck of dust and working with acid to make sure there was no buildup," says Davidson, who went on to build a "carbon-copy" clean lab at Carnegie Mellon despite workers who told him it couldn't be done.

Many others were converted to Patterson's way of thinking and became equally zealous in their pursuit of the perfect clean lab. Although he had first met Patterson in Woods Hole in 1963, Bill Fitzgerald really got to know him at the 1972 International Decade of Ocean Exploration Baseline Conference at Brookhaven. At that time, Fitzgerald was so disillusioned with the state of science he was on the verge of giving up chemistry for medicine. Patterson relit the fires of Fitzgerald's scientific passion. "He was a hero," says Fitzgerald. "He reinvigorated me. I saw a person who was uncompromised, dedicated, and wanted to do things right. I decided I wanted to do work as well as he did, and I had to get a clean lab." The lab he built at the University of Connecticut helped him do for mercury measurements what Patterson had done for lead.

The range of Patterson's work was unusual. He measured lead in a wide variety of materials: bones, seawater, ice, tuna, and mice. Usually, his students were expert in only one area, but they quickly learned that the whole was greater than the parts. Schaule, the nuclear physicist who came to Pasadena to measure lead in seawater, found himself calling around Los Angeles one day to find bait with which to catch weasels in Thompson Canyon (they never did catch a weasel and settled for the pine martens). "It was unusual stuff that without wavering you just had to do," says Schaule. "Pat had a comprehensive vision of how things are linked. He steered his coworkers toward getting the complete story together."

In addition to criticizing everyone else's ability to measure correctly, Patterson did violence to one of the orthodoxies of science. He maintained that one good measurement was worth more than a thousand mediocre measurements. Given that it took him months just to clean his lab, sometimes one measurement was all Patterson had. Like Patterson, geochemist Jerome Nriagu studied the cycle of lead or its pathways through the environment. He first saw Patterson in the early 1970s at a geochemistry conference at which Patterson was defending himself as usual. "People who had published the wrong results didn't want to be told their numbers were wrong," says Nriagu. "Clair has his way of looking at things and usually a very strong opinion of his results. He was not very diplomatic, and he could turn a few people off that way. He didn't really have a lot of data either; most of it was based on conjecture. It takes a special genius to put yourself out on a limb with no data."

The lengths to which Patterson would go could leave people speechless. In the late 1970s, Patterson and Davidson, who was by then at Carnegie Mellon, were part of a new research project in Greenland. At one of the planning meetings, Patterson made his priorities clear. The group was planning to drill two miles through the ice to bedrock, collect samples, and then analyze them. They were discussing which drilling fluid to use. "The drill is going to burn up if you don't have a drilling fluid that is also a lubricant," said one of the drilling experts on hand. Then he added: "But the best lubricant is a really bad actor." That was because the lubricant was a highly toxic organic solvent. The drilling expert didn't know or care much about the environment or pollution, but said he wouldn't recommend that lubricant at all. "I wouldn't want to be anywhere near barrels of this stuff," he said.

It became clear, however, that this dangerous lubricant was as free of lead and metal as any lubricant could be. "I noticed Patterson sitting and listening to this conversation about which we should get," says Davidson. All of a sudden, Patterson stood up, and banged his fist on the table. "What are you all talking about!" Patterson exclaimed. "If you guys are not willing to give your lives up for science, then I'm not in this project. I give my life for science." Then he sat down.

"Even today, people talk about that moment when Pat stood up," says Davidson. Though Davidson still wrestles with how to respond to Patterson's demand (after all, he wasn't even thirty at the time and had a lot of life left to live), he appreciated what it meant for his mentor: nothing was more important than basic science and finding the truth. The others, however, thought Patterson's suggestion was folly. They chose the less dangerous lubricant. Anyway, says Davidson of the purer lubricant, "we would never have got permission to load it on the C-130s."

At every opportunity, Patterson delivered his message about the importance of accurate measurement. He hammered away at government, for which he was developing even less respect than he had for industry, if such a thing was possible. Industry, at least, was efficient in achieving its capitalistic goals, he maintained. Government could not say the same.

In May 1974, Patterson sent a raft of letters on the issue of accurate measurement and poor laboratory quality to the National Science Foundation, the Environmental Protection Agency, and his old ally Senator Edmund Muskie. He wrote to Muskie: "The health hazards associated with the burning of leaded gasolines now appears far more serious than had been previously supposed, and it appears that meaningful steps should be taken to reduce the manufacture of lead alkyls to zero levels as expeditiously as possible." Little progress could be made, however, argued Patterson, until the EPA was able to measure parts per million as well as Caltech did. It was "urgent" that the situation be changed and that money be found to improve the government's labs.

He said more of the same when he testified at the House of Representatives again in 1975. There were not as many fireworks as in 1966 when he took on Kehoe and company, but he still didn't mince words.

> This problem has been with us for more than 4,000 years . . . within the last fifty years half of all the lead which has ever been mined has been produced by man. . . .
>
> It so happens that these activities of man have resulted in a severe contamination and pollution of the entire earth. . . .
>
> Lead in the atmosphere today is about 500 times greater than that which existed in prehistoric times. . . .
>
> You should recognize that the average person's exposure can only be increased further by a very small amount, no more than a factor of five, before we will then exhibit symptoms of classical lead poisoning. . . .
>
> Trace metal concentration data [from other laboratories] . . . are erroneous and misleading. . . .
>
> The attitude at present . . . is that there are not sufficient funds to build the kind of hospital operating room type laboratories that

are needed. . . . [Other researchers] believe they can only deal with levels of metals [that] are overtly toxic. Then we go round and round when I try to explain that we are already at toxic levels.

## WASHINGTON, D.C., 1978

It was a hot August day when Clair Patterson opened the door of the office building at 2100 Pennsylvania Avenue and went into his first meeting for the National Research Council of the National Academy of Sciences. Finally, he was on the inside. He still refused membership in the academy, but he had accepted an invitation to be on its newly formed Lead in the Human Environment committee, which had been assigned to revisit the issue of lead and update the academy's flawed 1971 report. The pace of activity on lead regulation had steadily increased through the 1970s. Now the Department of Housing and Urban Development was asking the academy for a definitive report, mostly in hopes that it would pin some blame on gasoline and take a bit of pressure off HUD's lead paint abatement efforts.

"The read we got on Patterson was that he was an excellent scientist, had a terrific mind, but was not a committee person in any way," says Ned Groth, who coordinated the committee and report for the National Academy of Sciences. Academy officials were warned that Patterson would be "abrasive and disruptive," but as Groth saw it, the main criticism of the previous report was that Clair Patterson wasn't on the committee. This time, they would have Patterson and would try to ensure a balanced representation of views. "The unspoken knowledge is that no one is unbiased," says Groth. "The goal is to have the biases cancel each other out." For instance, Cliff Davidson, who at twenty-eight was already well respected, was included in part for his scientific ability and in part because he was considered "an environmentalist." Jerome Nriagu, Patterson's friend, was also on the committee. Closely allied to industry were Emil Pfitzer, who was a toxicologist in the pharmaceutical industry, and Lloyd Tepper, who was by then the medical director of a Pennsylvania chemical company but had spent years as a researcher in the Kettering Laboratory with Robert Kehoe.

Patterson's friends were amused to think of him working from the inside out. One sent him a mock press release in which Patterson announces to Washington that the making of lead was the original sin: "It was not the apple after all, that caused the fall!" said the headline. Patterson knew how to take a joke. He wrote back: "You are more perceptive than you may think..." And he enclosed a *B.C.* comic strip in which a prehistoric man stands on a pedestal engraved TRUTH and intones "Wisdom is gained through the experience of mistakes." To which the audience responds: "Remind us never to ask you up there again."

At the very first meeting, Patterson made his presence felt. Committee Chairman Ben Ewing of the University of Illinois had taken the unusual step of granting him the opportunity to make a presentation on the issue of natural lead levels. Patterson laid out his view that underlying most work on lead were "erroneous assumptions" such as that lead in most people is normal or that lead can be readily and accurately analyzed. He reviewed the work of his Caltech group in detail and said the committee must upend the old assumptions if it had any hope of producing a useful report. In response, it was immediately clear who some of Patterson's antagonists would be. Geochemist Nord Gale said the committee should focus on lead levels that had already been proved toxic. Tepper repeated his old boss Kehoe's view that although Patterson was a respected geochemist, he didn't know much about biology and shouldn't presume expertise in that field.

The second committee meeting was an exhaustive workshop on all the issues of lead. Experts of all stripes were brought in, including T. J. Chow, Herb Needleman, Phil Landrigan, and David Schoenbrod on one side and Julian Chisholm and DuPont's Emmett Jacobs on the other side. As usual, they disagreed. Chisholm, for example, emphasized that much research remained to be done, that it was not yet known whether any neurological effects were permanent, and that living conditions in some areas presented near-insurmountable obstacles to minimizing the presence of environmental lead. It was "unrealistic," he said, to think that children in the inner city could achieve average blood lead levels below 40 micrograms.

Needleman followed Chisholm and began by saying that although his remarks might sound "polemical," he felt they were supported by the facts. "We have enough data to act effectively now," he said. In his view, the argument had developed into a classic passing of blame: "The tetraethyl lead producers blame the paint in old housing; the Department of HUD blames lead in auto exhaust; and the paint manufacturers blame historic, not current, use of leaded paints." It was not an 'either-or' situation, said Needleman. "Children are in the middle, exposed to all sources.... Judgments will always have to be made on imperfect knowledge." (As if to buttress Needleman's blame-shifting argument, Ethyl Corporation's Gary Ter Haar wrote to Ned Groth after the workshop to literally list the comments of the many panelists who cited paint as the most important danger for children. Ter Haar left out the fact that many of those same panelists also mentioned the hazards of leaded gasoline.)

At this conference and several that had come before, Patterson and Needleman had found in each other kindred spirits. When he first heard Patterson speak, a few years earlier, Needleman admits, "I thought he was so extreme. I believed lead was bad for you but not that bad." Needleman, however, was edging closer to Patterson's lead-soaked view of the world. By 1979, Patterson singled Needleman out among the medical experts as "a friend." He was happy to see him at the workshop, and glad to meet some of Needleman's allies, such as Schoenbrod.

But Patterson wasn't happy with the overall results of the workshop. In his view, the committee was already moving in the wrong direction by failing to structure the planned report around the issue of natural lead levels. Month after month, as the process wore on, he became more and more disgruntled. At meetings, Patterson paced around the room, waved his arms for emphasis, and got worked up over disagreements. During lunch breaks, he would not eat with the rest of the group.

The feeling was mutual for some. Kathryn Mahaffey, then a thirty-four-year-old toxicologist responsible for the FDA's program addressing lead contamination in food, found Patterson impossible to work with and thought his personality limited his effectiveness. They disagreed about the concentration of lead in the blood that would bring on adverse health effects: he thought it necessary to get to zero; she thought that position extreme. Mahaffey believed that an inordinate concern with levels too low to be achieved would discredit the report. "He had a lot of techniques to dismiss people he did not agree with," she says. "During one meeting, he was losing an argument with me, and he started addressing me as 'honey.'" Her response was: "You have a choice. You can call me Kathryn. You can call me Dr. Mahaffey, or just plain Doctor. But you cannot call me 'honey.'"

The explosion came in April 1979 when the committee discussed Patterson's draft section on natural and background levels of lead. The information was important and useful, the committee agreed, but the draft was too long, too detailed, and too extreme. Emil Pfitzer suggested making the material part of the appendix. Others suggested condensing it. Deeply insulted, Patterson retreated to his room and drafted an angry reply in cramped handwriting on the only available source: the inside of the manila folder that held his meeting papers. It began with the word *Compromises*—underlined—and went on to express how "deeply opposed" he was to the planned "rational" approach to the report:

> The basic question that I felt should have been dealt with was: How did it happen that we disperse 2 million tons of a toxic substance into our environment annually that is accumulating in our cities, has contaminated our bodies, and will destroy lives in amounts that are almost too small to see? I wanted to delineate what is known about the historical development of the problem and the circumstantial factors that caused it.
>
> I compromised here in a very profound way and quietly accepted the rational approach scheme because I thought in exchange for this a basically important concept would be explained in the report; namely, that natural levels of lead in humans and their environment were very much lower than existing levels.

After impatiently detailing past failures of a "rational" approach, which in his view had allowed workers to be poisoned by lead and allowed tetraethyl to be put into gasoline, he insisted that he be allowed to break away from the group and, with staff support from Groth, write his own report. "I will not compromise and allow this section to be relegated to an appendix."

That night, Patterson had dinner with Jerome Nriagu. He wanted Nriagu and Davidson to join him in his separate report. The two considered it, but both felt that there wasn't enough time. Nor did they think the committee's report would be the abomination that Patterson predicted. The next morning, Patterson had a hasty meeting with Ned Groth and Ben Ewing. In vain, they tried to talk him out of leaving, but Patterson didn't attend another meeting. A few weeks later, he drew on Henry David Thoreau in a letter to Ewing about the interplay in science between established ideas and pioneering concepts: "In science, one investigator who is right in the midst of many who are wrong constitutes a majority of one."

When the final report was issued—after months of delay waiting for Patterson—the committee list included an asterisk next to Clair Patterson's name. "*Dr. Patterson does not wish to be associated with this report." The main report begins with a favorite industry line: "Lead, a useful but toxic metal, is an integral part of the economy of the United States." Nonetheless, the committee had come a long way from the 1971 "whitewash" that claimed there was no harm from lead. It included many of Patterson's findings and distinguished between "typical" and "natural" levels of lead. In a measured tone, it called for action in several areas despite imprecise scientific knowledge: general reduction of exposure, expanded efforts to identify at-risk children and to remove lead paint, improvement of measurement capabilities, and further study on all fronts.

Patterson's chapter, which came at the end, was called "An Alternative Perspective." It included a note from Cliff Davidson and Jerome Nriagu saying that joint authorship was not feasible, but that they endorsed "most" of Patterson's ideas. The chapter offered all the strengths and weaknesses of Clair Patterson. He wasted no time on notions of usefulness and began: "Sometime in the near future it probably will be shown that the older urban areas of the United States have been rendered more or less uninhabitable by the millions of tons of poisonous industrial lead residues that have accumulated in the cities during the past century." Then he dismissed the long discussion of controls of various exposures that had filled the preceding pages. There was only one solution: Get rid of the lead industry entirely. "The mining and smelting of lead and dispersal of manufactured leaded products within the human environment is actually a monumental crime committed by humanity against itself." Get rid of the engineers, too, he said, for they are the ones who can't see the big picture and the necessity of dismantling an industry to which they are closely tied.

Such radical statements wouldn't win over anyone who disagreed with him, but the formidable marshaling of evidence that followed had prosecutorial power. He included what would become a famous image. Known as the "measles" picture, it showed three human torsos in outline and compared relative levels of lead body burden in dots, each of which represented three micrograms per seventy kilograms of body weight. The figure on the left was "natural" man; he had one dot in the middle of his belly. In the middle, the "typical" man for 1970s America had five hundred dots and what looked like a bad case of chicken pox. On the right, a poisoned figure had two thousand dots; he was awash in black, as full of dots as a pointillist painting. Lead isotopes, lab contamination, polar ice cores, seawater samples, meadow mice, canned tuna, ancient Peruvians—they were all mentioned.

Patterson had been absorbing such evidence for nearly twenty years. When he tried to tell the world what he'd found, he felt as if he hadn't left his soundproof office: no one could hear him. The alternative perspective amounted to Patterson's attempt to yell as loudly as he could the inevitable question: How could we have done such a thing to ourselves?

CHAPTER SIX

# *Reluctant to Relent*

CALTECH, 1980

"Put these on." Clair Patterson handed Herb Needleman a plastic gown, cap, and shoe covers. Patterson slid his own feet into a pair of old slippers that he called "my lead-free shoes." They were on the third floor of Mudd, the building that was home to Caltech's geology department, where Patterson now had both his office and his lab. Needleman had come to Los Angeles for a meeting, and Patterson had invited him to lunch.

But first, Patterson gave Needleman a tour of his clean lab. Dressed in the protective clothing, they entered the lab through the antechamber. Inside, Patterson described the water and air filtration systems he had built. He showed Needleman the hoods under which he and his colleagues did much of their work. In truth, it didn't look all that special with its epoxy floor and utilitarian wood cupboards. There wasn't a lot of fancy instrumentation. (The mass spectrometer was in the basement, with bird droppings taped to the side to remind users of the fallibility of machines.) "Part of it looked like an ordinary chemistry lab," remembers Needleman. Patterson was used to that reaction. Visitors envisioned a gleaming high-tech wonder, and most were disappointed. "It ain't how it looks that counts," was his stock response.

Needleman knew as well as anyone the quality of the work that went on here. While collecting teeth from Chelsea and Somerville, he had asked Patterson to run an analysis on some of them as a reference. "Herb, do you know what it costs me?" said Patterson. In the end, they agreed that the amounts Needleman was measuring weren't small enough to require Patterson's level of precision.

Although they hadn't collaborated in the laboratory, they were now allies in a larger sense. Needleman's 1979 study had made national news just as Patterson's work had in the 1960s. Patterson had shown that the extent of lead pollution was unnatural; Needleman had shown how harmful that lead was to children's brains. Patterson was pleased that Needleman's work had helped put a human face on his own findings. In previous letters to Needleman, Patterson had called his work as well as that of Shapiro and Piomelli "outstanding" and expressed the hope that it would lead to the elimination of childhood lead poisoning.

Now the two men, on opposite coasts and in ostensibly unrelated fields of study, had become a scientific one-two punch on lead. Though they weren't the only people studying lead, the importance of their work and the insistence of their voices put them in the center of the nation's conversation on the subject. In national newspapers and magazines, on radio broadcasts, they echoed one another. "Why does the problem of lead continue to be debated?" Needleman asked in one article, just a few months before his visit to Pasadena. A few paragraphs later, the same reporter quoted Patterson: "It is intrinsically wrong to mine and smelt millions of tons of a highly toxic, poisonous substance such as lead each year and disperse it within human environments."

The lead industry didn't like Needleman's message any more than it had Patterson's. Needleman was emblematic of the new generation of scientists formed by the environmental movement and politics of the '60s and '70s. This generation questioned authority and had a fundamentally different view of toxicity than its predecessors. As historian Samuel Hays noted: "Sharply different political positions were maintained between those scientists associated with industry who demanded high levels of proof before action and those who argued that reasonable inferences based on new knowledge provided a sound basis for a regulation."

Clearly, industry's old strategy of controlling the science was no longer working. So industry was developing a new one: attack the science and the scientists. In a letter to the *New York Times,* Jerome Cole, who worked for both the Lead Industries Association and its offshoot, the International Lead Zinc Research Organization, called Needleman's study "flawed and irrelevant." In no way, argued Cole, did the study prove that lead in gasoline posed a health hazard. Cole and others regularly maintained that Needleman was an antilead fanatic who couldn't be trusted; they viewed environmentalists in general and the public who supported them as emotional and prone to overreaction.

Ethyl Corporation's Gary Ter Haar was less personally dismissive (he even found Needleman "gracious" on occasion) but no more persuaded by his work. "Needleman was strongly of the view that very slight differences of concentrations had effects on children," says Ter Haar, who headed Ethyl's health division after years in the company's chemistry laboratory. "We had enormous numbers of people working in our lead plants with levels in the forties and fifties. The evidence from our workforce was that as long as blood leads were held under 80, we didn't have any health effects in workers. I think [Needleman was] absolutely wrong." Of course, Ethyl's workers were adults, not growing children, and they weren't being tested for subtle changes.

When Needleman and Patterson were together, they compared notes. After the tour of the lab, over lunch at the Athenaeum, Caltech's faculty club, they talked about lead and the fine points of research methodology. But they didn't agree on everything and could be combative even with each other.

"We have to ban lead mining and extraction entirely," Patterson said, repeating the solution he now proposed regularly.

"Pat, that's extreme," Needleman replied.

"Herb, it's a crime," Patterson insisted.

Patterson was emphatic and grew agitated when he couldn't convince Needleman on this point. But it was "a minor tiff," says Needleman, and they were friendly again as they walked back across campus. The strong June sun lit up the pale yellow walls of the Moorish buildings on Caltech's campus. Patterson pointed out a dorm room window. "See that room there? The student who lived there had a hi-fi, and I used to stand under his window and shout at him: 'Turn it down, you bastard!'" Needleman laughed. It wasn't hard to picture Patterson carrying on in the courtyard.

After his trip, Needleman sent Patterson a note of thanks. In a nod to their new bond, he wrote, "Now when somebody calls me an 'environmental extremist' you can defend me, as I do when they call you a 'nut.'"

Like Patterson, Needleman was always looking to add to his evidence. The work in Somerville and Chelsea had broken new ground, but much remained unknown. The battle over the 1978 criteria document had persuaded everyone involved of the need for unassailable epidemiological studies. Needleman was one of the first of several researchers around the world to plan a prospective study that would follow children over several years measuring their lead levels and their cognitive development.

To help him, Needleman hired a young psychologist named David Bellinger. A mild man with a full beard and glasses, Bellinger had just finished a postdoctorate fellowship at Boston University. The two men hit it off from the start. They spent the interview discussing Needleman's newly published *New England Journal* study and a recent article in *Science* on "the nefarious workings of the tobacco industry," remembers Bellinger. "It was the best interview I ever had." Even so, he thought that the lead study was going to be his day job and that he would eventually return to his primary interest, psycholinguistics.

Needleman's energy and engagement in lead, in politics, and in the wider world proved inspiring and infectious. Keeping up was demanding. "One of the assistants told me she always had to be sure to read the newspaper when she [would be working] with Herb," says Bellinger with a laugh. At lunch in the Children's Hospital cafeteria, Needleman introduced Bellinger to a wide range of physicians, most of whose work he knew well. Clearly, he fit in much better here than at Temple. And once, when Bellinger was working in the library, he found an issue of *Pediatrics* in which a doctor who had trained at Harvard attributed one of his most valuable lessons to Needleman's teaching. "He said that when trainees were presenting cases to Herb, they would be going through the history and so on, and Herb would say: 'What does the child look like?' Usually the trainee had no idea," says Bellinger. "Herb was really concerned about the whole person, not just numbers on a page." Soon Bellinger had a new sense of purpose. "It was so exciting to work with him. I found that I loved the environmental work," he says. In his quieter way, Bellinger, who is still at Harvard, has since become one of the leaders in the field in his own right.

In the prospective study, known as the Boston Study, Needleman and Bellinger followed 249 children from birth. Their first round of funding from NIH allowed for two years of work. They recruited women who had just given birth at Brigham and Women's Hospital. Based on lead levels in umbilical cord blood, the subjects were sorted into low-, middle-, or high-lead groups. These were relative terms. In this reasonably affluent and educated population, low lead equaled less than three micrograms per deciliter, and high was ten micrograms or higher. With umbilical cord blood as the starting point, they would then periodically measure blood lead levels and development, using the Bayley Scales for Infant Development in the early years and age-appropriate IQ tests as the children got older. In the first two years, they did evaluations every six months.

By its nature, the prospective study was a long-term project. But their early results were striking. As with Needleman's previous study, the data analysis was done on the big computers at the Harvard School of Public Health. "We were flipping through the printouts, and there was an inverse relationship between cord blood and development at six months," says Bellinger. "At that time, the CDC guideline was thirty micrograms per deciliter of blood and our high group was above ten. We thought we were well into the safe zone. No one had ever shown an effect at such low levels."

• • •

Needleman was getting noticed at Harvard, and new invitations came his way. One was from the university's dean of development, who was holding a dinner at Boston's St. Botolph Club, an elite haven for Boston's leaders of which John Quincy Adams was the first chairman. "It was very swanky," says Needleman. "All the stars of Harvard Medical School were there." They washed down the shrimp, lobster, and rack of lamb with expensive French wine. As Needleman remembers it, around 10 p.m., the dean rose to speak. He began with a story. The president of MIT and the president of Standard Oil found themselves sitting next to each other in the first-class section of a plane flying across the country, said the dean. Their conversation turned to research. Both agreed that pollution was here to stay. Wasn't it time, they said to each other, that the best scientists in the country focus not on getting rid of pollution but on studying ways to make the host, the human body, more resistant to environmental toxicants? Industry was willing to put substantial amounts of money into such work.

"One by one," says Needleman, "these stars got up and said this was the way of the future, that they had to work with the oil industry." He couldn't quite believe what he was hearing and began to feel very uncomfortable. Mindful that he did not yet have tenure, Needleman says, "I kept telling myself to shut up. I knew if I spoke up, I'd pay for it. But if I didn't, I'd pay for it in other ways. It would haunt me. One has to live with oneself." He raised his hand and stood. "I depend on research support and hustle grants as much as anyone here, but what I've heard tonight goes against the grain of one hundred years of public health history," he said. "The first step in dealing with environmental toxicants is to stop their production; the second is to build barriers between the toxicant and the host; and, finally, when those two have been accomplished, to strengthen the resistance of the host to the agent."

He sat down to silence. Then an epidemiology professor said that he'd been in on the funding discussions and that they involved not just millions of dollars but hundreds of millions. Finally, one pathologist spoke up in Needleman's defense: "We should listen to what

Herb said," she suggested. But if anyone else was so inclined, he or she didn't say so.

The question of funding was never far from Needleman's mind. His research money had always come from the federal government; he believed that that was the only way to avoid the conflicts of interest inherent in industry money. "Science is hard to do even if it is uncluttered by this other stuff," he says. Others argue that without corporate money there wouldn't be enough funding to go around, that such support helps research proceed faster and speeds its application, that it boosts the economy. The risk, however, lies in the cost in independence to the researchers who accept it.

"Gifts, grants and contracts do not come to universities without some benefit to the corporate donors," argues Sheldon Krimsky in his book *Science in the Private Interest.* Furthermore, corporations are most interested in knowledge that serves their private, commercial interests rather than broader knowledge that serves the public. Clair Patterson's need to show how his basic research would help find oil is an example. Another is the fact that it is generally harder to get funding for work that looks at environmental causes of cancer rather than cellular or genetic causes; the latter might result in a valuable treatment, but there's little for companies to gain from the former—and plenty to lose for those who may be contributing to environmental pollution.

Historically, the country has tacked back and forth on this issue. Robert Kehoe's Kettering Laboratory was a prime example of the cozy relationship between research and industry in the first half of the century. But by the 1960s, Americans were uncomfortable with that arrangement and distrustful of its results. By 1965, no less than 60 percent of all research and development in the United States was financed by the federal government, with the bulk of the money coming from the National Science Foundation and the newly created National Institutes of Health. Today, the pendulum has swung back the other way. Private interests fund 65 percent of research and development. To what effect? Health policy expert Lisa Bero of the University of California San Francisco has done extensive research on the quality of industry-funded research. She found that researchers with industry ties were 88 times more likely to find no harm from secondhand smoke. In studies comparing the efficacy of cholesterol drugs, work funded by drug companies was twenty times more likely to favor the drug of the sponsor.

Corporate funding was not the only issue on which Needleman was at odds with his Harvard colleagues. He had disagreements with two members of his research team, psychologist Charles "Tink" Gunnoe and toxicologist Phyllis Mullenix, who was doing animal research under Needleman's NIH grant. "Herb does come on strong, and he doesn't suffer fools gladly," says Leviton. "There comes a point where he feels 'Enough. I cannot continue to work with this person.'" Both Gunnoe and Mullenix left, but they had allies in the psychiatry department, and their departures tarnished Needleman's star.

By 1981, Needleman realized that he never would get tenure at Harvard. "They drummed me out," he says. Leviton agrees with that interpretation. "My feeling was that he wasn't treated well and that what he was pushed out for didn't warrant it." Around the time of this realization, Needleman got a call from Thomas Detre, then head of the Western Psychiatric Institute and chairman of the Department of Psychiatry at the University of Pittsburgh Medical Center. "He told me the streets were paved with gold," says Needleman. At Pittsburgh, he thought he would get tenure quickly and carry on his lead research.

He and Roberta moved Josh and Sara, then in high school, to western Pennsylvania. Roberta, still a social worker, worked in Pittsburgh as head of social services for the Allegheny County Health Department. (Sam, his son with Shirley, had recently completed his medical training at the University of Pennsylvania and a residency at the University of Iowa.)

Before he left Harvard, Needleman had developed a cordial relationship with a psychologist named Claire Ernhart, who he thought was an ally. She was then at Hofstra University on Long Island, where she did one of the early studies on neuropsychological effects of low-level lead exposure. She and her graduate student Joseph Perino followed eighty black preschoolers in Queens, none of whom had been diagnosed with lead poisoning, and found that as lead levels increased, scores on tests of cognitive, verbal, and perceptual-performance abilities decreased. Among the controls that Perino and Ernhart imposed were controls for socioeconomic status and parental IQ. Though the study involved only a small group of children, Needleman was impressed with it. "It showed quite persuasively that lead was a bad business," he says. He cited it in his own 1979 study. At one point, when Ernhart was seeking a position at Case Western Reserve University in Ohio, she gave Needleman as a reference for the strength of her work. Later, as a tenured professor at Case Western, Ernhart sent her vitae to Needleman at Harvard and said she would like to be considered for his group. He wrote back to say that she was a bit too senior.

Ernhart had originally planned to be a social worker. "I was like other idealistic teenagers," she says. "I thought I was going to solve the problems of the world." But in her first job doing relief work for the city of Cleveland, Ohio, she found herself drawn to psychology and research. "I got interested in asking 'How do you know?'" After she earned her Ph.D. and before moving to Hofstra, she worked with psychologists at Washington University in St. Louis studying, among other things, the effects of family ideology on children. That early work would inform much of what she did later, especially her sense of the importance of home environments on children's development.

"We regarded Claire as a colleague," says Irving Shapiro, who wrote two papers with Ernhart in addition to the papers on dentine lead that he published with Needleman. That changed at a symposium on lead in Toronto in 1981. Needleman was on a panel with Jerome Nriagu, Rob Elias, Kathryn Mahaffey, Ellen Silbergeld, and Jerome Cole. After the presentations, Claire Ernhart got up from the audience. Her piercing blue eyes and large glasses gave her the appearance of an old-fashioned schoolmarm. She said she was about to publish a paper in which she followed up on the children from her study with Perino and no longer found a neuropsychological effect from lead. "I was puzzled," says Needleman. "Her '74 paper was the best one on the subject at the time."

After the Toronto conference, Ernhart did publish her follow-up study in *Pediatrics.* But she didn't limit herself to reporting her own new conclusions; she included what she considered a "carefully worded" critique of Needleman's 1979 paper. "I made comments about methodology," she says. "I thought I made them nicely and gently." Her "most serious" complaint was that Needleman and his colleagues had not adequately considered all confounding variables, though she didn't say specifically what they had left out, and she admitted that they had included the variable she considered most critical: parental IQ. She also questioned the issue of multiple comparisons, saying that with so many outcomes under consideration, the odds were that Needleman had been bound to turn up an effect somewhere just by chance. Her reanalysis of her own work actually still resulted in statistically significant effects from lead, but she dismissed those as due to "methodologic difficulties" inherent in such work.

The sum of her argument was that it would be nearly impossible to be sure that cognitive problems were caused by lead and not something else; there could never be enough proof. She tempered that conclusion with the caveat that her change of view did not amount to a call for decreasing screening programs or dismantling deregulation efforts. "Even if low to moderate levels of lead do not produce developmental deficits, they serve as warnings of exposure that can lead to the serious consequences of high lead levels."

Scientific disagreements generally play out in the letters columns of the relevant journals. Accordingly, Needleman, Leviton, and Bellinger responded with a commentary in *Pediatrics.* They argued that Ernhart had not actually shown how their study failed, that her own first study was good, that her new one still showed effects from low-level lead, and that she couldn't throw out all research on the subject. "Because real-world problems are complex, epidemiologic investigations cannot be expected to totally end debate on difficult questions," they wrote. "In the past decade a consensus has been forming, however, around one well-studied and unarguably vital question. That question is the effects of low doses of lead on brain function, and the consensus is that these lesser doses are indeed neurotoxic." Then Needleman and colleagues called the critique by Ernhart and colleagues "tendentious and incorrect."

It escalated from there. In her next letter, Ernhart was more pointedly critical and added to her list of dissatisfactions with the 1979 paper. "Research on this topic is not easy and if things can go wrong they will," she said. "Needleman and associates appear unable to see the difficulties in this area of research and cling tenaciously to a poorly supported conclusion. We can't."

Around the same time, Ernhart accepted a grant from the International Lead Zinc Research Organization, the research arm of the Lead Industries Association. The money enabled her to add lead testing to a large study on the effects of maternal alcohol use she had under way. That grant ultimately totaled $375,000 over several years and paid a substantial part of Ernhart's salary. (The March of Dimes provided much of the rest of her funding.) Needleman thought Ernhart had gone over to the other side. Although her initial critique predated her industry grant, he was highly suspicious. "She became the academician for the industry," he says.

As the debate intensified over the coming years, some of the specific issues Ernhart questioned evolved, but her basic complaint was always that Needleman's work was a poor job of statistics and that he was unwilling to admit it. Needleman and his colleagues agreed that epidemiology is an imperfect science. "Epidemiology is deceptive," says Bellinger. "It consists of a few simple-sounding principles, but the implementation can be fraught with pitfalls." Nonetheless, Needleman argued strenuously that any errors in his study didn't change the outcome: low levels of lead had a negative effect on children's brains. As Leviton put it: "Our understanding was this is proof of principle. Despite all our limitations we still saw an effect."

Needleman and Ernhart each took root in their opposing positions and could not be pulled from the ground they'd claimed. As soon as word of Ernhart's grant emerged, Needleman dismissed her as a tool of industry. She insists that she took on Needleman on her own and that her industry grant has nothing to do with it. It is clear that her view of his work is deeply held. Those on the other side of the table, however, could see no difference between her position and industry's. "She represented their view at meetings," says Paul Mushak, the toxicologist who helped to write the first EPA lead criteria document. "She sat with them and was only chummy with industry spokesmen. She would yell to high heaven that all this stuff is nonsense."

Significantly, once she did have industry funding, Ernhart stopped calling for continued regulation of lead. She began to say that Needleman's work should not be used as the basis for federal policy. "Lead is a useful metal," she says. She believes there are far worse problems afflicting inner-city children, such as poor education opportunities. If effects from low-level lead exposure exist, she says, they are small and can't be separated from issues of genetics and home environment. "That all this attention has been paid to lead is a travesty," she says. "The money should be spent on any of the other things that put a zap on these kids."

To some extent, Needleman and Ernhart were like Patterson and Kehoe: they were looking at the same evidence but interpreting it differently. Ernhart repeatedly said that if there was an effect from low levels of lead—and she could not say there wasn't—it was minimal. Needleman said if there was an effect from low levels of lead—and his work showed that there was—it was criminal. "Why do we have this?" he thought from the beginning. "This is a manmade disease."

The argument quickly got personal. Or perhaps there had been a personal element all along. Joseph Perino, coauthor of Ernhart's 1974 paper (it was his dissertation), thought highly of Ernhart at Hofstra. He was more interested in clinical work than research, but he recognized Ernhart's abilities. "She was very smart and a brilliant, exacting researcher," says Perino. But he also remembers that Ernhart was not happy about Needleman's high profile throughout the 1970s. "She was annoyed after we did our study that he seemed to be getting more of the credit," he says. She wanted their paper to be published in a medical journal rather than a psychology journal. (As noted, Needleman's early papers with Shapiro were published in the prestigious *Journal of the American Medical Association* and the *New*

*England Journal of Medicine.*) "We got rejected all over the place," says Perino. "No one wanted to hear from two psychologists." Finally, he gave up on medical journals and placed the paper in the *Journal of Learning Disabilities.* Later, Perino demurred from speaking out with Ernhart against Needleman. "I didn't agree with her. I felt that whatever was good for lowering the lead levels was a good thing."

In 1983, two years after the angry exchanges in *Pediatrics*, the stakes got higher. The EPA's first criteria document on lead had been published in 1978. Since a new document was required every five years, the next one was due. The EPA faced a difficult situation. Two respected researchers were making opposite claims. One said there was an effect from lead; the other said there wasn't. Each criticized the other's work. "There wasn't a hell of a lot of other work out there to rely on," says Mushak.

Two other recent studies were also being hotly contested at the time. Industry was actively promoting new research from Germany that claimed to show a critical role for low levels of lead in the body—the very issue of essentiality that had so infuriated Sergio Piomelli. In addition, there was a significant piece of new information from the CDC.

At the request of Kathryn Mahaffey, then at the FDA, the CDC had included blood lead levels in its second National Health and Nutrition Examination Survey. From 1976 through 1980, CDC researchers had sampled more than twenty-seven thousand Americans between the ages of six months and seventy-four years. When the results came back, the analysts thought there was a mistake. Blood lead levels had moved steadily downward each year of the study; overall, the mean had dropped 36.7 percent. After ruling out error in the lab, they concluded there must really be a significant downward trend nationally. (The data nonetheless indicated that even though levels were falling, 9 percent of preschoolers, or 1.5 million children, had lead levels over 25 micrograms, and among black preschool children the rate was 24.5 percent.)

But why had the levels dropped? Together with EPA analyst Joel

Schwartz, who had data on the monthly amounts of lead used in gasoline, the CDC created a striking graph. In six-month increments across the four years, the graph compared average blood lead levels from the study with total lead used in thousands of tons. From a high of about 190,000 tons of lead early in 1976 and an average blood lead of about 15 micrograms, the two plotted lines stay in remarkable sync, moving slowly down, then briefly up again until late 1978 when regulations tightened. At that point, as if they were riding in the same car on a roller-coaster, the two lines plunged downward together. In just over a year, they dropped to 90,000 thousand tons of lead and an average blood lead level just below 10 micrograms. As EPA met to begin its deliberations, these results were about to be published.

Lester Grant had left academia to head the EPA's criteria document office full time. It fell to him and his staff, which included Patterson's protégé Rob Elias, to referee the debate. They began with what was now their standard operating procedure: a workshop at which to review the latest science. Needleman and Ernhart were both invited. The premise that the science was unclear worked to industry's advantage. "They were trying to create an alternate reality that lead wasn't really such a problem," says Mahaffey. "We ended up with dueling experts."

The sides were clearly drawn. The meeting room was set up with a large rectangular table. On one side, Needleman sat among allies such as Ellen Silbergeld, who marshaled the evidence from animal studies, and Phil Landrigan, who describes his role as "tactician." Ernhart sat opposite them with Julian Chisholm, Jerome Cole, and other industry representatives. Grant and his EPA staff tried to keep order from the middle. As soon as the discussion turned to possible health effects, sparks flew. Needleman and Ernhart accused each other of duplicity. She said he had not been fully accurate or honest. He questioned her motives. "They had pretty intense, brutal exchanges," says Grant. When Needleman pointed out errors in her own study, Ernhart began to cry. But she was unbowed.

"One day, Claire Ernhart informed us that a little lead poisoning in poor children didn't matter because their life was of little value anyway," remembers Landrigan. That was too much for Julian Chisholm. Although he was conservative by nature and agreed with industry on the risks of "overinterpreting" the data, he had also treated thousands of lead-poisoned children in Baltimore through his career. "Chisholm got up from the industry side and said, 'Every child's life is of value,'" says Landrigan. "Then he came around the table and sat with us."

The tension spilled out of the meeting room. Workshop participants were staying at the Governor's Inn. After a long day of hearings, they returned to the inn for dinner. When two of Needleman's friends and allies, Jane Lin-Fu and Carol Angle, a professor of pediatrics from Nebraska, went into the ladies' room, they found Ernhart brushing her teeth. "You should wash your mouth out with soap," said Angle.

The battle with Ernhart brought out the bare-knuckled fighter in Needleman. "I was proud of the work and when people criticized it, I got mad," he says. "Stubbornness runs in my family." Even friends describe him as formidable and occasionally huffy. Though everyone who weathered this storm agrees that Ernhart was equally vicious, some thought Needleman's aggressive behavior limited his effectiveness and polarized the discussion. "If you insult people, or argue from the point of view that you're smarter, you're not going to convince them," says one.

No matter how much Needleman liked a good fight, this one took a toll on him. At lunch in Washington, D.C., with his son Sam a few months later, Sam was struck by his father's appearance. "He had a nervous twitch, and he looked twenty years older," says Sam. "I could see it was hurting him." When Sam dared to suggest that his father step back from the front lines, Herb was aghast. "They're wrong!" he said. At times, Needleman's manner hardened his enemies' resolve and cost him some would-be allies, but his certainty also sustained him and gave him the will to take on a rich and powerful industry. "He has a backbone of steel," says his medical school friend Bob Phillips. Sometimes that helped stiffen the spine of his friends. Says Silbergeld: "When Herb Needleman looks you in the eye and asks whose side you're on, you have to answer him or answer to your God when you die."

It was clear there would be no resolution at the workshop. "In the office, there was never any time when we had any serious doubts about Herb's work," says Rob Elias. But to be able to use the work as part of the argument in the criteria document, they had to defuse some of the criticism.

The EPA decided to appoint an Expert Committee to assess the work of both Needleman and Ernhart. (The agency also appointed similar committees to examine the German research on lead's essentiality, which was ultimately dismissed, and the health and nutrition survey from the CDC, which was endorsed.) Paul Mushak, whose expertise was in measures of exposure, was named to the committee, but he was the only member with experience in lead research. The other five were primarily experts in statistics and research methods. One, Lawrence Kupper, was a well-known biostatistician who did research on the causality of lung cancer for the tobacco industry. Another, who would prove important, was Sandra Scarr, a child development psychologist at the University of Virginia who was brought on for her methodological expertise. Among other things, Scarr studied twins and child-care environments. "She was a strong proponent of nature over nurture," says Mushak. "Her sense was that a lot of cognitive dysfunction was genetic."

Grant and the committee arranged to spend two days with Ernhart and two days with Needleman reviewing their original data and asking questions about their respective studies. Ernhart met with the committee in North Carolina. Needleman asked them to come to Pittsburgh. He had two reasons: first, the volume of raw data from his study was so large it would be difficult to transport; and second, he was concerned about who had access to his work.

Accounts of the visit to Pittsburgh differ. "We had what seemed like an affable meeting," Needleman says. "Scarr had a cold, so I gave her some cough drops." He brought out the stacks of computer printouts for the committee to examine. The questions focused on how subjects were chosen for the high- and low-lead groups, how well Needleman controlled for confounding variables, and—the most serious question—whether he knew the subjects' lead levels before they were ruled in or out, thereby introducing bias. Needleman explained the design of the study, how it had worked in practice (a computer code made the exclusions, not him) and the decisions that had been made as the study evolved.

Needleman described changing the classifications of high- and low-lead groups from cutoffs of six and twenty-four parts per million to the final cutoffs of ten and twenty parts per million. Although the published report was in error, the change itself was standard practice. "You can modify your measurement criteria so long as you don't fundamentally change your testing hypothesis," says Mushak. "You can't go fishing for a hypothesis. His fundamental hypothesis was not that high-lead kids have twenty-four and low-lead kids have six. It was that low-dentine-lead kids are better off." If anything, the shift to ten and twenty probably made it harder to find an effect because it would tend to dilute the difference between the two groups. "The fact that he did find an effect is significant," says Mushak. "It met the rigor of the *New England Journal of Medicine*. That's pretty damn tough to get into."

When it came time for the group to leave Pittsburgh, however, committee members knew that there was at least one error, and they did not yet feel their questions were answered. They wanted more time with the data. But Needleman said that although he would answer every question to the best of his ability and that they could have as much time with the material as they liked in Pittsburgh, they could not take copies with them. "That left us in a quandary," says Grant. It wasn't possible for committee members to stay on, or even return as a group, to Pittsburgh, but they wanted to see the data for themselves. At least two of the committee members, including Scarr, later said that Needleman was uncooperative and that his behavior had raised their suspicions. Grant, however, wrote Needleman a friendly note of thanks after the visit. Although Needleman did send some further material, they mostly had to work with what they had.

Ernhart's study was much smaller. Her paper with Perino included eighty subjects, and the later paper followed sixty-three of those. The committee found a data analysis error in the Perino paper and believed that Ernhart may not have adequately controlled for confounding variables in that study. In the 1981 follow-up, they believed the blood tests she used were unreliable, and again they suggested she had not adequately controlled for confounding variables. (After the review, Ernhart reclassified one subject as a possible case of undiagnosed lead poisoning whose dramatically lower intelligence affected the results. With that "outlier" removed, she saw no association between lead levels and cognitive ability.)

Late in 1983, the Expert Committee drafted a report declaring that neither study sufficiently supported the conclusions that had been drawn. They criticized both and said they could not accept the results without some reanalyses. In Mushak's view, that decision was ascribable to lack of time for a more thorough evaluation and the fact that the larger Clean Air Science Advisory Committee was going to have to review the studies anyway. "For sure, a number of panel members felt they hadn't had an opportunity to finish the job," says Grant.

Needleman was incensed. He and Grant had agreed that he would receive a draft of the report with ample time to review it. Instead, he got it on the same day it went to the EPA press for printing. ("There wasn't much time," says Grant.) In the draft, Needleman found twelve errors of fact, some of which were more important than others, but all of which tended to lessen the strength of his work. For example, the report said that his team's rate of error in entering data was seven in one thousand when it was actually seven in ten thousand. The committee report also said, "Of the myriad statistical analyses, the committee came away with the impression that most runs led to non-significant findings." Needleman shot back: "Of the 66 outcomes we measured, 65 favored the low lead group. The odds of this happening by chance . . . are formidable." The report also got wrong the dentine lead levels of the groups, the type of dental tissue analyzed, and the IQ test he used.

After Needleman complained, Grant pulled the report from printing. A corrected draft went to the Clean Air Science Advisory Committee's subcommittee on lead, the eminent group of experts that would have the final say. The advisory committee scheduled meetings for two days at the end of April 1984 in Research Triangle Park.

In the meantime, the EPA sent two analysts, Joel Schwartz and econometrician Hugh Pitcher, to Pittsburgh to review Needleman's work further and report to the meeting. "The analysis really held up," says Pitcher. "I know lots of people whose work I would not trust for one second because I know they are advocates, and they twist analysis. Herb does not fall into that category. Regardless of what one's perception might be of him being an advocate, the results held up."

Needleman did prepare a reanalysis based on some of the committee's suggestions. He reclassified subjects on the basis of mean tooth lead level (to make it clearer who should be included and who excluded), controlled for age and father's socioeconomic status, and used multiple regression analysis, a more sophisticated technique. He also replaced subjects who had been excluded during the study for discordant tooth lead levels. The results did not change: children with more lead in their bodies did worse.

The scheduled April meeting came, and tempers had not cooled. The advisory committee plowed through all the issues and questioned both Needleman and Ernhart. It also heard from Pitcher, who had assessed Needleman's original study and the reanalysis in detail and found it supported the published conclusions. Finally, the advisory committee backed Needleman. "It would have been easy enough to ignore what Needleman had to say," says Mahaffey, who was a member of the panel. "But we believed that Needleman's work was plausible, and he clearly was finding in the direction of the general findings. This committee definitely defended what Needleman had done." Committee Chairman Morton Lippman, a professor of environmental medicine at NYU Medical Center, wrote: "Our committee was unanimous in finding [the charges against Needleman] groundless. No study is perfect, or fully and perfectly presented in scientific papers, and Dr. Needleman was cooperative and convincing in addressing all of the concerns raised."

The unanimity was significant. The twenty-three members of the committee included some who had been friendly to industry, such as Paul Hammond and Julian Chisholm. Members of the smaller group who had evaluated Needleman and Ernhart (some were also on the advisory committee) had a chance to raise objections, but no one did. One, Lloyd Humphreys, even acknowledged that Needleman had been responsive to the committee's criticisms in his reanalysis.

The lead industry responded in two ways. Its International Lead Zinc Research Organization wrote to individual members of the Expert Committee (the smaller group) and tried to solicit private criticism of Needleman's work. The letter asked if committee members felt that the advisory committee had paid enough attention to their report. The industry group also hired the public relations firm of Hill and Knowlton, which copied the Expert Committee's draft report. The firm removed the stamp REVIEW DRAFT: DO NOT QUOTE OR CITE and the admonition that the document should "not be considered to represent Agency policy." It clearly was not agency policy at that point, given that the advisory committee had ended up endorsing Needleman. But Hill and Knowlton sent it to science journalists and investigators across the country with a cover letter calling Needleman's work "worthless as a peg for government policy."

The final Air Quality Criteria for Lead Document, released in 1986, came out strongly on the side of Needleman—and Patterson, too. It said that there were unnatural levels of lead in the environment, that air lead levels were directly linked to blood lead levels, and that the case for health effects from lead was stronger than ever. Much of the section on lead in the environment drew on Patterson's work. As for Needleman's study, the document called it "pioneering," and, after describing the statistically significant results, it noted that methodological problems had been noted and addressed in three reanalyses and that they confirmed the published findings. He had defended his work and he had won. Needleman thought that the fight was over.

At the same time that the EPA was developing a new criteria document, the agency was being forced to reconsider its phase-down of lead in gasoline. Before he joined the EPA in 1979 as an economic analyst, Joel Schwartz trained as a theoretical physicist and worked on congressional economic policy. His job at the EPA, as he saw it, was to defend the agency against attempts to get rid of environmental regulations. "The best defense is a good offense," he says in his fast-talking, fast-thinking style.

The first go-round had come as lead regulations took effect at the end of the 1970s, and gasoline refiners had to reduce the amount of lead in their product. Initially, they were allowed to average leaded and unleaded gasoline, which gave them wiggle room. By the time Schwartz arrived at the EPA, however, the average amount of lead allowed had ratcheted down, and some refiners now felt it as a binding constraint. "One of the things the Department of Energy did was agree that EPA had to relax the rule because of the energy crisis," says Schwartz. To stop that, he came up with a novel way of looking at the problem: he combined data on children's blood lead levels in New York City through the 1970s with data on the amount of lead in gasoline sold on a quarterly basis. (The amount of lead required changed with the temperature.) The result was a pair of wavy lines that rose and fell almost in lockstep. "It's kind of like there's an association there," says Schwartz with a grin. "That worked. It stopped DOE."

But that was the '70s, and Ronald Reagan was elected in 1980. One of Reagan's campaign goals was to deregulate business. His administration drew up a list of what the U.S. Chamber of Commerce called the "terrible twenty" regulations most offensive to American business. For the one hundred–plus gasoline refiners at the time, lead regulations were near the top of the list. Schwartz was asked to figure out how much money relaxing the regulations would save the oil industry. "What about the health stuff?" asked Schwartz. He was told: "What are you going to do? The fix is in."

Frustrated, Schwartz dug for data to mount a counterargument. In addition to expanding his earlier work on the relationship between blood lead levels and lead in gasoline, he looked at how to tie the health effects to economics. He planned to speak the language of the pro-industry administration for which he was working. And he thought he could use Needleman's study to help make his case.

A policy office team, including Hugh Pitcher, was assigned to help Schwartz develop what would turn out to be the first major cost-benefit analysis for health policy. It took the five of them eighteen months. First, they did a meta-analysis of every related study they could find in order to better assess statistical significance. "We were saying, 'What are the odds that you would see this set of results?'" says Pitcher. "Everything was going in the same direction. The odds of that happening, if you were looking at significance due to random effects, were very small. The results were so important because they got at something that is a very clear, definite health effect that, as far as we knew, was not reversible."

Then they took the four IQ points Needleman showed were lost from lead and linked them to lower educational attainment and earning power to show that every point change in IQ equaled a 1 percent change in the wage rate. They included the powerful graphs from the CDC's second National Health and Nutrition Examination Survey showing how dropping blood lead levels were tied to dropping lead use. Schwartz did not neglect his original assignment. He showed that letting refiners put all the lead in gas they wanted would save about 2 cents per gallon for a total savings of $100 million (in 1983 dollars). If lead were dramatically reduced or removed, the cost to industry would be $500 million to $600 million. On the other hand, the benefit to society, in terms of what all the lost education and wages and increased health care would have cost, was close to a billion dollars. "The benefits of getting rid of lead way, way outstripped the costs," says Pitcher.

The lead industry "went berserk," says Schwartz. At the EPA hearings, Ethyl's vice chairman Lawrence Blanchard said Schwartz and the agency were guilty of "intellectual fraud." "They called me some of the same names they had called Herb," says Schwartz. In a company statement, Ethyl insisted the issue of lead emissions from cars was a "fictional problem . . . being exploited by scare tactics." Blanchard told the *Washington Post* that the EPA was taking a "juvenile and simplistic approach" and using "absurd hypothetical examples." Says Schwartz dryly: "I think he was upset."

But the cost-benefit analysis was a powerful tool. Even the champions of deregulation at Reagan's Office of Management and Budget admitted as much. Christopher DeMuth, the OMB's regulatory chief—the very man who had instructed the EPA to relax its lead standards—ultimately called Schwartz's study "a model of how regulatory issues in the health care area ought to be approached." As a result, although the EPA had begun by considering relaxing its regulations, it ended by tightening them even more.

The agency's policy chief, Joseph A. Cannon, had also had a change of heart. He originally believed in the power of the market to solve the problem—more and more cars requiring unleaded gas were entering the market, and those using leaded gasoline were on the way out. But when he was shown Needleman's work and Schwartz's related study, Cannon decided the market couldn't do the job fast enough. When he saw that the problem primarily affected poor inner-city children, he reached a conclusion exactly opposite that of Claire Ernhart and Robert Kehoe, who argued that lead was an inconsequential contributor to the overwhelming hardship of these children's lives. "You've got kids who are disadvantaged and then you're adding another layer of disadvantage," Cannon told the *Washington Post*. "The effects were clear and observable and the victims were mostly children who can't protect themselves. If left on its own, the market would not achieve this goal. The health studies are so compelling that you can't look away. You just can't look away."

In August 1984, the EPA administrator William Ruckelshaus first officially proposed speeding up the lead phase-down and said there was "overwhelming evidence" of the harm being done to children's brains by lead. The next year, the EPA made the rule final and determined that the amount of allowable lead would be 0.1 gram per gallon as of January 1, 1986. In effect, the EPA was removing lead entirely, although it was left to Congress to ban it outright in 1995. By the time the new regulations were announced, Ruckelshaus had left government, but the new administrator, Lee Thomas, echoed his predecessor: "There is no doubt in my mind that lead in the environment is a major public health problem and that gasoline is a major contributor to that problem."

• • •

Sixty years after it was added, lead was taken out of gasoline. But plenty of lead remained in the environment, and researchers weren't done specifying the harm that had been done. Through the last half of the 1980s, scientific support continued to solidify behind Needleman. "Those further studies are the ones that really help pin it down," says Lester Grant. In 1985, the CDC, using much of the same material the EPA had relied on for the criteria document, moved the level of concern down from 30 micrograms to 25. In 1987, the American Academy of Pediatrics published a comprehensive statement on the issue calling for widespread screening of preschool children, continued vigorous abatement of lead hazards, and mandatory reporting of lead poisoning in all states. Two European studies had results similar to Needleman's: one showed an IQ decrement of 4.6 points, the other found significant differences in IQ and reading ability. A review of all studies by other researchers found it "highly implausible" that consistent IQ decrements could have arisen by chance. The review's conclusion was that the modern urban environment causes a mean IQ decrement of 2 to 5. "The body of prospective studies were remarkably similar in what they showed," says Paul Mushak. "Certain domains of functions were affected whether in Australia, America, or elsewhere."

It was a favorite argument of Needleman's critics to say that a few IQ points did not matter much. After all, studies have found that reading to children regularly can affect IQ far more. Confronted with such an argument at a meeting at Harvard, Needleman once observed: "I know people at this university who would kill for four IQ points." But the true significance lay in the dramatic effect that a population-wide movement of four points had at the far ends of the spectrum. "A downward shift of this magnitude is associated with a threefold increase in the number of children with IQ scores below 80 and a threefold reduction in the number with IQ scores above 125," wrote Phil Landrigan in 1987. "In the population of American children with elevated blood lead levels, the aggregate effect of this silent loss will be immense. The attainment forgone and the societal disruption engendered are incalculable."

Needleman also believed that IQ was not necessarily the most critical of the effects he had found. It was simply the easiest to measure. Of far more importance in daily functioning would be poor reading skills, attention deficit, and disruptive behavior. "It translates into living life," says John Rosen, who has overseen the treatment of tens of thousands of lead-poisoned children at his clinic at Montefiore in the Bronx. "It affects memory, learning, language skills, verbal concept formation, planning and organizing. It's the difference between being able to understand a complex historical movie or book, being able to understand a manual for fixing a bike, and being able to interpret two- or three-dimensional diagrams."

Needleman and Bellinger continued to publish papers on the children in their Boston study. After Needleman moved to Pittsburgh, Bellinger became principal investigator. They got grants to continue the work until the children were ten years old. As the years went by, they found that the inverse association between lead exposure and cognitive development continued up to two years of age. As the children aged, however, the effect from lead diminished. Their final analysis was that the blood lead level passed on from mothers (ironically, in some cases, probably from renovating bedrooms for their coming babies) had a temporary effect on development. It was strongest at two years of age, and the lead level at two was associated with a child's IQ at ten years of age.

Around this time, a new front opened in the battle over lead. The families of lead-poisoned children went to court. Some of the first cases involved children who lived in the Boston area.

One concerned two-year-old Janette Christopher, who had lived in Chelsea, where Needleman had done his landmark study. In fact, Janette was born in June of 1979, just three months after Needleman's article appeared in the *New England Journal of Medicine*. When she was two, Janette was diagnosed with lead poisoning during a screening at a neighborhood health clinic. Under state law, her parents had seven days to have their apartment cleansed of lead. The contractor did a poor job of removing the lead paint and added to the problem by creating more lead dust. Janette's lead poisoning got worse, not better. A month after the cleanup, Janette was admitted to Boston City Hospital to undergo chelation. While she was undergoing the treatment, Janette contracted a staph infection from which she never recovered. A month later, she was dead.

The Christopher family sued the contractor, but it was also among the first plaintiffs to try to hold paint manufacturers liable for the toxicity of their product, on the grounds that Janette would never have been in the hospital exposed to the staph infection if not for the lead poisoning. That case did not succeed, but it and others like it served notice to companies who had manufactured lead pigment for paint that the legal landscape was changing.

Lawyers on both sides sought out Needleman and Claire Ernhart to be expert witnesses. For Needleman, the most memorable case came in 1988. It concerned Deneta Ruffin, a girl in Ohio. At the age of two, Deneta was described as "playful and bright." She sang nursery rhymes, ran, jumped, and talked in short sentences. All that changed in May of 1984. Deneta's family noticed she was eating paint chips, and she was treated several times for sporadic vomiting and abdominal pain. In July, she was admitted to a hospital. "Although she opened her eyes when called, she was unable to speak," according to her case history. There was evidence of massive brain swelling. In the operating room, her blood lead level was 100 micrograms per deciliter. She required six courses of chelation to bring her lead level below 40. At age six, when Needleman reviewed her case, she was in remedial education and had an IQ of 74.

The landlord of Ruffin's building was sued for improperly handling the lead paint present in the home. Needleman testified that a lead level of 100 probably affected Ruffin's IQ. But Ernhart, who had previously agreed that high levels of lead were indisputably dangerous, argued that Deneta's low IQ could be attributed to a combination of her race (Deneta was black) and the fact that her mother had died and that she did not go to nursery school. Deneta won a settlement from the landlord, who then launched a protracted suit against his insurance company.

• • •

In 1988, Needleman and Bellinger realized that the subjects from the Chelsea and Somerville study were now in their late teens. They decided to try to find out what had happened to them. They tracked down and enrolled 132 of the 270 subjects they had initially classified as falling into the high- or low-lead groups. (In the 1979 study, that group was reduced to 158 when they excluded subjects for such reasons as discordant tooth lead levels. After the EPA reanalysis, in which it was found that those exclusions were unnecessary, they decided to include the entire group of 270 in the follow-up.)

"We found that if they had high lead levels in their teeth in 1976, they were seven times more likely to fail out of high school and six times more likely to have reading difficulties," says Needleman. As the study reports: "Higher lead levels in childhood were also significantly associated with lower class standing in high school, increased absenteeism, lower vocabulary and grammatical-reasoning scores, poorer hand-eye coordination, longer reaction times, and slower finger tapping." Again, the results were published in the *New England Journal of Medicine,* appearing in January 1990. "The effects of early lead poisoning are permanent," says Needleman. "People don't get better."

The only solution was to not be exposed to lead in the first place. As Landrigan put it, "no therapy can replace dead neurons." Now Needleman spoke of complete eradication of lead poisoning. And he was not alone. He and a few like-minded others founded a nonprofit group called Alliance to End Childhood Lead Poisoning. Lead in old paint was the group's main concern. The oldest paint could contain as much as 50 percent lead by weight. One gram of such paint contained 500 milligrams of lead, or twenty thousand times the permissible intake for a child according to the standards of the late 1980s.

In addition, researchers were beginning to understand that paint had more subtle ways of reaching kids than they had previously thought. It wasn't only kids who chewed paint chips who were unduly exposed. "The role of dust was becoming clearer," says Suzanne Binder, who headed the CDC's lead-poisoning prevention program. Regular household dust, even in neat and tidy homes, can contain lead particles from paint on windows and doors, or that are tracked in from outside. Today, house dust is considered the most common exposure pathway for children.

That new knowledge added a new complication to the resistance from industry: fear of litigation. On some levels, industry representatives had come a long way. "They started to say, 'Tell us how clean it has to be,'" says the EPA's Rob Elias. But now they saw more than just the costs of cleaning it up. "It really wasn't just blood lead levels coming down," says Binder. "There was the potential to hold various polluters responsible. The lawsuits were starting because the science was getting there." Tackling the problem of old paint and household dust was going to take as much or more political will as was required for the reduction of lead in gasoline. Now a whole new range of industries were involved: real estate developers, landlords, construction contractors, and insurance companies.

For a time, it seemed the will could be found. The vision that Needleman had back in North Philadelphia while he looked out at the children in the Kenderton school—"I'll do this, and they'll get rid of lead poisoning"—was going to come true twenty years later.

In 1991, the CDC's Vernon Houk set up a meeting with James Mason, who was assistant secretary of health in the George H. W. Bush administration. Mason was a politically conservative Mormon who had dedicated his life to public health. All of the top environmental health officials were there. So was Herb Needleman. They reviewed the situation, and Mason asked what Needleman thought were "penetrating" questions. On the wall, Needleman noticed a plaque commemorating the end of smallpox in the United States. "There's room for another plaque," he told Mason. At the end of the meeting, Mason was unequivocal. "I want a plan to eliminate childhood lead poisoning, and I want it on my desk in six months," he told the group. Needleman's mouth dropped. "It's happened!" he thought and floated out of the room.

## CHAPTER SEVEN

# *What Have We Done?*

CALTECH, 1979

The office door was closed and had been for days. A photo taped to the door showed a highway exit sign pointing to "Patterson" and there were some aging newspaper cartoons. Russ Flegal was a young geochemist newly arrived in Pasadena to spend six months working in Clair Patterson's famous laboratory. He'd left his young family in Santa Cruz, thinking that the opportunity to work with Patterson was worth some hardship.

Staring at a closed door, however amusingly decorated, was not what Flegal had in mind. "I worked with Dorothy Settle, but Patterson wasn't available to talk to me," says Flegal. "After a week of being there to work with the great Patterson, I hadn't seen him." He was getting angrier by the day. Flegal had a personality nearly as strong as Patterson's—so much so that his advisor at Santa Cruz bet the two wouldn't last a month together. Finally, he banged on Patterson's door.

"I've come here to work with you," he said, shouting to be heard through the double door. "I expect to see you."

"I have terminal cancer," came a voice from inside.

Aghast, Flegal left the man in peace. The next day he went back and knocked again.

"Are you seeking treatment?" he asked. "Can I help?"

It turned out that Patterson had diagnosed himself and didn't really have cancer. "He didn't die for nearly another twenty years," says Flegal, "and not from cancer." But Patterson, who was then nearing sixty, behaved like a man with little time left. When Flegal finally was admitted to the inner sanctum of Patterson's office, he noticed that Patterson kept a newspaper clipping framed on his desk. It showed a UC Berkeley professor in his nineties marching up the stairs to his office. "Pat really wanted to get as much done as possible," says Flegal.

Patterson was increasingly desperate to make the world see lead as the scourge he believed it to be. Locked in his office, he spent his time thinking and writing, searching for a way to communicate the enormity of the problem. Flegal had arrived in Pasadena just as Patterson was finishing his "Alternative Perspective" chapter for the National Academy of Sciences report on lead. It had been no small feat to get his chapter included, but the battles with the committee left him frustrated, spent, and talking of "futility." Although the report was a clear step forward from the previous one and the last five years had brought the banning of interior lead paint and the first reductions of lead in gasoline, Patterson wasn't satisfied. The conversation shouldn't be about "control" of lead, he said, it should be about the immediate and total elimination of lead. "It was clear to him," says Dorothy Settle. "He didn't understand why it wasn't clear to everyone. 'Here it is. What's the matter with them?'"

Patterson spent a lot of time talking with Rob Elias at the EPA. "His ultimate goal was for everybody to see things the way he saw them," says Elias. "The only way that could happen was if you knew him and you understood. So many would meet him and not understand. It was the job of the rest of us to communicate. It was not going along as fast as Pat wanted, and he was getting older. He was worried about the rest of the world. He couldn't sleep with those worries."

He was not just desperate; he was depressed. Being steeped in the facts of lead pollution for twenty years had darkened his perspective. "My world has been made lonely and dreadful by the knowledge I have gained and by my inability to communicate with others," Patterson wrote. He despaired over the state of the planet and over the human role in its ruination. "We poison ourselves with lead; we spoon it in," Patterson told Canadian radio. "There isn't a single blade [of grass] or a mouse anywhere in the Northern Hemisphere of this earth that doesn't contain ten times more lead than its prehistoric ancestors did."

By now, Patterson's scientific questions had little to do with chemistry and everything to do with humanity. He wanted to know how we could have done this to ourselves. The answer is as intricately bound up in man's propensity for the latest technology as lead is with silver in the earth. At every turn, we looked for new uses for lead—in part, because it was there. When the ancient Greeks adopted silver coinage, they created a lot of lead waste in their efforts to get at silver: four hundred tons of it for every one ton of silver. Soon, they found uses for the lead in their plumbing, kitchenware, and tank linings, and celebrated their propensity for innovation as well as the wealth and success it brought. In their heyday, the Greeks were producing an estimated ten thousand tons of lead per year.

The Romans, who exploited the silver and lead they found in Spain, raised that to sixty thousand tons per year. They lined their wine casks and extensive system of water pipes with it. (Patterson helped analyze bones of ancient Romans for Colum Gilfillan, who initiated the controversial idea that the Roman nobility had poisoned itself with lead and thereby brought about the "loss of Roman genius." To that theory, which Patterson thought possible, Patterson added his own: that the fall of Rome was actually attributable to the depletion of their lead and silver mines.) Lead production plummeted during the Dark Ages, but the exploration of the New World brought new lead mines from Peru and Mexico, and later the United States, that helped spur the Industrial Revolution and a wide new range of uses for the metal. From Patterson's work in Greenland and Antarctica, we know what happened next: a 750 percent increase in environmental lead concentrations between 1750 and 1965.

Patterson saw the increasing use and development of lead as a series of bad decisions and wondered if that decision-making was rooted in something as fundamental as the way our brains were wired. He developed a theory that divided the world of science into two distinct groups: the classical scientists and the engineers. Engineers used "utilitarian thinking" and scientists "nonutilitarian." As Patterson saw it, the goal of utilitarian thinking was to apply scientific knowledge in an effort to progress technologically. Classical scientists, on the other hand, explored the basic questions that defined the world and sought knowledge for its own sake. It wasn't hard to guess how Patterson judged the two groups. He found the mind-set of the engineers "abhorrent," whereas he believed classical scientists understood the beauty and preciousness of humanity. In Patterson's own terms, scientists and artists were *homo sapiens sapiens* (*sapiens* is Greek for "wise" or "knowing"), and engineers were *homo sapiens android* (*android* derives from Greek and describes a robot designed to look like a man), though sometimes he used *homo sapiens sapiens* to refer to everyone.

It was harsh language to express harsh judgments, but the essential question still resonates: Why did we fill our environment with a known toxin? We did it, in part, because we didn't know just what a bad idea it would turn out to be. Patterson came to that understanding far earlier than most. It pained him to wait for the rest of the world to catch up; his anguish and anger were the result of his clear reading of the evidence.

Patterson asked the next logical question, too: How can we learn from our past mistakes? With his split-personality view of science, he thought the classical scientists were the only hope. Clearly, they needed to fight their side, to prove the consequences of man's actions. More than that, they needed to make the world understand what had been done and heed the lessons. Patterson hoped to write a book that would help to do just this. But first, in 1980, he found a surrogate, a master communicator who would tell his story better than he could.

In the early months of 1980, the writer Saul Bellow followed his fourth wife, mathematician Alexandra Ionescu-Tulcea, to Caltech, where she was teaching. While he was there, he taught a course on the early-twentieth-century novel. "The students who signed up for it were as mystified by Joseph Conrad as I was by jet propulsion," Bellow wrote. But the "boy prodigies," as Bellow called them, were not the only ones in the classroom. There was also a "white-haired, close-cropped man" close to Bellow's own age who sat at the center of the classroom and never missed a lecture. "He was lean and tall, rather Western looking." Bellow correctly took him for a member of the faculty auditing the class—it was Clair Patterson.

Bellow wondered if Patterson could help bridge the gap between himself and the young scientists who were his students. One day they walked together to lunch at the faculty club. During that stroll, Patterson couldn't actually provide much translation for the students, but he described his own work in terms that Bellow found fascinating and insightful. Their friendship grew around lunches and walks such as that first one, and Patterson told Bellow of his despair over the gradual lead contamination of the planet. "I was dazzled by the originality of his researches and by their scope," wrote Bellow. "Moving to conquer nature as the Enlightenment had told us we must, man had fatally damaged the earth, had poisoned its air and its waters. Already our brains were affected by the lead wastes we had ingested . . . our conquest of nature, from Patterson's standpoint, was therefore not a triumph but a defeat. I was always inclined to view Patterson's account as prophetic revelation."

For Patterson, the friendship with Bellow was a lifeline—"one of the great pleasures of his life," Laurie Patterson told Bellow. He felt a keen kinship with Bellow's artistic mind. Indeed, he thought artists, musicians, writers, and poets were wired like classical scientists. Together, the artists and scientists were society's only hope. He believed a man like Bellow had the capacity to understand. ("Pat used to say consolingly that I had done remarkably well for a man of my lead-poisoned generation," wrote Bellow.)

Patterson knew the world mostly saw him as "an aging zealot." But perhaps the world would listen to an artist like Bellow. Initially, Patterson asked Bellow to prepare a series of articles, perhaps for *Harper's* magazine, which would explain the problem of lead contamination in the terms Patterson felt it deserved. "Your interest in this important matter makes one hope that you might transform my failure into something good for people," he wrote to Bellow.

Bellow was willing to consider such a project. They began with a long interview at Caltech, during which Patterson laid out his case for why Bellow should take this on. Then Patterson recorded a series of monologues, which he sent to Bellow to amplify his argument. Instead of an article for *Harper's,* Bellow wrote a novel, *The Dean's December.*

The Dean of the title is Albert Corde, a Chicago academic and journalist who has recently published a controversial series of articles in *Harper's.* Throughout the novel, Corde considers the plea of an eminent scientist called Sam Beech (a name Patterson's friends all assumed was purposefully close to "son of a . . ."). Beech wanted him to reveal to the world the dreadful story of lead and had presented Corde with piles of evidence: his own work plus "Needleman's neuropsychiatric findings."

> Beech somehow inspired respect. There was a special seriousness about him. He was even physically, constitutionally serious. His head, for a body of such length, was small, his face devoid of personal vanity. Light hair, grizzled and cropped Marine style, gave him an old-fashioned hayseed look. His cheeks were austerely creased, his glance was dry. Corde had checked on his credentials. He was indeed an eminent man of science. That was unanimous. He had authoritatively dated the age of the earth. . . . Corde was beginning to think that with pure scientists, when they turned their eyes from their own disciplines, there were, occasionally, storms of convulsive clear consciousness; they suffered attacks of confusing lucidity. . . . What he had learned by listening to his tapes with the closest attention was that the geophysicist had incorporated the planet itself into his deepest feelings, as if it were a being which had given birth to life. Beech was shocked by *Homo sapiens sapiens,* by its ingratitude and impiety. *Homo sapiens sapiens* was incapable of hearing earth's own poetry, or, now, its plea. Man would degrade himself. . . . [The biological language was Beech's own.]

• • •

Most researchers who have spent time studying lead agree with many of Patterson's conclusions. "We tend to underrate the future. People just don't think about the consequence," says Hugh Pitcher, the econometrician who helped produce the EPA's 1985 cost-benefit analysis on leaded gasoline and is currently senior staff scientist for the Joint Global Change Research Institute. "What we learned about lead was if you put it in gasoline, you're going to expose everybody in the country. It took a long time for us to understand just how persistent some of these things are, but it tells me a lot about what I don't want in gasoline. We are going to face this question about how conservative we are about things we put into our environment."

Proving the persistence and penetration of pollutants like lead continued to occupy Patterson. Though privately despairing, he was not about to give up. "Pat wanted to get the lead problem fixed, and the way for him to fix it was to show the global magnitude of the problem, to show this wasn't a local problem but that everybody's got it," says Russ Flegal. Neither would Patterson admit his despair to his critics, for whom he had little regard. "He sorted them into two types," says Flegal, "those who were incompetent and those who had an economic interest in disputing his values." And he was determined to continue strengthening his case. "I know the answers to these questions," he wrote, "but the scientific community requires that measurements of all kinds be made before *they* become convinced that *they* know the answers."

### Te Paki, New Zealand, 1983

The tower on Ninety Mile Beach was more than sixty feet high. Climbing the stairs to the top while hauling sampling equipment was a challenge. Patterson didn't care what the weather was. During a test run on a smaller tower, he and Dorothy Settle had stayed at the top changing samples while lightning crashed around them. Some rain was good because they wanted to sample the rainwater to assess the amount of lead it was carrying through the atmosphere. At other times of year, they wanted "dry fallout" samples, a measurement of the lead in the dry air. "If a storm was coming, we'd have to scramble to the top of the tower and cover the dry filters," says Settle.

When they had the precious samples, they triple-bagged them for protection and carried them back down the tower to the mobile clean lab they had constructed on the ground. At night, they returned to their camp on a remote sheep station. They slept in small trailers that rocked in the dark as the horses that shared the field butted the metal intruders.

On this quiet northern tip of New Zealand, Patterson found lead from the tailpipes of cars in Los Angeles, Tokyo, and cities in South America and Australia. The experiments were part of a collaborative effort called SEAREX, which stood for Sea/Air Exchange. A group of trace element chemists and oceanographers—many of whom could get funding more easily than Patterson—was measuring various trace elements. Patterson and Settle were looking at lead, while others looked at mercury, pesticides, and other toxins, both natural and manmade. Before they got to New Zealand, they had already taken samples at Enewetak in the Marshall Islands and in American Samoa. In 1985, there was a cruise of the North Pacific for shipboard sampling. Since Patterson had sworn off boats, he usually sent Bernhard Schaule or Russ Flegal on any cruises.

Patterson's goal was to use isotopic measurements to provide an accurate breakdown of the sources of lead. "Many people said, 'Lead is just a natural element in the air and all this business of pollution is crazy,'" says Settle. Volcanic emissions and silicate dusts were among the natural sources that the naysayers cited. Patterson knew different. To prove it, he collected samples of volcanic gases and of rain and air across the South Pacific and used isotopic measurements to separate one source from another.

Although Bob Duce, then at the University of Rhode Island, was the organizer of SEAREX, he and the others regarded Patterson as the project's "spiritual leader." They had learned their vigilance from him, but he still had something to teach them. He wouldn't let the team light the steep paths at night: light bulbs would attract insects, and insects could contaminate the samples.

Age hadn't mellowed him. One day, while they were at Enewetak, he and Dorothy Settle had to stay behind on nearby Sand Island to finish an experiment. The others left a boat for them, which they had to maneuver back out through the surf by themselves—something at which neither excelled. "I wasn't doing something right and we were having difficulty getting the boat off the island," remembers Settle. Patterson, being Patterson, was yelling. Just then, a message came over the radio asking what was going on. "I was in tears and at the end of my rope," says Settle. So she answered: "There's a madman on the beach here!" When the two returned to the main camp in their little boat, the military police were waiting on the dock, blue lights flashing. They were afraid that Settle had been attacked by a rogue Navy man who might have been driven mad by the isolation of his post. "It was one of the worst experiences of our life," she says. "It was almost the end."

But they carried on. To measure volcanic emissions, Patterson also traveled to Mt. Etna, to New Zealand's White Island, and to Hawaii. They measured the lead in the volcanic fumes emitting from the craters and in the ambient air. The work was as dramatic and hazardous as anything Patterson had ever done. In Hawaii, for example, a helicopter dropped Patterson, Settle, Bill Fitzgerald, and Todd Hinkley at the top of the volcano. "It was just black lava and fumes, no plant life," says Settle. "Fitzgerald put his backpack down on the ground. The next thing we knew, it was on fire because he'd put it on a crack." Patterson got a blast of sulfuric fumes in his face, burning his eyes and making it difficult to breathe. (Laurie Patterson believes that he never fully recovered from that experience.) But they got the answer they were seeking. "The amount [of lead in volcanic emissions] was insignificant compared to smelters, automobiles, and other things putting lead in the air," says Settle.

Patterson had indeed strengthened his case. "He could tell where the pollution was coming from," says Duce. On Enewetak, for instance, the measurements they took in April showed that lead had blown east from China and Japan. But the following August, the wind patterns had changed and so had the isotopic signature of the lead. It was now blowing across the Pacific from North America. Patterson could even go so far as to say that only 2 percent of the lead in his samples came from seaspray, but that 90 percent of the lead in the seaspray was of industrial origin. "It was the first time anybody had ever proven the source," says Duce. "We know now that pollutants and natural material are transported sometimes thousands of kilometers from its source. That was the first clear evidence."

By the end of the 1980s, even Patterson admitted to some victories. "The people in the lead industries thought because they had all this power they could stop [or] effectively inhibit the actions of a single person who wasn't very powerful," he said in 1988. "They thought that that's the way they could solve their problem. What they didn't understand was that you can't get rid of, or win in the face of, developing knowledge. If you work long and hard . . . [if] you keep adhering to the development of scientific knowledge concerning this matter, you'll win." From inside the EPA, Rob Elias kept Patterson focused on the progress rather than the protracted delays. "It was going in the right direction," Elias says. "I encouraged him to be a little more patient, to take what we could get."

One clear victory was on the issue of lead in food. After his work on tuna, the Food and Drug Administration became one of Patterson's regular governmental targets. As the rest of the country battled over lead in gasoline, Patterson took on lead in food. Food was proof of the multifaceted nature of lead. Ethyl Corporation and others maintained that lead in food was the primary source of lead in people. But Patterson argued, and his work showed, that most of the lead in food originated as lead in gasoline or contamination in processing and packaging.

He thought the FDA was nearly as wrongheaded in its approach as Ethyl Corporation had been; and was guilty, in effect, of the same "tragic misconception." That misconception was that his measurements of lead in tuna, and their own inability to duplicate them, did not matter as much as determining the threshold levels above which poisoning occurred. A long series of letters between Patterson and FDA officials followed.

He also sought help from U.S. senator Alan Cranston of California. In a seven-page letter to Cranston in 1980, Patterson wrote, "I can challenge the [FDA] commissioner to prove that the concentration of lead in fresh tuna muscle is not less than 1 part per billion as reported in CIT studies, but is instead 400 parts per billion as reported in studies approved by the FDA, and offer to resign from Caltech if he is right, if he and the heads and assistants in the food section will offer to resign from the FDA if I am right." Pragmatically, he noted that, while he was "willing, in fact, eager" to do just that, it made more sense to have a third party weigh in. Of course, there were only three labs (at that time) he trusted to do the work: Mitsunobu Tatsumoto's at the U.S. Geological Survey in Denver (where Todd Hinkley was also working), George Tilton's at the University of California, Santa Barbara (where he had moved in the late 1960s), and his colleague Gerry Wasserburg's at Caltech. Or finally, he proposed that the FDA send someone to work in his lab to be "educated."

The main culprit in food contamination was the lead solder used to seal cans during processing. That lead solder slowly migrated into the food inside; the longer a can sat on a shelf, the more lead ended up in the contents. Like that in gasoline exhausts, the amount of lead in food was rarely enough to bring on clinical symptoms of lead poisoning, but it added to the overall accumulation of lead levels in Americans. In 1971, a lead intake of 300 micrograms per day from food was deemed safe. But that was questioned within a year. With the debate over health effects at low levels simmering, food cans were an obvious source that had to be addressed. Ethyl Corporation and others in the petroleum industry made sure of it by trying to pin the blame for higher blood lead levels on food.

Unlike Ethyl, the food industry was not prepared for a bare-knuckles fight. When FDA focused on getting lead out of food cans in earnest, a campaign that began in the mid-1970s, some segments of the food industry made voluntary changes. "We got food manufacturers into a situation where they did not want to publicly not co-operate," says Kathryn Mahaffey, who, as a toxicologist for the FDA in the 1970s, headed that effort. That was particularly true for makers of infant formula and baby food manufacturers. "The baby food industry cares enormously about [its] image," says Mahaffey. If representatives of the industry had argued when the FDA told them their products presented health problems, she said, "they might win the battle, but they would clearly lose the war."

After a brief argument over the potential risk of botulism if they changed their packaging, those industries changed to welded cans quite quickly, in about a year. The FDA didn't actually ban lead solder in cans until 1995, but by then American food processors had all switched to welded technology. In 1979, the FDA lowered the acceptable daily lead intake to 100 micrograms, and by the early 1980s, when many cans had already been changed, most Americans were getting less than 10 micrograms per day from their food.

In fact, the FDA had much to be proud of and Patterson acknowledged the agency's good work after a meeting with FDA officials at the end of 1981. "I was astonished, gratified and pleased with the reception [you] gave me . . . and at the progress made by FDA chemists," he wrote in an unusually gracious letter. In an amusing twist, the welded can industry considered Patterson a hero and showered him with samples of their wares. But Laurie Patterson keeps a lead-soldered can of Campbell's Soup on the shelf in her office as a reminder.

On nearly every aspect of lead in the environment that Clair Patterson investigated—oceans, ice, soil—it is his protégés who are developing new knowledge today. Russ Flegal is one of them. It turned out that Flegal's advisor was wrong. Once Patterson opened his office door and the two began talking, they got along beautifully. Flegal was awed by Patterson's grasp of lead. Once, when Flegal came in to report on an isotopic measurement of water from Peru, Patterson predicted the ratio of Lead 206 to Lead 207 down to the decimal point. "He just had this sense of where all the lead in the world was," says Flegal. Instead of staying for six months as planned, Flegal collaborated with Patterson for the next twelve years. "It was exhilarating to work with him," says Flegal. "Literally everything we did was new. In my case, we showed that previous analysis was wrong by two, three, and four orders of magnitude."

Since then, it has been particularly gratifying to Flegal, who is at the University of California, Santa Cruz, to show that the very oceans that first launched Patterson on his lead crusade are recovering from the toxic abuse heaped on them. Just as blood lead levels have dropped in people, so too do the oceans evidence decreasing lead levels, according to research by Flegal and MIT's Ed Boyle. "They've done an elegant job of showing, in both the Atlantic and the Pacific, that as we cut out lead additives in gasoline, the oceans are cleaning themselves up," says Ken Bruland. "It's a beautiful story."

French researcher Claude Boutron initially infuriated Patterson with his inaccurate reports of lead concentrations in ice and snow. Patterson finally decided that the only solution was to bring Boutron to Pasadena and teach him how to do it right. Boutron was quickly converted. After he returned to France, he regularly wrote back to Patterson and Settle for advice on where to find the proper equipment for the ultraclean lab he was building. In 1991, Boutron returned to Greenland and documented a drop in lead concentrations there after lead was removed from gasoline. In 1993, he showed through isotopic measurements that the bulk of the lead that was in Greenland came from the United States. (The research camp in Greenland is now underwater because of global warming.)

When Cliff Davidson first worked with Patterson at Caltech in the 1970s, his Ph.D. research involved measuring lead in soil in the Los Angeles basin. In the last few years, he and one of his students, Allison Harris, have revisited the freeways of L.A. In such an urban area, the news isn't as good as it is in the oceans and the ice caps. Although we are no longer adding to the lead in the soil, the lead that is there isn't going away. "All of that enormous amount of lead that was emitted from Los Angeles tailpipes is now in the soil," says Davidson. "When wind kicks up the soil, there is lead in the air. The lead story is far from over. The legacy that we have from all of that leaded gasoline is going to continue in pretty much any urban area."

At the tender age of twenty-five, Allison Harris testified on the significance of her doctoral work in front of the EPA's latest Clean Air Science Advisory Committee as it prepared to release yet another criteria document (which was published in October 2006). That experience is still a bruising one, Davidson notes, akin to being cross-examined in court. "It's not the kind of thing you'd want to do if you could choose," he says. But like a gene passed from generation to generation, Harris has inherited the desire to solve this problem even as she recognizes how difficult that will be. "The question I'm asking," she says, "is can the soil emit pollutants, and the answer is yes, it can." Although there are no large-scale solutions, she says, there are some plants that pull lead out of the soil and phosphates that can be applied to soil to make it innocuous. "The thing about lead is that we can't ever get rid of it," says Harris. "The lifetime of lead in the soil is several hundred years."

Ten years after Patterson's "Alternative Perspective" chapter appeared at the end of a National Academy of Sciences report that Patterson disavowed, Russ Flegal was asked to be on the agency's committee for the next report on lead. "The first thing they do is say, 'Are you going to act up like Patterson?'" says Flegal. John Rosen, the Bronx pediatrician, also served on the committee, as did Joel Schwartz.

The deliberations were not without disagreement, but the report, published in 1993, began not with a nod to lead's usefulness but with the line, "Lead is a ubiquitous toxicant." On the next page, it reprinted the "Measles Figure" that had featured in Patterson's minority chapter, showing the lead burdens borne by the bodies of ancient, contemporary, and poisoned humans. The report cited infants, children, and pregnant women as the populations most at risk from lead exposure. Together with many suggestions on health effects and research, its recommendations included "rigorous trace-metal clean techniques" and "that mass spectrometry with stable isotopes be used to investigate sources of environmental lead, as well as to examine lead metabolism in humans." Says Flegal: "Among ourselves, we call it Patterson's Revenge."

Even before these successes, Patterson had begun to soften on some scores. By the mid-'80s, Flegal told the powers that be that Patterson would accept election to the National Academy of Sciences and wouldn't make a scene. When he was finally elected, Barclay Kamb, who had been Patterson's boss as head of geology and later provost of Caltech, said: "His thinking and imagination are so far ahead of the times that he has often gone misunderstood and unappreciated for years, until his colleagues finally caught up and realized he was right."

On tenure, too, Patterson changed his mind. In 1989, thirty-six years after arriving at Caltech and only three years before he retired, he finally accepted an appointment as professor of geochemistry. "My recent appointment is the result of concern by my faculty colleagues for me and is an attempt by them to lift my spirits. They personify the type of human activity I hold sacred, and I am grateful and pleased to accept their offer." He even went so far as to say he had been wrong to refuse tenure and wrong to criticize others for accepting it. "It is regrettable that I have been so ruthless to my family, to my colleagues, and to the Institute, and that it has taken me so many years to recognize this."

Patterson finally retired from Caltech in 1992. In his honor, his former colleague Thomas Church, who was by then an oceanographer at the University of Delaware, organized a symposium on Patterson's work for December of that year. It included nearly everyone who had worked with Patterson as well as allies from related fields, such as Herb Needleman. Given Patterson's habitual dislike of honors, Church and his chief conspirator, Patterson's longtime Caltech colleague Lee Silver, kept the symposium a secret from Patterson for months and then enlisted Laurie to "break the news" to him and persuade him to see it through. "This is as much for us as for him," Church wrote to Laurie. Patterson did not make trouble and used his speech at the end of the symposium to celebrate the "fellowship" he had found with his colleagues. He told them, "I am grateful for the way you have enriched my life as a scientist."

There were a few awards Patterson was willing to accept over the years, including honorary degrees from the University of Paris and from Grinnell, an award from the National Academy of Sciences in 1975, and a prestigious medal from the American Geochemical Society in 1980. The society later named an award in his honor. It is given to scientists in recognition of recent innovative breakthroughs in environmental geochemistry. Recipients have included Ed Boyle, Bill Fitzgerald, and Ken Bruland. Much to his delight, Patterson also had an asteroid, Number 2511, and a peak in Antarctica named after him.

But his friends and colleagues wanted larger recognition for his accomplishments. Cliff Davidson organized and edited a scientific book of tribute called *Clean Hands* in which colleagues contributed chapters on Patterson's life and work. Todd Hinkley and Mitsunobu Tatsumoto launched a campaign in the early 1980s to have Patterson awarded the Nobel Peace Prize. They chose the Peace Prize because Patterson's work didn't fall neatly into any of the scientific categories like chemistry or medicine. "Patterson's work is an example of a man's effort to untie a difficult scientific problem related to the well-being of people all over the world," wrote Hinkley and Tatsumoto. "[He] has devoted his career to making this a clean world to live in." They asked Linus Pauling, Edmund Muskie, and Saul Bellow to nominate him. Bellow obliged, but that campaign failed.

Beginning in 1986, Hinkley and Tatsumoto turned their attention to the Tyler Prize, the premier international environmental award first given to Arie Haagen-Smit in 1974 for his work identifying and reducing smog. It took nine years, but in 1995, Clair Patterson was awarded the Tyler Prize. Having finally accepted tenure and election to the National Academy of Sciences, Patterson also accepted this honor, though he gave most of the prize money to Caltech. Knowing that his colleagues had worked so long on his behalf cheered him. "I have no sense of personal gratification about this matter," he wrote. "Rather, I am lifted out, for awhile, from my despair over the futility of my efforts."

The Tyler banquet took place on the evening of Friday, April 25, 1995, in the apricot silk-walled dining room of the Four Seasons in Beverly Hills. Dressed in black tie, Patterson was by then stooped and thin, clearly not the robust scientist who had conquered Antarctica and the South Pacific. But he was, for him, relatively gracious. He acknowledged that the reductions in lead in gasoline and in soldered cans would benefit "hundreds of millions in future generations."

• • •

Patterson set up an office in the retirement home he and Laurie built in the Northern California community of Sea Ranch. There he planned to carry on with his thinking and writing, and he told friends the book he was producing on brain wiring and the importance of classical science would be more important than anything he had done yet. He hoped it would inspire young people to lives in science, but more than that to inspire them to lives in which they understood the relationship between scientific understanding, personal integrity, and responsibility to human society.

But the book was not to be. In the early morning hours of Tuesday, December 5, 1995, Clair Patterson died suddenly of an asthma attack at the age of seventy-three. At the memorial held at Caltech the following March, Laurie Patterson chose to reprint on the program the poem she'd found pinned to Pat's bulletin board. It was "Unfinished Business," by Auschwitz survivor and chemist Primo Levi, and Pat had used a black marker to outline the last few lines:

*Above all, dear sir, I had in mind*
*A marvelous book that would have*
*Revealed innumerable secrets,*
*Alleviated pain and fear,*
*Dissolved doubts, given to many people*
*The boon of tears and laughter.*
*You'll find the outline in my drawer,*
*In back, with the unfinished business.*
*I haven't had time to see it through. Too bad.*
*It would have been a fundamental work.*

## CHAPTER EIGHT

# *A Professional Death Sentence*

PITTSBURGH, 1990

It was early when Herb Needleman arrived at the law offices of Jones Day in downtown Pittsburgh to give a deposition. He had already served as an expert witness in several lead poisoning cases, so he knew the general routine. He would explain how his work showed that lead was an environmental hazard that caused neurological deficits in children. There would be hours of questions designed to help the corporate lawyers find ways to weaken the strength of his testimony. This case was a little different, however. He wasn't testifying on behalf of any one child. He was testifying for the U.S. government in a Utah Superfund trial.

In a suburb of Salt Lake City called Midvale, a tailings pile covered 260 acres between South Main Street and the Jordan River. The pile was the complicated legacy of the United States Refining and Mining Company, which closed down its smelting and steel-mill operations in 1971. Once the beating heart of the town ("you could set your watch by the shift-change whistle," remembered a neighbor), United States Refining and Mining was one of five lead and copper smelting operations in Midvale. It left an estimated 15 million to 20 million tons of refuse or, as a city official put it, "19 Great Pyramids" worth of material, on the ground.

Ten years after the site was abandoned, investigations by state and local authorities and the EPA found toxic amounts of lead, arsenic, copper, and zinc in the tailings—of those, lead was by far the most prevalent. When it was windy, lead-laden dust from the tailings blew across the neighborhoods on the west side of town and settled into the soil around at least a thousand homes. Lead had also seeped into the groundwater under the site. In 1984, the EPA declared the area a Superfund site. (Midvale has the dubious distinction of having two Superfund sites within city limits. The other is the Midvale Slag site.) By then the land was known as the Sharon Steel site after the company that bought the old steel mill in 1982 in hopes of reusing the tailings. Under the Superfund law, the EPA would clean up the site, but the agency thought the companies that had owned the site or had helped contaminate it should contribute.

The companies disagreed. So in 1989, the Department of Justice, acting for the EPA, filed suit against Sharon Steel, UV Industries Inc. Liquidating Trust (the remaining entity of the old owner, United States Refining and Mining), and Atlantic Richfield Co. (ARCO), which had dumped waste at the site for thirteen years. The companies argued that the cleanup was not their responsibility and, further, that lead in the area had not been hazardous to the children of Midvale. They hired Bob Bornschein of the Kettering Laboratory to do a study of local children, which showed average blood lead levels no higher than were typical of children living in downtown Salt Lake City.

That's where Herb Needleman came in. To bolster the government's case, he would discuss his own work and the many other studies that had since added to the knowledge of how and at what low levels lead was affecting children's brains. He had a lot of material with which to work. The accumulating evidence, particularly from the prospective studies begun in the 1980s, now suggested that the threshold for adverse health effects from lead was as low as 10 to 15 micrograms per deciliter. The CDC was about to lower its level of concern again, this time from 25 to 10 micrograms.

As Needleman made his way through the Jones Day offices, the place struck him as "luxurious in the coldest way." In the conference room, there were about a dozen defense lawyers gathered around a conference table "as long as a bowling alley." Claire Ernhart was there, too. She had been hired by the companies to help in their defense.

"I didn't expect Ernhart," says Needleman. "I had never heard of an expert witness for the defense attending a deposition." The two didn't speak. For three hours, through the morning and into lunch, the attorneys asked about the methodology of his studies. What other factors could be causing the observed deficits? How had he accounted for them? What errors of measurement had he made? Ernhart never asked a question, she just took notes. Needleman assumed she was there to identify any potential flaws in his testimony. When it was all over, he returned to his office at Pitt, puzzled but not overly concerned.

In some respects, that was the end of it. Needleman never did have to testify. Before the Midvale case got to court, Sharon Steel, which was now bankrupt, and UV Industries settled. Atlantic Richfield waited until the first day of trial in October 1990. ("Lead is a product of civilization," the company's attorney argued. "In every city, there is lead in the soils.") But Atlantic Richfield settled, too. In all, the EPA received $63 million from the three companies to help pay for the cleanup, which included capping the tailings and removing the top layer of soil at the thousand affected homes.

But the case turned out to have ramifications as potentially poisonous and permanent for Needleman as the tailings pile in Midvale. Claire Ernhart and the corporations for whom she was testifying saw the case as an opportunity to get a look at Needleman's raw data from the 1979 study—now more than ten years old. They asked the court to allow her to study the material as part of discovery for the defense.

Ernhart was joined in the request by Sandra Scarr, the psychologist who had been critical of Needleman when she served on the EPA panel that reviewed his work in 1983. That was her only connection to lead research, but on the strength of it, she, too, had been hired as an expert witness for the defense in Midvale. "They came to me and said, 'You've looked at Needleman's research before. Would you be willing to do it again?'" says Scarr. Needleman tried to block the effort in court, but he lost. Ernhart and Scarr had to be allowed to look at his printouts.

In September 1990, Ernhart and Scarr arrived in Pittsburgh with an attorney. Hostility filled the air. "What I told my people was these are not my friends, not my colleagues," says Needleman. He provided what was required of him and no more. "They can use the bathroom down the hall," he told his staff, "but I'm not going to offer them coffee. Ignore them." The raw data were made available in a small empty office. They were allowed to look at it, take notes, and copy material by hand.

Ernhart and Scarr were offended by what they perceived as Needleman's lack of manners and grace. "He could not have been meaner or nastier," says Scarr of the entire experience. They thought the room they were given to work in was unnecessarily bare and suggested later that the pictures had been purposefully removed from the walls. "It was weird," says Scarr. She also commented later that she thought she saw the ceiling panels move—implying that they were being watched. They also thought it rude that Needleman wouldn't allow their attorney in the room with them. A chair was provided for him in the hall for the day and a half that the two psychologists spent examining the data. "I'm not letting industry look at my work," was Needleman's response.

On the second day, U.S. attorney Benjamin Fisherow, chief counsel for the government in the Midvale case, presented Ernhart and Scarr with a confidentiality document that Needleman wanted them to sign. Again, accounts differ. In a talk a few months later at Harvard Medical School, Scarr described her response as dramatic: "I picked my notes up, my yellow pad, and I put them in my briefcase. I zipped them up and said, 'Gentlemen, I'm out of here and if you want to stop me you have to assault me.'" Fisherow says it didn't happen like that. His version of the event was far less confrontational. "After I presented, at Dr. Needleman's request, the proposed confidentiality agreement to the two doctors and their lawyer, they conferred in private and then left for lunch," Fisherow wrote in a statement on Scarr's factual errors. "[They] did not return to Dr.

Needleman's office. There was no discussion of or reaction to the proposed agreement directed to me by Drs. Scarr and Ernhart after I presented it to them."

Using the notes they took during their day and a half studying Needleman's data, Ernhart and Scarr wrote up a sixty-four-page critique, which quickly turned up in the hands of defense lawyers in lead-poisoning cases. Needleman received a copy from a plaintiff's attorney in Philadelphia, and that was the first he knew of its existence. In August 1991, Needleman got a call from a reporter at *Science* magazine who told him that Ernhart and Scarr had filed their report as an allegation of misconduct against him with what was then called the Office of Scientific Integrity at the National Institutes of Health.

They had also distributed the report to conservative journalists. Needleman was criticized first in the *Wall Street Journal* in an essay by Eric Felten whose argument was summed up in the headline: "Lead Scare: Leftist Politics by Other Means." (Felten also attacked Ellen Silbergeld, then at the Environmental Defense Fund.) Felten's political argument ignored the fact that in 1991, as he was writing, the Republican administration of George H. W. Bush was leading the effort against lead and that the final reduction of lead in gasoline had been promulgated by the Reagan administration.

Felten's essay was followed by a series of attacks by conservative syndicated columnist Warren T. Brookes. Like Scarr's speech at Harvard, Brookes's work was riddled with factual errors. He said that the EPA's 1983 panel had two hours, not two days, to review Needleman's work and accused the EPA of withdrawing the panel's critical report without ever consulting its authors. (In fact, three out of six of the panel members were present at the advisory committee meeting at which it was debated, including Scarr, and not one objected to the endorsement of Needleman's work.) But accurate reporting wasn't the point. Brookes, who passed away shortly after these columns were written, accused Needleman of "potentially the most significant fraud case in U.S. history." Almost in the same breath, he called the work of lead activists an "overreaction." His chief complaint was the high cost of lead abatement for what he considered questionable health benefits. (The Reagan Republicans had considered the same issue and been swayed by the cost-benefit analysis prepared by Joel Schwartz, Hugh Pitcher, and their colleagues.)

On November 8, 1991, Herb Needleman received a memo from George Bernier, dean of the University of Pittsburgh School of Medicine. "An allegation of research misconduct has been made against you," wrote Bernier. "[It] concerns the potential improper selection and exclusion of data [in the 1979 study]." The charges were not laid out specifically, but they amounted to roughly the same complaints Ernhart had made about his work in 1983, nearly ten years earlier: improper control of confounding variables, improper selection of cases, and running multiple comparisons so that the results could have been due to chance. In accordance with the policies of the Office of Scientific Integrity and the University of Pittsburgh, a panel of university professors had been appointed to "inquire into the substance of the allegation."

Misconduct is the most serious accusation one can make in the world of science. Needleman likened it, if proved justified, to a professional death sentence. In 1991, when Scarr and Ernhart lodged their complaint against Needleman, the high-profile case of alleged scientific misconduct involving Thereza Imanishi-Kari and her Nobel Prize–winning professor, biologist David Baltimore, was in the news, and the scientific community was in the midst of rethinking its approach to the issue. "We were at a crossroads," says Mary Scheetz, a professor in the Center of Biomedical Ethics at the University of Virginia who observed the Needleman case when she was a graduate student at Pittsburgh and went on to spend thirteen years on the staff of the Office of Research Integrity. "Institutions were not really well-oiled machines that knew how to do these things, and the public wasn't used to questioning scientists."

The University of Pittsburgh defined misconduct as "fabrication, falsification, plagiarism or other practices which seriously deviate from those that are commonly accepted within the scientific community for proposing, conducting, or reporting research." Ernhart and Scarr were suggesting that Needleman had deliberately manipulated his data so as to present as true a result that may not have been

—their allegations seemed to fall in the vague category of "other practices." The definition specified that misconduct did *not* include "honest error or honest differences in interpretations or judgments of data."

Jane Schultz, an associate professor of pathology, was Pittsburgh's research integrity officer, a new position. Schultz thought the accusations "nonsense" and said so in internal memos. "I think really it was a scientific debate," she says. But the university's attorney, Lewis Popper, pushed for a full investigation. "It was in the press, the public knew about it," says Schultz, who is now director of research development at the University of California, Riverside. "It became clear they were going to have to do something about it." In accordance with the policy, Schultz put lock bars on Needleman's filing cabinet and kept the only key. When he needed access to prepare his case, she sat with him in the room doing paperwork while he reviewed the data.

The Inquiry Panel spent a month considering Needleman's data and delivered its report in December 1991. Members had discovered the same errors that had come up before, and had continuing questions about inclusions and exclusions. They noted that there was no evidence of misconduct, and that the errors "strongly suggest[ed]" a lack of scientific rigor rather than misconduct. Nevertheless, there were enough open questions that they felt a further investigation was warranted. "We cannot rule out misconduct," they wrote.

Schultz suggested to Needleman at the time that part of the reason for the panel's decision was that he had made its members angry, though she didn't specify how. Certainly, he was angry himself. He repeated, as he had said in 1983, that the reporting errors did not affect the outcome of the study and that the panel had found no evidence of misconduct. He got support from statistician Joel Greenhouse, a professor at both Carnegie-Mellon and Pittsburgh, who didn't disagree with every aspect of the panel's report but arrived at a different conclusion. "There are no hard-and-fast rules" when it came to choosing variables or statistical models, he said. "Reasonable statisticians will differ." Needleman responded point by point in detail, but he made clear that he was angry: "The analysis . . . is superficial, incomplete, tendentious, shallow in its scholarship, naive and incorrect in its application of statistical principles and wrong in its conclusions."

It was hard for Needleman and for many observers to see how his work could be called fraudulent when science had in fact coalesced around his findings. By this time, twelve more published papers had shown a similar association between lead and IQ, and five additional studies had been done but were as yet unpublished. Nearly all of those, including his own Boston study, had improved on the methods Needleman used in the 1970s and were considered stronger proof. "The train had left the station in terms of proving the association," says Paul Mushak. "It was never the case that lead and neurocognitive health would stop at what Ernhart and Needleman had to say."

If anything, concerns about lead had broadened. An influential *Newsweek* cover story in 1991 titled "Lead and Your Kids" pointed out that it wasn't just poor black children who were affected. Middle-class children in the suburbs were being poisoned when their parents unwittingly exposed them during home renovations.

*Newsweek*'s article featured the Tackling family of New London, Connecticut. Jessica Tackling was a toddler and her brother, Nicholas, was a baby when their parents, thrilled at the prospect of creating their dream home, moved them into an old house. Their father, Bruce, quickly set to work scraping old paint and sanding walls. Soon, Jessica was complaining of stomachaches, and Nicholas never stopped crying, "his voice sometimes locking into a continual eerie scream," said *Newsweek*. Tests revealed that both children had been lead poisoned by the dust stirred up by Bruce's handiwork. When their mother, Helene, vacuumed up paint chips, she had actually put more dust into the air. "Odds are," said the article, "Jessica and Nicholas will not be quite as intelligent as they were born to be." Helene was anguished. "I'm living it every single day, every single day," she told the reporter. "I just think of this nightmare. I look at my children and wonder what I've taken away from them."

Conservative critics accused *Newsweek* of exaggerating the problem and relying too much on Needleman's work. Steven Waldman, who wrote the story, said in response: "'Debunking' the lead threat by criticizing Dr. Needleman is like saying, 'Those Ford Model T's really had some problems; therefore cars clearly can't work.'" He also pointed out that *Newsweek's* story had been prompted in large part by the George H. W. Bush administration's labeling of lead as the number one environmental health threat to kids.

"Needleman's study was not the only thing we were relying on," says Suzanne Binder, who, as chief of the CDC's childhood-lead poisoning prevention branch from 1990 to 1995, oversaw the lowering of the level of concern to 10 micrograms per deciliter. "He was one voice—a strong voice—but we were being led by the data. It's like watching your child and worrying about behavior. The first time you say it's because he was hungry and tired. But if you see it again and again, you know there's something going on here. There's no perfect study but if you have multiple kinds of data that all point to the same answer you know the data are telling you something. The investigation over whether Herb had falsified data was so much wasted time and energy that really was distracting from [answering the question]: What's the right thing to do?"

Clearly Ernhart and Scarr thought differently. They seemed to believe that if they could destroy Needleman's credibility, they would yank the keystone out from under the edifice of lead research and that the walls would come tumbling down. At several conferences in 1991, Ernhart and Scarr questioned the dangers of low-level lead exposure and criticized the use of Needleman's study as a basis for public policy.

Did industry put them up to it? "The question is what motivated Claire Ernhart to try to discredit the work when she didn't have to," says Rob Elias. "She only had to present her information and say it disagrees. That's the correct scientific method." To Needleman, there was no question that Ernhart spoke for the lead industry.

Ernhart resents that assertion. "Every time I turn around Needleman throws industry in my face," says Ernhart. "People from industry in no way directed what I said and did. I was trying to do the right thing by blowing the whistle on that man." Like Robert Kehoe, she does not concede that there could be a conflict of interest, even though she got industry support for her research—at least $375,000 worth—and even though she and Scarr both served as expert witnesses on behalf of industry and landlords being sued by the families of lead-poisoned children. "They are entitled to expert opinion," says Scarr. "You testify to what you know, not for or against one side or the other." But it's hard to see how regularly appearing on behalf of one side in an ongoing argument—for pay—does not advance the interests of that side.

Scarr had the smallest role in this drama and it is not as personal for her as it is for Ernhart. "I'm not in favor of lead in the environment," she says, but she has a conservative view on how to deal with it. "The question is, how much do you want to spend and how much trouble do you want to go to. There have been political decisions that are quite irrational and expensive. Is a lead level of 10 really damaging to children?" Furthermore, the body of her research in psychology has focused on inherited traits and the role of genetics. "You can't unconfound life," she says. But for a researcher who claims her only part in this was to call for honest science, she is prone to casually critical statements that don't hold up to factual scrutiny and that undermine the strength of her argument. She once said that the District Court in Utah "had their doubts about Needleman too." The court said no such thing. It simply held that he couldn't and shouldn't prevent Scarr and Ernhart from looking at his data. She also says that Needleman "ultimately had to retract and restate some of his results." That is not true, either. Every time his work was reanalyzed, the results were the same.

For Ernhart, on the other hand, the fight to bring down Needleman became a crusade. She spent days at a time reviewing his published work trying to find the errors in it. She sought out his disgruntled former employees and interviewed them. She wrote to the CDC to try to have him removed from its advisory committee. Her efforts have cost her. "I lost out on getting grants because of this," she says. "I lost out on a big chunk of my time." Not surprisingly, her relationships with other lead researchers suffered. Industry representatives became her allies.

Even some of those who share Ernhart's conservative interpretation of the research find her position hard to support. In Britain, Marjorie Smith did several studies on lead and IQ and believes many factors are more important to children's health than lead is. She has tussled with Needleman at conferences, does not agree with his interpretation of the level of the problem, and has testified on behalf of industry and landlords. He accuses her of focusing on "phantom variables." And yet, Smith says of the 1979 study that Ernhart has spent so much time taking apart: "It was groundbreaking for its time, and I don't think we should underestimate the contribution." Of Ernhart, she says, "She was an important influence in that she questioned the work when others didn't, but Sandra Scarr's view was a much more balanced one."

The lead industry capitalized on Ernhart's personal antipathy for Needleman. It considered support of her research a priority because she was the only researcher challenging Needleman. Industry representatives enlisted her as an expert witness, and her presence at Needleman's Jones Day deposition indicates that she strategized with them over how to work against him. The sixty-four-page report she submitted to the NIH's Office of Scientific Integrity may have been the maturation of her personal crusade, but it was born as part of a legal strategy by the lead industry to avoid paying for environmental cleanup.

While the allegations were pending, lead industry representatives hired Edelman Public Relations to push their case. Edelman set up an 800 number through which callers could receive a package of materials criticizing Needleman, Ellen Silbergeld, and other environmental researchers. It infuriated Needleman, but also reconfirmed his view of industry's historical role. "If there is a jewel in the scientific misconduct toad's forehead," he wrote, "it illuminates the industry's attempts to slow action on a problem well enough understood to have been eradicated years ago."

• • •

After the Inquiry Panel left open questions, the University of Pittsburgh decided to proceed with a larger investigation. The university had just come through two embarrassing and bruising cases of misconduct. First, Stephen Breuning, a psychologist at the university, was found guilty of fabricating and falsifying study results. Second, Dr. Erdem Cantekin accused his colleague Dr. Charles Bluestone, an authority in ear infections, of conflict of interest. According to Cantekin, Bluestone solicited funds from pharmaceutical companies for research they had conducted jointly on the effectiveness of amoxicillin on children's ear infections and had then reached conclusions that were beneficial to the companies. Bluestone was found not guilty of misconduct, but his research center was put under a five-year monitoring plan. As a result of both cases, says Jane Schultz, "there was some reason for [the university] to be jumpy."

Furthermore, Needleman wasn't the most popular man at the university. As at Harvard, he had become entangled in the politics of academia—a realm in which his hard-charging style often sent him crashing into conflict with other big egos. "I can be a little abrasive," he says. His relationship with Thomas Detre, the man who had brought him to Pittsburgh, had soured. Needleman says it was because he refused to do the research that Detre wanted him to do. "I came here with the understanding that I would study lead and other neurotoxicants," he says. "No one said no to Tom." When Needleman came up for tenure, someone at Pittsburgh solicited comment from Claire Ernhart. She wrote a highly critical letter, which was shown to Needleman with the letterhead cut off. His tenure was refused. (At least one Pittsburgh colleague complained to Ernhart that he "was a one-issue person who didn't carry his load," she says.) On his second try, tenure was granted, but by then he was no longer the "golden boy." By the time the misconduct hearings were held, Needleman believed and Schultz confirms that there was a group within the medical school who wanted to get rid of him.

Faced with the inevitable, Needleman demanded that the hearings in his case be open to the public. His friends rallied around. Alan Leviton came to Pittsburgh to testify on Needleman's behalf.

"My thought was that Herb was right all along," says Leviton. "They really were out to get him. I think they wanted to diminish his ability to testify against them and to say bad things against the lead industry."

David Bellinger came along for moral support, and he and Leviton stayed with the Needlemans while they were there. "It made me angry that Ernhart and Scarr, based on a very minimal exposure [to the work], had drawn such strong conclusions," says Bellinger. "The whole proceeding seemed kind of nonsensical to me. The issues being discussed were scientific issues, like whether age had been adjusted in the covariate model." (Needleman's allies were not the only ones who felt that way. In *Newsweek,* science writer Sharon Begley likened charging Needleman with misconduct for such possible offenses to "charging a jaywalker with a felony.")

Irving Shapiro, Needleman's colleague from his earliest lead work in Philadelphia, was one of the leaders of the effort to have scientists sign a petition supporting Needleman and try to raise money for a defense fund. Clair Patterson sent $150 and a letter of encouragement that detailed his own run-ins with industry, saying: "I managed to survive. You are an investigator of integrity and first class ability, and should be able to weather the harassment you have been subjected to."

Needleman also lined up support from influential scientists. Morton Lippmann, the NYU professor who had led the Clean Air Science Advisory Committee that had already reviewed and then endorsed Needleman's study, wrote to NIH to complain: "It is indeed a shame and waste of time, talent and taxpayer expense that Dr. Needleman is the subject of a continuing vendetta by persons and parties who seem consumed with a need to punish an early messenger of unpleasant news about the role of lead on the health of children."

The hearing was held over two days in April 1992 in a large classroom at Pittsburgh's School of Public Health. Positioned at either end of a large U, Needleman and his two attorneys faced Ernhart and Scarr and their attorney, David Geneson, whose firm, Hunton and Williams, had also represented the lead industry. The five members of the Hearing Board sat across the base of the U. Needleman regarded the hearing as a trial with himself as both defendant and defense attorney (his lawyers were there as advisors). But the university, still feeling its way on how to handle such a proceeding, resisted his interpretation. The head of the hearing board was part moderator, part judge. Needleman was given the opportunity to question his two accusers and he did so with relish, making use of the space between them to pace back and forth and present them with documents. But because of the rules of the hearing, they didn't have to answer him. Mostly they said that whether or not he was guilty of misconduct was a matter for others to decide; they had simply raised questions.

The result was a quasi-judicial piece of scientific theater. "It was like a dissertation defense, but nastier," says Mary Scheetz, who sat in on the hearings because of her interest in the issue of research integrity. In his opening statement, Needleman laid out the historical context:

> Not just my reputation and academic future is at stake.... One highly placed Capitol Hill staff member said that: "The EPA based their lead standards on Needleman's work, and if Needleman's work is invalidated, much government policy concerning lead will need revision...." I don't think EPA based its work entirely or in a large part on mine, but it does show that people do believe that; and what happens here will affect more than just my own destiny....
>
> This hearing did not rise *de novo* out of pure air. This hearing is taking place today because of a long standing campaign by the lead industry and its spokespersons to camouflage the health effects of lead, and to attack my work.... To ignore the progress in this rapidly moving field and the place my group's work has occupied in contributing to new knowledge, is to voluntarily blindfold yourself and then examine this elephant called scientific misconduct with your bare hands...to discover whether I looked at na-

ture and pictured it honestly, you have to know what nature looks like. In this case, the entire scientific world, excluding the lead industry and its defenders, believe that lead is toxic at low dose.

In her statement, Ernhart acknowledged that her latest review of Needleman's work had been at the behest of the industry lawyers for whom she was working in the Midvale case. "We believe that in several aspects of the decision making that is part of doing research, the investigators acted in ways that are contrary to accepted practice. Furthermore, the strategies used appear to greatly enhance the likelihood of finding support for the hypothesis that low levels of lead are associated with deficits in neurobehavioral outcomes." She described her visit to Pittsburgh with Scarr and the flaws they believed serious enough to warrant the misconduct charge.

They were essentially the same criticisms she had made previously: improper control of confounding; improper exclusions of data from the final, published analyses; and the assemblage of data for too many outcome variables, which increased the possibility of finding a significant effect by chance. "This continues to be a widely cited study. It has clearly had major influence in a number of policy decisions that are costly and detrimental to the welfare of children and others," she said. "We continue to be confident in our conclusion that this work is seriously flawed and that it does not establish any basis for claims that low levels of lead exposure have detrimental effects on child development."

On the issue of whether or not he should have controlled for age (the principal confounding variable the two accusers said was missing), Needleman repeated his assertions that the IQ test he used was normed for age, which would have made adding age as a separate variable a case of overcontrolling. He also pointed out that Ernhart was guilty of the same thing.

NEEDLEMAN: In your 1981 paper... did you put age into the model?

ERNHART: My study is irrelevant to the issues here today.

NEEDLEMAN: I'm just asking a question. It's easy enough. I'll answer it for you.

ERNHART: I'm sorry, sir, I do not wish to be harassed in this manner. That question is irrelevant...

NEEDLEMAN: The question is: Did I conduct my research according to generally accepted scientific standards? And what I'm trying to demonstrate here is that this accusation was brought against me by people who did not subscribe to those strictures themselves.

(The chairman of the board agreed with Ernhart that her work wasn't relevant.)

On the issue of exclusions, Needleman exhibited the raw data sheets, which included a piece of computer code at the top that instructed the software to include or exclude cases based on several predetermined variables such as English as first language or previous diagnoses of lead poisoning.

ERNHART: I don't recall having seen this...

NEEDLEMAN: Let me state that on the first page of the first data sheet in the first volume of my printouts you will find that. You will find it 24 times throughout the six volumes. It occurs at the beginning of every data analysis of 160 subjects.... Does this give you any cause to reconsider your charge of selection of cases in a biased fashion?

ERNHART: No.

NEEDLEMAN: So you are not amenable to instruction?

ERNHART: I am not amenable to your instruction.

And so it went. Alan Leviton testified to his role in designing the 1979 study (for which he has never been criticized despite the fact that many of the charges concern the epidemiological approach). "Let me make it clear," he said at one point, "that changes in the study along the way are considered good practice." Mushak testified to his role on the 1983 EPA panel and questioned Scarr's version of events. Hugh Pitcher testified to his review of Needleman's data.

"These results are very robust.... We have had four different investigators look at this data set. It has been pretty intensively looked at for a data set of this kind."

Joel Schwartz, one of those who had reanalyzed the data set, had added in age and the contested excluded cases. He testified to finding the same result as Needleman. "Making those exclusions and making those funny classifications of lead exposure, which you may or may not like, were probably not motivated by the need to do that in order to find a significant association between lead and full scale IQ," said Schwartz. "Because, in fact, if you don't do any of those things, there's a significant association between lead and full scale IQ." Two other statisticians testified to the fact that most of what was in question consisted of debatable points between scientists.

Pitcher says that he was surprised the issue of Needleman's work had come up again at all. "I thought this was really trumped-up stuff," he says. "It was the last gasp of what I consider to be one of the least responsible [trade] associations on the face of the earth. They suppressed evidence. They [did] not deal with the consequences of what they've created. I have a bias. I understand why they are the way they are. But I think sometimes you just have to stand up and say, OK, I make [lead], and I've got a problem with [lead] poisoning." He also points out that by 1992, there could be little question that Needleman had been right. "The bulk of the evidence is that even at very low levels lead disrupts the biochemical processes in the body—the calcium and iron pathways. You don't want that happening, particularly in developing children."

Ernhart and Scarr had resisted Needleman's call to make the hearings public, and both women describe the experience as awful. "He was at his rancorous best," says Ernhart. In Needleman's view, he was defending his work and reputation. If they made accusations, they should have to defend them publicly. He felt he succeeded. "We destroyed Scarr and Ernhart," he said.

At least one journalist found Needleman too self-righteous and indignant, saying, "He was awfully quick to say: 'How dare you!'" But most everyone else, whether they liked his approach or not, thought he effectively dismissed his critics. Philip Hilts covered the story for the *New York Times* and found the case against Needleman unconvincing. "This was a landmark study, and if there was really a serious question, it looked like a key moment," he remembers. "I thought I was going to see at the hearing that something was wrong. As the testimony went on, it became clear that the critics didn't have a good case. He was being quite clear. It wasn't like he was trying to hide things or say 'We didn't make mistakes.' In the end, the data still stands up. So what's your point? I thought 'There's some other agenda here.' He was a strong personality and aggressive, but you have to look past the personality to the data. On the data alone, there wasn't a real good reason to hold this hearing."

The Pittsburgh Hearing Board took another month to complete its investigation and issued its report at the end of May 1992. They found Needleman not guilty of misconduct. "What is particularly important is that we found no evidence of deliberate falsification of data, procedures or analysis that would bias the results," said the report. "The board is also confident that these data reveal a harmful effect of lead.... The Board found that most aspects of this study that were being disputed by the complainants and Dr. Needleman's other critics were honest differences in how such studies should be conducted or in interpretations and judgments of data."

But the board didn't find Needleman entirely blameless. It simply couldn't believe his claim that the mistakes in reporting were honest error. The report called them "deliberate misrepresentations." The board did agree that those mistakes had not biased the results and acknowledged that, if anything, the revised cut-offs for inclusion would have diluted the effect. But it nonetheless found the reports misleading and called for him to publish a correction to the scientific record. (That correction appeared in the *New England Journal of Medicine* in 1994.)

According to policy, the panel report went to the federal authorities for review. By then, the Office of Scientific Integrity had been restructured, removed from NIH, and renamed the Office of Research Integrity. It took two years for the federal office to release its own report, but it finally did so in 1994. It, too, found Needleman not guilty of misconduct but culpable for misrepresentations. Even though that report, too, found Needleman not guilty, Ernhart thought the criticisms in it were "devastating."

For Needleman, however, it was well and truly over, and he declared victory. "It took three years out of my professional life," he says. "I pretty much didn't have a new idea for three years. The anger was not healthy." His wife, Roberta, agrees. "He likes a good fight, but this has been more of a fight than he wanted. I thought he was going to die. He was so angry. We had several years where we didn't know if he'd have a job." When it was done, the Needlemans went to Sanibel Island in Florida to recover. "He must have slept eighteen or nineteen hours a day," says Roberta. "It was clear that he was recuperating and regenerating."

In 1995, Needleman got to enjoy congratulations instead of condemnations when he received the Heinz Award for the Environment, one of a group of prestigious annual awards established by Teresa Heinz in honor of her late husband, Senator John Heinz, and intended to recognize "the power of the individual in American society." Needleman was in good company. Other honorees that year included his old mentor C. Everett Koop; opera singer Beverly Sills; and Marian Wright Edelman, founder of the Children's Defense Fund. The award came with $250,000, with which Needleman paid his substantial legal bills. "That's when I knew it was really over," says Roberta Needleman.

New ideas started popping. Needleman and Phil Landrigan coauthored a book called *Raising Healthy Children in a Toxic World.* He started up new research. "If you listen to parents with lead-poisoned kids, they tell you that the biggest thing is that the kids' behavior changes—they become dangerous," he says. So he decided to look at juvenile delinquency. His first study, done in the mid-1990s, found that kids in the high-lead group had more aggression; they had not been arrested or diagnosed with lead poisoning but had more self-reported bad behavior.

The next step was to see if youths who had run-ins with the law also had high lead levels. Needleman compared bone lead levels in a group of adjudicated juvenile delinquents and a group of control subjects. The amount of lead in the bones of delinquents was seven times what it was in the controls. Based on his data, Needleman figured the odds: kids with high lead were four times more likely to be delinquent.

Others have continued with this line of research. In 2001, Kim Dietrich and his colleagues at the University of Cincinnati found a striking increase in the arrest rate for both males and females based on blood lead levels at age six. In October 2007, the *New York Times Magazine* ran an article about research by Amherst economist Jessica Wolpaw Reyes. "Reyes found that the rise and fall of lead exposure rates seemed to match the arc of violent crime, but with a twenty-year lag—just long enough for children exposed to the highest levels of lead in 1973 to reach their most violence-prone years in the early '90s, when crime rates hit their peak," said the *Times*. The theory of a link between lead and crime has met with healthy skepticism because it is so hard to prove. (Claire Ernhart wrote a critical letter to the *Times* about this article, though it went unpublished.) But a look back at how the work of Clair Patterson and Herbert Needleman was originally received is a reminder that an initial critical reception doesn't mean the idea is wrong.

### Pittsburgh, 2007

Herb Needleman celebrated his eightieth birthday at the end of 2007. Like the Berkeley professor that Clair Patterson didn't get the chance to emulate, he still works several days a week in a cluttered office near the University of Pittsburgh Medical Center. His latest NIH grant—to study a possible connection between early lead exposure and Alzheimer's—won't run out for a few more years. He periodically tries to cull the accumulated books and files in the office, but without much visible progress. A cartoon on the office door shows cowboys debating the toxicity of lead bullets under the title: "Environmental Scientists in the Wild West." A few awards hang on the wall. A photograph of him receiving the Prince Mahidol Award from the king of Thailand in 2003 has pride of place on the desk. Along with photographs of his wife and grandchildren, there is a picture of one of his heroes, Randolph Byers, whose 1943 study on lingering effects of lead poisoning started him thinking. There is also a signed photograph of C. Everett Koop. It reads: "To Herb Needleman, my nominee for a Nobel Prize."

His accomplishments are certainly worthy. By the 1990s, it was clear just how pervasive the effects of lead in gasoline had been. It took its absence to clearly define its presence. We will probably never be able to tease out how much lead in our bodies came from gasoline and how much from food, but the disappearance of lead from both sources had a stunning effect on the health of Americans.

The first hint came in the CDC's 1976–1980 National Health and Nutrition Examination Survey results, which showed a drop in blood lead that mirrored the drop in gasoline nearly to the month. When the CDC repeated that study between 1988 and 1991, the results were much more powerful: the mean blood lead level of all Americans had declined 78 percent since 1976, to 2.8 micrograms per deciliter of blood. Back in 1978, nearly 15 million children had undue levels of lead exposure. By 1991, the estimated number of children ages one to five with blood lead levels of 10 or greater was 8.9 percent, or 1.7 million children. By 2000, that number had dropped again, to 4.4 percent, or about 890,000 children. By 2007, the total was 310,000 children. Millions of children had been spared. That drop is one of the great public health success stories of the twentieth century.

For Needleman, that success has certainly been gratifying. "He's often said how wonderful it is to earn your living doing something you love," says Roberta. But he is still not entirely satisfied.

How to deal with the lead that remains is still a politically and economically charged question. Take lead out of gasoline and food cans and that's that. But paint can live on the walls of old homes for as long as those walls exist. It is not a hazard if it is sitting unreachable under layers of lead-free paint. But if that lead-free paint peels or is chipped, the lead paint underneath becomes exposed. This is most likely to happen where there is frequent movement and friction, such as windows and doors. In one study, Joel Schwartz found that children with lead paint in their homes were ten times more likely to be lead poisoned. Removing lead paint improperly adds to the problem: if it is sanded off, for instance, lead that was once on the wall becomes suspended in the air and the dust.

The CDC's 1991 strategy to eliminate lead poisoning, the plan that James Mason demanded, called for "primary prevention." An example would be putting in new lead-free windows instead of repainting old windows. But that is no longer a government goal. Shortly after the CDC plan was published, in response to Congress's passage of a bill addressing lead paint, HUD and the EPA set up a task force that delivered a report on lead paint hazard reduction and financing in 1995. The thirty-nine-member task force included two parents of lead-poisoned children. It also included Ellen Silbergeld, the only environmental health scientist, and Don Ryan, executive director of the Alliance to End Childhood Lead Poisoning, the advocacy group Needleman had helped found. Far more heavily represented were real estate, insurance, and mortgage companies.

The report drew distinctions between those properties that contain lead paint, which at that time were estimated to be half of the entire U.S. housing stock, and those in which there were "lead *hazards*" (emphasis original). They put the latter category at 5 million to 15 million units. The report emphasized the need for more information and guidance for landlords and others to properly "adhere to the standard of care and thereby avoid liability" and focused on the need to reform insurance and liability claims in this area.

Notably, Silbergeld and all the representatives of parents and tenants dissented or disagreed with most of the report. "Almost all the discussion . . . is about property owners, insurance companies, banks, owners, realtors, and contractors," wrote Maurci Jackson, a mother of a lead-poisoned child who became an activist on the issue. "Everyone seems to forget the real reason for this Task Force: to protect children from lead poisoning—to prevent the human tragedy of lead poisoning. . . . I know that lead-based paint is a 'problem' to landlords, bankers, insurance companies, health departments, etc. But no one can truly understand and know what a problem lead paint really is until it's *your* child who gets poisoned." Silbergeld and the tenants' representatives argued that in their experience landlords acted not out of ignorance, but out of neglect. In their opinion, the task force recommendations "knuckle under to what the controlling interests will agree to." They considered the promotion of "interim control" as a substitute for permanent abatement and protection from liability to be "morally repugnant."

Needleman was outraged that Don Ryan endorsed the report, and that endorsement led Needleman to resign from the board of the Alliance to End Childhood Lead Poisoning. He didn't stop there. Still determined to say exactly what he thought, Needleman publicly criticized Ryan and the alliance, saying essentially that they had sold out. Sadly, he has also had a falling out with some of his most ardent early allies. Sergio Piomelli, the Italian doctor who manned the conference room barricades with Needleman at his first EPA hearing, believes it wasn't necessary to drop the lead level below 25. David Schoenbrod has publicly supported Piomelli. Needleman lambasted them in print.

Although not everyone adopts Needleman's blistering style of attack, many others agree that prevention should be the focus. Before he died in 2001, Julian Chisholm, sometime adversary of Needleman, Patterson, and the other environmental advocates, argued in *Pediatrics* about the need to focus on prevention and long-term low-level effects.

Bruce Lanphear, professor of children's environmental health at the University of Cincinnati and one of Needleman's scientific heirs, puts it another way. If we don't focus on prevention, but wait for children to get exposed, he says, we are treating our children like the canaries who served as early warning systems in coal mines. "If they stop singing or die, you know not to go down there," says Lanphear, who keeps on his office wall a photograph of one of the cages used to lower canaries into the mines. "It's an absurd way to protect kids from lead poisoning. Despite dramatic declines, lead toxicity remains a major public health problem. It remains an environmental justice problem and a major epidemic in some places."

• • •

By 2000, there had been eight major prospective studies on lead conducted around the world, including Bellinger and Needleman's Boston Study. Six of them resulted in evidence of a harmful effect of lead at very low levels. One conducted in Sydney, Australia, found no effect from lead. The eighth was Claire Ernhart's Cleveland Study, which looked at effects of both lead and maternal alcohol use, and, although she doesn't like to say so, did result in some statistically significant lead effects.

Bruce Lanphear decided to try to see what the results would look like if all the studies were put together. He organized the first international pooled study of lead effects. Unlike a meta-analysis, which compares study results on a given subject, a pooled study throws together raw data from multiple studies and recalculates the results. "It allows you to look at the problem in a larger way," says Lanphear. Seven of the eight principal investigators, including Ernhart, agreed to participate. (Researchers in Sydney never returned Lanphear's calls.)

Combined, they were able to assemble data on 1,333 children with a mean blood lead level of 12.4 micrograms per deciliter. The group met twice to hammer out the best strategies for handling differences in design and methodology among the studies. That meant Lanphear had the distinction of being one of the very few to succeed in putting Herb Needleman and Claire Ernhart in the same room. "We put them on the same side of the room, at the corners of the table, so they wouldn't have to look at each other," he says. The two never spoke.

But Ernhart did complain to Lanphear about the statistical techniques the group chose. Ultimately, she removed her name from the final paper (her colleague Tom Greene did not), though she could not remove her data from the pool. While Ernhart is not as critical of Lanphear, Bellinger, and other current researchers as she is of Needleman, she insists that there are serious methodological problems with every study that has shown low-level lead effects, including the group effort.

"I suppose she participated because she thought it might validate her life's work," says Lanphear. It did not. The pooled analysis showed a decline of 6.2 IQ points for an increase of ten micrograms of blood lead. Furthermore, it showed that the steepest decrements in IQ—that is, the biggest step changes—came at the lowest levels of exposure. So, for instance, the differences between 1 and 7 micrograms per deciliter might be greater than the difference between 11 and 17 micrograms per deciliter. "There's quite a bit of evidence," says Lanphear. "Most would say it's definitive, as definitive as you can get from combined observational studies."

In addition to these new epidemiological results, the EPA criteria document released in October 2006 devoted hundreds of pages to reviewing the many other studies that have been done on health effects from lead since the 1986 document and its 1990 addendum. It noted that deficits in academic achievement have an enduring effect on success in "real life." It also said that effects of lead on behavior and mood may extend to increased risk for antisocial and delinquent behavior. In adults, it described symptoms of clinical lead poisoning beginning at 40 micrograms per deciliter (well below the level of many Ethyl Corporation employees over the years). It also found poorer performance in lead-exposed adults on cognitive tasks, reaction time, verbal learning, and reasoning ability that reflected involvement of both the peripheral and central nervous systems.

The report covered more than just cognitive effects. It noted that researchers have found an effect on kidney function at blood lead levels as low as 2 or 3 micrograms per deciliter. They have found increased lead is associated with increased blood pressure, hypertension, and cardiovascular morbidity and mortality. In animal research, the biochemical effects of lead are "immediate" and "convincing" at the cellular level. The new criteria document notes that several studies have shown no clear evidence of a threshold for adverse health effects. That is, there may be no point at which lead is not harmful.

Just as Clair Patterson maintained, it may be necessary to go to zero.

### CHICAGO, 2007

Bearded and shuffling a bit, in a tweed jacket, Herb Needleman enters the hotel ballroom looking exactly like the aging academic he is. He still travels for conferences and meetings, and was in Chicago to make a presentation to a lead litigation conference. What used to be an event primarily for corporate lawyers is now more evenly split between industry attorneys and plaintiff attorneys. Until recently, most litigation on lead poisoning has been personal injury suits filed against landlords for poorly maintaining properties. All larger efforts to hold industry accountable, specifically manufacturers of lead pigment that was added to paint, had failed. Courts held that product liability statutes either had run out or could not be applied if it was not clear which company made the paint in a specific home.

That changed in Rhode Island in February 2006, when a jury declared three lead paint manufacturers (Sherwin-Williams, Lyondell, and NL Industries, formerly National Lead) liable for the lead poisoning of tens of thousands of the state's children. It was the first time anyone had held lead producers accountable for the harm done by their product.

Lawyers from both sides of the Rhode Island case were in the ballroom with Needleman in Chicago. A year later, in July 2008, the Rhode Island Supreme Court overturned the jury's verdict, but during the Chicago conference, appeals were pending and passions were high. Each side took umbrage at the presentations and comments of the other. The discussion was heated but it was tamer than in the past. It used to be that Needleman and Ernhart regularly shared the dais at these events, duking it out on a panel on health effects. At one of the most memorable conferences, Ernhart likened searching for low-level lead effects to looking for the Loch Ness monster. Needleman replied: "She wouldn't know the Loch Ness monster if it sat on her shoe." But Ernhart has retired to South Carolina now, and no one has assumed her place. Industry relies more and more on consultants to make their case in court.

But Needleman still comes. He's treated like a hero by half the room. Some are old friends with whom he's been in the trenches for years. Others have never met him and want to shake his hand. "I just want to say thank you," they say. "We stand on his shoulders," says Neil Kelly, deputy attorney general of Rhode Island. The other half of the room mostly ignores Needleman though they do admit to frustration that there is no one on the panel with him to rebut. "There are two sides to every story," says David Governo, a Boston-based attorney whose firm specializes in defending against lead-poisoning claims.

This time, Needleman gets to tell his story. He has a standard Powerpoint presentation for these events. He shows pictures of the Australian Lockhart Gibson and of Randy Byers. He talks about Clair Patterson's work. He runs through his own research and updates it with others including the newest studies looking at links between lead, attention-deficit/hyperactivity disorder and Alzheimer's. Although he's quieter about it, Needleman is still angry. He couldn't care less about the "lead head" and "junk science" labels thrown at him by the other side. "That's trivial," he says. He's angry that there are still several hundred thousand American children with elevated blood lead levels. He's angry that the CDC has yet to lower the threshold below 10. He's angry that, in his estimation, lead abatement efforts have mostly stalled.

He has a suggestion that he keeps making when he speaks, and he makes it in Chicago to this roomful of lawyers. Look at almost any urban map, on the East Coast anyway, and draw three circles: one around the area with highest blood lead levels, one around the area of highest unemployment, and one around rundown old housing. They overlap. Why not train the unemployed in those neighborhoods to abate lead paint and solve three problems at once?

Nobody has yet taken him up on this idea. Many people argue that lead is no longer a problem. It's a problem of the past. Which brings him to his closing remarks. He has found a quote that aptly sums up his life experience with lead. It comes from American psychologist and philosopher William James, who said:

> When a thing was new, people said: "It's not true." When it was shown to be true, people said: "It's not important." And when its importance could no longer be denied, people said: "Anyway, it's not new."

# *Acknowledgments*

First and foremost, I want to thank the Needleman and Patterson families for supporting this project from the beginning. Herb Needleman spent hours with me on multiple visits to Pittsburgh and allowed me to follow him around in Chicago. He opened up his files and his life to me. Thanks also to Roberta Needleman, Sam Needleman, Josh Needleman, and Sara Needleman Kline. Laurie and Cam Patterson were gracious and welcoming. Laurie let me pore through her bookshelves and filing cabinets and even made me lunch, twice. I was pleased that in some cases, my digging around in the past helped to reconnect old friends and colleagues.

I spoke to many people during the two years I spent working on this book, several of them more than once. Most people I interviewed are named in the book, a few are not, but I'd like to thank all of them here for their time and patience. It was clear why so many of these people make such excellent teachers. Thank you to George Tilton, Joe Dykstra, Lee Silver, Bob Phillips, Charles Reilly, Evelyn Bouden Wilson, Patrick Pasquariello, Dorothy Settle, Russ Flegal, Ken Bruland, Bernhard Schaule, Rob Elias, Lester Grant, Ken Bridbord, Harold Rutenberg, John Balaban, Cliff Davidson, Allison Harris, Todd Hinkley, Paul Mushak (who had to put up with extra phone calls and emails because he proved to have such complete files and to be able to lay his hands on anything at a moment's notice), Bill Fitzgerald, David Bellinger, Alan Leviton, Anthony Fedelli, Patricia Hallion, Joel Schwartz, Neil Maher, Peter Barrett, David Rosner, Gerald Markowitz, Neil Leifer, Richard Lewis, Neil Kelly, Fidelma Fitzpatrick, Jerome Nriagu, Ned Groth, Kathryn Mahaffey, J. Haworth Jonte, Melvin Hill and his daughter Candace Morris, Gary Ter Haar, Sandra Scarr, Benjamin Fisherow, Marjorie Smith, Ellen Silbergeld, Phillip Landrigan, Bruce Lanphear, Hugh Pitcher, Joseph Palca, Philip Hilts, Suzanne Binder, Jane Schultz, Mary Scheetz, Joseph Perino, and Beth Landa. I would also like to say a heartfelt thank you to Claire Ernhart, who graciously welcomed me into her home even though we disagreed.

I made use of many libraries and learned the ways of archives during this project. Thanks to Charlotte Erwin, Bonnie Ludt, and the staff at the Caltech Archives, Bill Stout at Temple University, Cheryl Neubert at Grinnell College, Doris Haag and Sue Riddell at the University of Cincinnati, Diane Koch at Muhlenberg College, Wendy Chmielewski at the Swarthmore College Peace Collection, and Laura Kissel at the Polar Archives at Ohio State University. Also thanks to Joey McCool at Children's Hospital of Philadelphia, and to Ken Powell and Cheryl Henderson in the EPA Docket Office.

A sincere thank you to my agent, Russell Galen, who believed in me and in this book. He asked all the right questions and gave me the guidance I needed to make it a reality. Brian Halley and everyone at Beacon Press also believed in the book right away and saw what I saw in the story. I thank them for that and for helping to make it an even better book.

Thank you to all the friends who listened to me work through my ideas, supported me when I was down and cheered with me when I was up. Marcus Mabry and Alex Prud'homme gave valuable advice early on. Amy and Tom Jakobson and Elizabeth Schwarz listened and had the drinks ready when needed. Susanna Wenniger was a steady support (now I can run!). And thanks most especially to Moira Bailey—sounding board, soul mate, and reader extraordinaire.

Thank you to my mother, Joanne Denworth, for the idea. And for everything else.

Any parent, but especially any mother, of young children who is crazy enough to try to write a book, especially one requiring the level of reporting and travel that this one did, knows that it would not have been possible without help on the home front. So let me say a heartfelt thank you to all those who have helped keep me sane during this process: Jessica Barthel, Katharina Zubrzycki, Ramona Freismuth, and Lobsang Dolma.

To my three boys, Jake, Matthew, and Alex, thank you for sharing me with "the book." You are a precious reminder of why we must care about what we put into the world. In you, I see the curiosity and mental leaps that come so easily to children and that are the hallmark of great scientists and great thinkers. Hang on to that.

And finally, to my husband, Mark Justh, without whose love and support I would neither have started nor finished. Thank you.

# *Timeline*

**1839:** First comprehensive study of lead's neurotoxic effects published in France.

**1904:** Australian physicians link childhood lead poisoning to paint.

**1920s:** Twelve countries ban lead from interior paint.

**1923:** First gallon of leaded gasoline sold in Dayton, Ohio.

**1923–1924:** Fifteen workers die and hundreds are hospitalized after exposure to tetraethyl lead at Standard Oil, DuPont, and GM plants.

**1924:** Ethyl Corporation created by General Motors and Standard Oil to make and market tetraethyl lead as a gasoline additive.

**1925:** After hearings and safety studies determine "no good grounds" not to sell it, a suspension of sales of tetraethyl lead is lifted, and it goes back on the market as a gasoline additive.

**1943:** Researchers at Boston Children's Hospital publish first study showing poor school performance and other cognitive problems in previously lead-poisoned children.

**1952:** Clair Patterson builds at Caltech the first ultraclean lab to combat lead contamination.

**1953:** Patterson uses lead isotopes to determine the age of the Earth as 4.55 billion years.

**1957:** Herb Needleman treats his first lead-poisoned patient at the Children's Hospital of Philadelphia.

**1960:** Ethyl Medical Director Robert Kehoe sums up his research on lead, calling lead levels in the environment "natural" and levels below 80 micrograms per deciliter in people "harmless."

**1963:** Patterson publishes paper linking lead contamination in oceans to leaded gasoline. American Petroleum Institute cancels his funding.

**1965:** Patterson argues in *Archives of Environmental Health* that people are subjected to a "severe chronic lead insult," and he estimates that Americans carry 100 times more lead in their bodies than did their preindustrial ancestors.

**1965:** Tri-City Study, produced by the federal government and industry, shows no increase in environmental lead levels.

Patterson begins studies in Greenland and Antarctica that will show environmental lead to have increased by 750 percent between 1750 and 1965.

**1966:** Senator Edmund Muskie's subcommittee hearings on air pollution specifically address concerns about lead.

**1970:** Needleman begins his first study of lead in teeth with Irving Shapiro in Philadelphia.

The U.S. Public Health Service establishes blood leads above 40 micrograms per deciliter as a "level of concern" for children.

Widespread screening of American children reveals that, in some cities, 25 percent of those tested have blood lead levels above 40 micrograms per deciliter.

The Environmental Protection Agency is formed. Passage of amendments to the Clean Air Act require the EPA to take action on lead.

**1971:** The National Academy of Sciences releases its first report on lead, which does not find a health risk from airborne lead.

Congress passes the Lead-Based Paint Poisoning Prevention Act. For the first time, lead paint is banned from federally funded housing.

**1972:** David Schoenbrod and the Natural Resources Defense Council sue the EPA for failure to act on lead in gasoline, and they win.

The EPA links lead in the air to blood lead levels in children and proposes reductions of lead in gasoline.

Jane Lin-Fu publishes an article in *New England Journal of Medicine* suggesting that childhood lead poisoning is far more common than thought.

**1974:** Schoenbrod and the Natural Resources Defense Council sue the EPA for failure to list lead as a criteria pollutant, and they win.

**1975:** First EPA ruling on lead takes effect: all new cars must have catalytic converters, which do not work with lead.

Average blood lead level in America is 15 micrograms per deciliter. The CDC lowers the pediatric level of concern to 30 micrograms per deciliter.

**1976:** After EPA wins legal battle with industry, reduction of lead in gasoline begins.

**1978:** First criteria document on lead is released. The EPA calls for an ambient air quality standard of 1.5 micrograms of lead per cubic meter.

Interior lead paint banned in the United States.

**1979:** Needleman publishes landmark study in *New England Journal of Medicine*. For the first time, there is strong evidence of the link between low-level lead exposure and cognitive impairment.

**1980:** National Academy of Sciences releases second report on lead, "Lead in the Human Environment," which includes Patterson's minority report.

**1983:** The EPA assigns a special committee to evaluate the conflicting work of Claire Ernhart and Herb Needleman.

**1984:** The EPA's Clean Air Science Advisory Committee endorses Needleman's work.

**1985:** The CDC lowers pediatric level of concern to 25 micrograms per deciliter.

**1986:** The EPA removes lead from gasoline.

The EPA's second criteria document on lead endorses Needleman's work and calls for stricter standards on lead.

**1991:** The CDC lowers the level of concern for lead to 10 micrograms per deciliter and calls for a plan to eliminate childhood lead poisoning by 2010.

**1992:** Needleman is accused of scientific misconduct in his 1979 study. He is found not guilty by the University of Pittsburgh's hearing board.

Prospective studies by Needleman and other researchers show cognitive effects from lead at lower levels than previously thought.

**1993:** Third National Academy of Sciences report on lead, "Measuring Lead Exposure in Infants, Children, and Other Sensitive Populations," released. Colleagues call it "Patterson's Revenge."

**1994:** Needleman is found not guilty of scientific misconduct by the federal Office of Research Integrity.

**1995:** Because of reduction of lead in environment, American average blood lead level falls to 2 micrograms per deciliter.

**2000:** Research published showing cognitive effects from lead below 10 micrograms per deciliter.

**2006:** Rhode Island jury finds three manufacturers of lead pigment—Sherwin-Williams, Lyondell, and NL Industries (formerly National Lead)—liable for the "public nuisance" of lead paint still present in the state's public housing.

**2007:** Millions of toys recalled because they contain lead paint.

**2008:** Rhode Island Supreme Court overturns 2006 jury decision. Manufacturers of lead pigment do not have to pay for cleanup of lead paint.

# Sources

There are many sources for information on how to prevent and recognize childhood lead poisoning. Two useful books are *Getting the Lead Out: The Complete Resource for Preventing and Coping with Lead Poisoning,* by Irene Kessel and John T. O'Connor (Cambridge, MA: Perseus Publishing, 1997), and *Lead Is a Silent Hazard,* by Richard Stapleton (New York: Walker and Company, 1994). The CDC also provides information and links at www.cdc.gov/nceh/lead. For information on other toxins, see *Raising Healthy Children in a Toxic World: 101 Smart Solutions for Every Family,* by Philip J. Landrigan, Herbert L. Needleman, and Mary Landrigan (Emmaus, PA: Rodale, 2001).

## Quotes

Comments that came from my interviews are indicated in present tense ("says" rather than "said"). Generally, the sources are named in the text.

## Primary Sources

I've provided sources for each chapter below, but there are some cited throughout that were most critical:

*Deceit and Denial: The Deadly Politics of Industrial Pollution,* by Gerald Markowitz and David Rosner (Berkeley: University of California Press, 2002).

*Brush with Death: A Social History of Lead Poisoning,* by Christian Warren (Baltimore: Johns Hopkins University Press, 2000).

*Clean Hands: Clair Patterson's Crusade against Environmental Lead Con-*

*tamination,* ed. Cliff I. Davidson (Commack, NY: Nova Science Publishers, 1999).

*Prometheans in the Lab: Chemistry and the Making of the Modern World,* by Sharon Bertsch McGrayne (New York: McGraw-Hill, 2001).

Clair C. Patterson Papers, 10135-MS, Caltech Archive, California Institute of Technology (referred to hereafter as CIT).

Archives of Robert A. Kehoe at the Center for the History of the Health Professions at the University of Cincinnati Medical Center (referred to hereafter as Kehoe).

The Scientific Misconduct Investigation of Herbert L. Needleman, Vols. 1 and 2, University of Pittsburgh Library.

*Beauty, Health, and Permanence: Environmental Politics in the United States, 1955–1985,* by Samuel P. Hays (Cambridge: Cambridge University Press, 1987).

## Introduction

The figure of 24 million homes has been widely used. One source is a federal report, "Eliminating Childhood Lead Poisoning: A Federal Strategy Targeting Lead Paint Hazards," President's Task Force on Environmental Health Risks and Safety Risks to Children, February 2000 (available at www.cdc.gov). Brooklyn statistics come from the U.S. Census Bureau. Information on the historic role of lead relative to other toxins came primarily from an article by Paul Mushak, "Defining Lead as the Premier Environmental Health Issue for Children in America: Criteria and Their Quantitative Application," *Environmental Research* 59, 281–309 (1992). Information on the changing CDC "levels of concern" is widely available but is fully recounted in *Brush with Death.* Information on the production of lead came from the Mineral Information Institute, www.mii.org.

Scott Armstrong at the Wharton School of the University of Pennsylvania conducted role-playing exercises based on the banning of Panalba, an Upjohn drug. That work is recounted in detail in *Protecting America's Health: The FDA, Business, and One Hundred Years of Regulation,* by Philip J. Hilts (Chapel Hill: University of North Carolina Press, 2003).

The 2007 toy recalls were heavily covered in the media. Two examples are: "Why Lead in Toy Paint? It's Cheaper," *New York Times,* Sept. 11, 2007, and "Mattel Issues New Massive China Toy Recall," Associated Press, Aug. 14, 2007. Discussion of government pamphlets on lead in the 1930s is in *Brush with Death,* 138–41. The 1957 Mattel statistic is in *Deceit and Denial,* 103.

A good summary of the Rhode Island public nuisance lawsuit is "The Nuisance That May Cost Billions," by Julie Cresswell, *New York Times,* April 2, 2006. Updated information on legal developments is available through the Alliance for Healthy Homes (www.afhh.org). The lead industry also maintains a Web site on the issue: www.leadlawsuits.com.

Statistics on chemicals in the environment come from the Environmental Defense Fund and the High Production Volume Challenge. More information is available at www.epa.gov/hpv/index.htm and www.environmentaldefense .org. For an interesting discussion on this issue, see transcripts of "Now with Bill Moyers," May 10, 2002, and "Trade Secrets: A Moyers Report," 2001 (both available at www.pbs.org).

## Prelude

The story of Celeste Felder is in *Brush with Death,* 168. I also relied on newspaper articles such as: "4 Diagnoses Wrong and Girl, 2, Is Dead," *New York Times,* Aug. 24, 1951, 22; and "His Little Girl Screamed in Pain for 6 Weeks But 4 MDs Said, 'Don't Worry'; Then She Died," *New York World-Telegram,* Aug. 23, 1951, 1.

## Chapter One: Every Conceivable Source

Biographical information on Clair Patterson is drawn from many sources, but the primary ones are Patterson's Oral History interview for Caltech, available at www.archives.caltech.edu (the source for many of Patterson's comments); a National Academy of Sciences biographical essay by George Tilton, available at www.nap.edu; and *Clean Hands.* A history of Oak Ridge National Laboratory and the Manhattan Project is available at www.ornl.gov and www.lanl.gov. I also drew on information at the Grinnell College Archives and the University of Chicago Special Collections. Information on lead and meteorites came from the Mineral Information Institute (www.mii.org) and the United States Geological Survey (www.minerals.usgs.gov).

Interviews with Laurie Patterson, Joe Dykstra, George Tilton, and Leon Silver helped to fill in the personal details of this part of Patterson's life and my understanding of the science involved. Additional information on Harrison Brown, including some of Patterson's comments, came from *Earth and the Human Future: Essays in Honor of Harrison Brown,* ed. Kirk R. Smith et al. (Boulder, CO: Westview, 1986). Details of Patterson's laboratory work came from some of his published papers, particularly his dissertation, "The Isotopic Composition of Trace Quantities of Lead and Calcium," 1951 (courtesy of Laurie Patterson); and his "Isotopic Composition and Distribution of Lead, Uranium, and Thorium in a Precambrian Granite," *Bulletin of Geological Society of America,* September 1955.

More detail on the history of the effort to date the earth is available in *The*

*Dating Game: One Man's Search for the Age of the Earth,* by Cherry Lewis (Cambridge: Cambridge University Press, 2000); and chap. 10 of *A Short History of Nearly Everything,* by Bill Bryson (New York: Broadway Books, 2003).

At the Caltech Archives, I referred to correspondence with George Tilton, Harrison Brown, Ralph Cannon, Mark Inghram, F. G. Houtermans, Argonne National Laboratory, and H. H. Nininger as well as the files on Patterson's dating of meteorites and the earth 1951–58 and the Project Progress Reports for the Atomic Energy Commission and American Petroleum Institute (CIT, Boxes 64 and 65).

Details of the Clean Lab construction came from *Clean Hands*; from interviews with Dorothy Settle, Cliff Davidson, and others; and from correspondence provided by Laurie Patterson. Clair Patterson described the work in some American Petroleum Institute project reports. His own account of his first geology field trip is in CIT, Box 66, folder 24, and Bob Sharp described the trip in *Clean Hands.* In addition to many of the sources above, details of Patterson's response to determining the age of the earth come from an October 1989 letter he wrote to Caltech president Thomas Everhart and from notes prepared for Saul Bellow (both courtesy of Laurie Patterson). Patterson wrote the lines about "true scientific discovery" in "Historical Changes in Integrity and Worth of Scientific Knowledge," *Geochimica et Cosmochimica Acta* 58: 3141, 1994.

## Chapter Two: The Faces of the Children

Biographical information on Herbert Needleman was drawn primarily from interviews with him and his family: Roberta, Sam, and Josh Needleman, and Sara Needleman Kline. Two magazine interviews were also helpful: "Houses of Butterflies," by Rebecca Skloot in *Pittmed,* January 2001; and "Standing Up to the Lead Industry: An Interview with Herbert Needleman," by David Rosner and Gerald Markowitz, in *Public Health Reports* 120 (May–June 2005). I reviewed newspapers and yearbooks at the Muhlenberg College Library. Information on his early medical career was drawn from interviews with Charles Reilly, Patrick Pasquariello, Evelyn Bouden, and Robert Phillips.

Material on the history of Children's Hospital of Philadelphia, including Stokes's comment on Needleman and details of the hospital's lead screening program, called "The Detection, Treatment, and Prevention of Lead Poisoning in a Children's Hospital Out-Patient Department," came from the papers of Joseph Stokes at the American Philosophical Society in Philadelphia. I found additional details in C. Everett Koop's memoir, *Koop* (Grand Rapids, MI: Zondervan Publishing House, 1992). Harold Rutenberg and John Balaban provided information on the Temple and COR years. More information on COR is in Balaban's book, *Remembering Heaven's Face* (New York: Touchstone, 1991), and in the COR Archives in the Swarthmore College Peace Collection.

I also referred to articles from *Temple News,* provided by Temple University Libraries.

Information on the deaths from tetraethyl lead at Standard Oil and DuPont came from *Deceit and Denial* and *Brush with Death.* Coverage in the *New York Times* began with a page 1 story, "Odd Gas Kills One, Makes Four Insane," published Oct. 27, 1924, and continued through Nov. 2, 1924. The paper's investigation of the DuPont plant was described in "Tetraethyl Lead Fatal to Makers," June 22, 1925, 3.

The history of childhood lead poisoning was drawn from many sources, but primarily *Deceit and Denial* and *Brush with Death.* At the New York Academy of Medicine Library, I was able to review Gibson and Turner's original article from the *Australasian Medical Gazette* (April 20, 1904), Blackfan and Thomas's account of the first American death attributed to childhood lead poisoning in *American Journal of Diseases of Children* (1914, 377–80), and many other early medical journals. Jane Lin-Fu's "Lead Poisoning and Undue Lead Exposure in Children: History and Current Status," in *Low Level Lead Exposure: The Clinical Interpretations of Current Research,* ed. H. L. Needleman (New York: Raven Press, 1980), was also helpful.

The Byers and Lord study was published in *American Journal of Diseases of Children* 66, 5 (November 1943). The quote from Felix Wormser is in *Brush with Death,* 149. The earlier study linking teeth to lead poisoning was Altshuler et al., "Deciduous Teeth as an Index of Body Burden of Lead," *Journal of Pediatrics* 60: 224–29 (1962).

## Chapter Three: That Nut at Caltech

For details of Patterson's work on sediments and seawater, I relied on interviews with Leon Silver, Ken Bruland, Bernhard Schaule, Russ Flegal, Bill Fitzgerald, and J. Haworth Jonte. I also referred to Patterson's published scientific papers on the subject, particularly "Concentration of Common Lead in Some Atlantic and Mediterranean Waters and in Snow," *Nature* 199 (1963): 350; and "The Occurrence and Significance of Lead Isotopes in Pelagic Sediments," *Geochimica et Cosmochimica Acta* 26 (1962): 263–308. A complete list of his publications is available in *Clean Hands.* I referred to correspondence with T. J. Chow (CIT, Box 5) and Progress Reports for API (CIT, Box 67). Details of industry representatives' visit to Patterson's lab came from my interview with Laurie Patterson, *Clean Hands,* and a letter dated March 9, 1979, from Patterson to Christine Stevens (CIT, Box 22).

The history of using tetraethyl lead as a gasoline additive comes primarily from *Prometheans in the Lab* (see primary sources); *A Short History of Nearly Everything* (see chap. 1); and *Ethyl: A History of the Corporation and the People Who Made It,* by Joseph C. Robert (Charlottesville: University Press of Virginia,

1983), an authorized history of Ethyl Corporation. The quote from Thomas Boyd on public health concerns is in *Prometheans in the Lab,* 88. There is an account of the surgeon general's hearing in *Brush with Death.* I also used the transcript of the meeting, Public Health Bulletin #158 (1925); and Jamie Lincoln Kitman, "The Secret History of Lead," *The Nation,* March 20, 2000.

Material on Robert Kehoe came from *Brush with Death; Deceit and Denial;* and the archives of Robert Kehoe (see primary sources). Two articles in *Environmental Research* 78 (1998): 79–85 were helpful: H.L. Needleman, "Claire Patterson and Robert Kehoe: Two Views of Lead Toxicity"; and Jerome Nriagu, "Clair Patterson and Robert Kehoe's Paradigm of 'Show Me the Data' on Environmental Lead Poisoning." In the Kehoe Archives, I also found Ethyl's internal memo to R.K. Scales describing Patterson as "vulnerable in both," DuPont's J.R. Sabina's comment, "When Dr. Kehoe speaks..." and correspondence on the Harben Lectures (Kehoe, Boxes 34, 56, and 87). The Harben Lectures were originally published in the *Journal of the Royal Institute of Public Health and Hygiene* in 1961.

Patterson describes biopurification in the CIT Oral History. I relied on interviews with Todd Hinkley and Rob Elias, and an article on the Thompson Canyon work, "Lead Pollution in the High Sierra," *Engineering and Science,* February–March 1975 (a Caltech publication).

Patterson's disputed article on lead pollution was "Contaminated and Natural Lead Environments of Man," *Archives of Environmental Health* 11, 3 (September 1965). I relied on Patterson's correspondence with Katherine Boucot and Harriet Hardy for details of peer reviews and reaction to the article (CIT, Boxes 2 and 34). Hardy also describes helping Patterson with the work in her autobiography, *Challenging Man-Made Disease: The Memoirs of Harriet L. Hardy, M.D.* (New York: Praeger, 1983). The account of Hardy's visit to Patterson's MIT office came from Laurie Patterson. I also used the Harvard Gazette Memorial Minute for Harriet L. Hardy from May 1, 1997. The *New York Times* stories on his work appeared Sept. 8 and 12, 1965, on pages 49 and 71, respectively.

A long account of Patterson's trips to Greenland and Antarctica, "Lead in the Natural Environment: How Much Is Natural?" by Clair C. Patterson and Joseph Salvia, was published in *Scientist and Citizen,* April 1968. Patterson described the work in the CIT Oral History and in "Lead Pollution in the High Sierra," *Engineering and Science,* February–March 1975. I also drew on material in CIT, Box 68, and interviews with Cameron Patterson, Sam Savin, and Hugh Kieffer. The cartoons are reprinted in *Clean Hands.* T.J. Chow's annotated notes from the Public Health Service meeting are in CIT, Box 5.

The Muskie Hearings began on June 7, 1966, and were held by the U.S. Senate Subcommittee on Air and Water Pollution of the Committee on Public Works.

## Chapter Four: Proof of Principle

Needleman, Irving Shapiro, and Bruce Dobkin described the first lead studies in interviews. The relevant papers were "Lead Levels in Deciduous Teeth of Urban and Suburban American Children," *Nature* 23 (1972): 434–35; and "Lead Exposure in Philadelphia Schoolchildren: Identification by Dentine Lead Analysis," *New England Journal of Medicine* 290 (1974): 245–48. I also used material from "Standing Up to the Lead Industry" (see chap. 2). The Amsterdam meeting is described in "Environmental Health Aspects of Lead (Proceedings of the International Symposium), Amsterdam, Oct. 2–6, 1972."

The history of the lead pigment (paint) industry is told in detail in *Brush with Death* and *Deceit and Denial.* Jane Lin-Fu's paper was "Undue Absorption of Lead among Children: A New Look at an Old Problem," *New England Journal of Medicine* 286 (1972): 702–10. Manfred Bowditch's comments to Kehoe and Kehoe's comments on poor parenting are in *Brush with Death,* 170 and 183. The quote from Christian Warren ("lead became a focus...") is in *Brush with Death,* 180.

I referred to "EPA's Position on the Health Effects of Airborne Lead," Nov. 29, 1972, and "EPA's Position on the Health Implications of Airborne Lead," Nov. 28, 1973 (both courtesy of Ken Bridbord). More detail is available in several Federal Register reports on the issue; see, for example, Federal Register 38, 6 (Jan. 10, 1973) and Federal Register 38, 234 (Dec. 6, 1973). Patterson's reply to the EPA is in CIT, Box 17, folder 15.

An example of Jack Newfield's articles is "Silent Epidemic in the Slums," *Village Voice,* Sept. 18, 1969. He also wrote about Janet Scurry and his experience covering lead in his memoir: *Somebody's Gotta Tell It: A Journalist's Life on the Lines* (New York: Macmillan, 2003), 121–24.

Details of administration arguments came from *Cleaning Up America: An Insider's View of the Environmental Protection Agency,* by John Quarles (Boston: Houghton Mifflin, 1976). Larry Blanchard's quote about witch hunts came from *Ethyl,* 307 (see chap. 3).

In this chapter, I also drew on interviews with Phil Landrigan, Ellen Silbergeld, Ian von Lindern, Ken Bridbord, Alan Leviton, David Bellinger, Neil Maher, Peter Barrett, Patricia Hallion, and Anthony Fedelli of Somerville, MA. In addition, Needleman discussed the 1979 study in "Standing Up to the Lead Industry" (see above). The published study was "Psychological Performance of Children with Elevated Lead Levels," *New England Journal of Medicine* 300, 1 (March 29, 1979).

For help understanding epidemiology, I relied on *Epidemiology: An Introduction,* by Kenneth J. Rothman (Oxford: Oxford University Press, 2002). Details on El Paso and Idaho came from interviews with Philip Landrigan and Ian von Lindern and from articles in *Low Level Lead Exposure* (see chap. 2).

David Schoenbrod provided extensive documentation on the legal battle between his organization and the EPA. The relevant cases were *NRDC et al. v. EPA* (No. 72-2233) and *NRDC v. Costle* (74 Civ. 4617). Industry's suit was *Ethyl Corp. v. EPA* (1976). A transcript of a roundtable discussion by all the participants, "Looking back at *Ethyl,*" held in April 1979 by the Environmental Law Institute, was also very helpful.

Details of the 1978 criteria document meetings came from interviews with David Schoenbrod, Sergio Piomelli, Lester Grant, and Paul Mushak and from EPA Docket OAQPS 77-1. Jerome Cole's comments were in "New EPA Lead Standard Could Cost $650 Million," by Larry Kramer, *Washington Post,* Sept. 30, 1978. The information on the Natural Resources Defense Council award for Piomelli and Needleman came from Schoenbrod's notes for the ceremony and Needleman's letter to NRDC (both courtesy of Schoenbrod). I also referred to Schoenbrod's book, *Saving Our Environment from Washington: How Congress Grabs Power, Shirks Responsibility, and Shortchanges the People* (New Haven, CT: Yale University Press, 2005).

## Chapter Five: A Majority of One

Information on Thompson Canyon came from interviews with Todd Hinkley, Rob Elias, Cliff Davidson, and Bernhard Schaule. I also used the "Summary Report to National Science Foundation Concerning Grant No. GB31038" (courtesy of Todd Hinkley) and "Lead Pollution in the High Sierra" (see chap. 3). At Caltech, I referred to the Thompson Canyon materials (CIT, Box 71) and correspondence with Elias and Hinkley (CIT, Boxes 8 and 12).

Details of Patterson's life at Caltech came from interviews with Leon Silver, Dorothy Settle, Russ Flegal, Laurie Patterson, Cliff Davidson, and Todd Hinkley, and from correspondence (CIT, Box 14). Patterson's letter to Brown about the National Academy of Sciences and his conversation with Bruce Murray about running for Congress are in Rebecca Adler's 2006 thesis, "Clair Patterson's Battle against Lead Pollution" (courtesy of Laurie Patterson). More information on the activity of the California Air Resources Board and Arie Haagen-Smit is available at www.arb.ca.gov. The quote about the "Pattersons of this world" came from a 1968 letter to Don Fowler of the Lead Industries Association (Kehoe, Box 61).

Information on measurement came from interviews with Cliff Davidson, Jerome Nriagu, Bill Fitzgerald, Bernhard Schaule, and Ken Bruland. The quote about "fortress sanctuaries" is in the letter to Christine Stevens (CIT, Box 22). Details of the water sampler came from Schaule, Bruland, and CIT, Box 21. The "down the hall" quote came from *Clean Hands,* p. 19. A full description of the changes in marine chemistry is in K.W. Bruland and M.C. Lohan, "Controls of Trace Metals in Seawater," *Treatise on Geochemistry* (Amsterdam: Elsevier, 2003).

Patterson and Settle's two articles on tuna are: "Occurrence of Lead in Tuna," *Nature* 251 (Sept. 13, 1974): 159–61; and "Lead in Albacore: Guide to Lead Pollution in Americans," *Science* 207 (March 14, 1980): 1167–76.

An example of Patterson's work on lead in bones is Jonathon E. Ericson, Hiroshi Shirahata, and Clair C. Patterson, "Skeletal Concentrations of Lead in Ancient Peruvians," *New England Journal of Medicine* 300 (April 26, 1979): 946–51.

Patterson's 1974 letter to Senator Muskie is in CIT, Box 16, folder 13. His testimony to the House Committee on Science and Technology was given Sept. 24, 1975.

Details of National Research Council meetings came from meeting summaries and correspondence (CIT, Boxes 89, 90, and 94) and from correspondence with Philip Handler of the National Academy of Sciences (CIT, Box 11, folder 23). I used interviews with Ned Groth, Kathryn Mahaffey, Cliff Davidson, and Jerome Nriagu. For more information, see chapter 10 in Philip M. Boffey, *The Brain Bank of America: An Inquiry into the Politics of Science* (New York: McGraw-Hill, 1975).

## Chapter Six: Reluctant to Relent

Needleman and Patterson appear together in many articles about lead in the 1980s. A few examples are: Jane Brody, "Lead Persists as Threat to Young," *New York Times,* May 13, 1980; "Lead: the Debate Goes On, but Not over Science," *Engineering Science and Technology* 15, 3 (March 1981), which was the source of the quotes; and "Ideas," a Canadian radio program on CBC, the Canadian Broadcasting Center, April 12 and 19, 1988. Additional lab description, including Patterson's quote ("It ain't what it looks like..."), came from Edmund Newton, "Lead Man," *Los Angeles Times,* Oct. 14, 1990. Jerome Cole's letter criticizing Needleman appeared in the *New York Times* on June 3, 1980.

Details of the dinner at the St. Botolph club came from interviews with Needleman. Description of Needleman's experiences at Harvard came from interviews with Needleman, Alan Leviton, David Bellinger, and Claire Ernhart. Lisa Bero's statistics on industry research and general statistics on funding for science were cited in Jennifer Washburn, "Science under Siege," *Discover,* October 2007. For an overview on the issues surrounding conflict of interest, I found one source particularly helpful: Sheldon Krimsky's *Science in the Private Interest: Has the Lure of Profits Corrupted Biomedical Research?* (Lanham, MD: Rowman & Littlefield, 2003).

For details of the disagreements between Needleman and Ernhart, I relied on interviews with them. Both provided access to their files. I also interviewed Sandra Scarr, Joseph Perino, Lester Grant, Paul Mushak, Kathryn Mahaffey, Joel Schwartz, Hugh Pitcher, Marjorie Smith, and others. Ernhart's first criticism of Needleman was in an article she cowrote: "Subclinical Levels of Lead and Developmental Deficit—A Multivariate Follow-up Reassessment," *Pediatrics* 67 (1981): 911–19. The exchange of letters continued in *Pediatrics* 68 (1981): 844 and 903–905. I also referred to correspondence between Needleman and Grant (courtesy of Needleman).

Much of the material from the 1983 EPA review of Needleman's work is available in the record of Needleman's 1992 Misconduct Hearing (see primary sources). Details of industry's responses to the EPA review came from letters industry sources distributed at the time (from Hill and Knowlton's James Callaghan to science journalists, dated Dec. 1, 1983; and from Jerome Cole to members of the Expert Committee, dated Nov. 1, 1984). I also referred to transcripts of the science advisory committee meeting (EPA Docket ECAO CD 81–82). In addition, I referred to press coverage such as Eliot Marshall, "EPA Faults Classic Lead Poisoning Study," *Science* 222 (Nov. 25, 1983): 906–907. Needleman's reanalysis appeared in *Science* 227 (1985): 701–704. For industry's view, I also relied on my interview with Gary Ter Haar.

The connection between Lawrence Kupper and the tobacco industry is documented in *The Cigarette Papers,* by Stanton A. Glantz, John Slade, Lisa A. Bero, Peter Hanauer, and Deborah E. Barnes (Berkeley: University of California Press, 1998). The book shows that Kupper received two grants from the Council for Tobacco Research, a research group founded by tobacco companies in 1954. One grant for $247,500 covered a large study from 1982 to 1987; the other, for $31,300, covered a pilot study on causality in 1984 and 1985.

For the story of the EPA's effort to reduce lead in gasoline, I relied on interviews with Joel Schwartz and Hugh Pitcher. President Reagan's list of the "terrible twenty" is described in Lou Cannon's *President Reagan: The Role of a Lifetime* (New York: Simon & Schuster, 1991). The Cost-Benefit Analysis and the 1986 Air Lead Criteria Document are available at www.epa.gov. The results of the CDC's second National Health and Nutrition Examination Survey were reported in J. L. Annest et al., "Chronological Trend in Blood Lead Levels between 1976 and 1980," *New England Journal of Medicine* 307 (June 9, 1983): 1373–77. Landrigan's comment on IQ loss is in a letter in *Pediatrics* 79, 8 (April 1987): 582–83. The *Washington Post* followed the EPA's attempts to reduce lead in gasoline closely, and there are many articles on the subject through the 1970s and 1980s. The quotes from Christopher DeMuth and Joseph Cannon came from Cass Peterson's article "How the EPA Reversed around the Gas Pumps," *Washington Post,* Aug. 1, 1984, A17. Lawrence Blanchard's comments on the Cost-Benefit Analysis came from Sari Horwitz, "Ethyl to Fight EPA Plan to Cut Lead in Gasoline," *Washington Post,* July 31, 1984.

Details of Janette Christopher's case came from Renee Loth, "When Will We Stop Poisoning Our Children?" *Boston Globe Sunday Magazine,* Feb. 21, 1988. Deneta Ruffin is a case history in H.L. Needleman, "The Persistent

Threat of Lead: Medical and Sociological Issues," *Current Problems in Pediatrics* 18, 12 (December 1988), which also is the source for statistics on the amount of lead in old paint. Claire Ernhart's view of the case is taken from her Nov. 20, 1987, letter to attorney Jerome S. Kalur and from interviews.

Needleman and Bellinger's follow-up of the children from Somerville and Chelsea is "The Long-Term Effects of Exposure to Low Doses of Lead in Childhood," *New England Journal of Medicine* 322, 2 (Jan. 11, 1990). Information on lead in household dust came from interviews with Rob Elias and Suzanne Binder and from "Eliminating Childhood Lead Poisoning" (see introduction.)

## Chapter Seven: What Have We Done?

More information on early lead use is in *Lead and Lead Poisoning in Antiquity,* by Jerome Nriagu (Hoboken, NJ: John Wiley & Sons, 1983). Colum Gilfillan's book is *Rome's Ruin by Lead Poison* (Long Beach, CA: Wenzel Press, 1990). I also relied on Patterson's work on early metallurgy: "Silver Stocks and Losses in Ancient and Medieval Times," *Economic History Review,* 2nd ser., 25, 2 (May 1972). Also helpful was Jane Lin-Fu's "Lead Poisoning and Undue Lead Exposure in Children: History and Current Status" (see chap. 2).

Transcripts of tapes and correspondence between Patterson and Saul Bellow came from Laurie Patterson and the Caltech Archives (CIT, Box 2). Patterson's comments on accepting tenure came from a letter to Caltech President Thomas Everhart, Oct. 13, 1989 (courtesy of Laurie Patterson). Barclay Kamb's comment on Patterson was in a Caltech press release, May 11, 1987.

Material on SEAREX came from interviews with Russ Flegal, Dorothy Settle, Bill Fitzgerald, Bob Duce, Cliff Davidson, and Todd Hinkley. At Caltech, I referred to Patterson and Settle's correspondence with Bob Duce, Tom Church, Bill Fitzgerald, Don Nelson, and Kevin Rosman as well as their field notes (CIT, Boxes 21 and 75–79). Some additional details came from *Clean Hands.*

For the disagreement with the FDA, I used correspondence between Patterson and Senator Cranston and the FDA's Jere Goyan and Mark Novitch (CIT, Boxes 6, 9, and 11). I also relied on interviews with Kathryn Mahaffey and Ned Groth as well as Groth's article, "Lead in Canned Food," in *Agriculture and Human Values* 3, 1–2 (Winter–Spring 1986).

Information on the Tyler Prize, Patterson's retirement symposium, and his memorial service was provided by Laurie Patterson.

## Chapter Eight: A Professional Death Sentence

Information on the Midvale, Utah, Superfund case came from a series of articles in *Deseret News* and an article in an EPA newsletter, "Midvale Slag Superfund Site to Become Bingham Junction Development," *Cleanup News,* April 2006, Issue 26. The reference to "19 Great Pyramids" came from Karl K. Cates, "Midvale Council to Meet with Residents Entitled to Toxic Soil Cleanup," *Deseret News*, April 1, 1992, B4. "You could set your watch..." is in "Historic Midvale Mill Will Soon Be History," by Karl K. Cates, *Deseret News*, July 14, 1992, B1.

Most of the correspondence and reports from Needleman's misconduct hearing can be found in "The Scientific Misconduct Investigation of Herbert L. Needleman, Vols. 1 and 2," at the University of Pittsburgh. Needleman's comment on "the jewel in the misconduct toad" was in a letter in *Pediatrics* 92 (September 1993): 3, 509. *Newsweek*'s cover story on lead poisoning was called "Lead and Your Kids," by Steven Waldman, July 15, 1991. The quote "like bringing a felony indictment for jaywalking" came from Sharon Begley, "Lead, Lies, and Data Tape," *Newsweek*, March 16, 1992.

There is a series of articles about the case in *Ethics and Behavior*. The first is an article by Ernhart, Scarr, and David F. Geneson titled "On Being a Whistleblower: The Needleman Case," 3 (1): 73–93. The second, by Needleman, is "Reply to Ernhart, Scarr, and Geneson," 3 (1): 95–101. The last is Scarr and Ernhart, "Of Whistleblowers, Investigators, and Judges," 3 (2): 199–206. Patterson's August 1992 letter to Needleman is in CIT, Box 17. Needleman's correction to the 1979 study appeared in the *New England Journal of Medicine* 331, 9 (Sept. 1, 1994): 616–17, as "Correction: Lead and Cognitive Performance in Children."

The 1995 report on lead poisoning was "Putting the Pieces Together: Controlling Lead Hazards in the Nation's Housing," published July 1995 by HUD (HUD-1547-LBP). Julian Chisholm discussed the need for prevention in "The Road to Primary Prevention of Lead Toxicity in Children," *Pediatrics* 107, 3 (March 2001): 581–83. Statistics on the drop in lead levels came from two related articles on the results from the CDC's third national health and nutrition study in the *Journal of the American Medical Association* 272, 4 (July 27, 1994). The figure for 2000 was taken from "Eliminating Childhood Lead Poisoning: A Federal Strategy Targeting Lead Paint Hazards" (see the introduction). Joel Schwartz and Ronnie Levin reported a tenfold increase in lead poisoning in children exposed to lead paint in "The Risk of Lead Toxicity in Homes with Lead Paint Hazard," *Environmental Research* 54 (1991): 1–7.

Needleman's criticism of the Public Health Service is "Childhood Lead Poisoning: The Promise and Abandonment of Primary Prevention," *American Journal of Public Health* 88, 12 (December 1998). Needleman has published several papers on juvenile delinquency. Two examples are "Bone Lead Levels and Delinquent Behavior," *Journal of the American Medical Association* 275, 5 (Feb. 7, 1996), and "Bone Lead Levels in Adjudicated Delinquents: A Case Control Study," *Neurotoxicology and Teratology* 24 (2002): 711–17.

Ernhart's paper that shows effects from lead on IQ is "Dentine Lead and Intelligence Prior to School Entry: A Statistical Sensitivity Analysis," *Journal of*

*Clinical Epidemiology* 46, 4 (1993): 323–39. The results of the pooled data were published by Bruce P. Lanphear et al. as "Low-Level Environmental Lead Exposure and Children's Intellectual Function: An International Pooled Analysis," *Environmental Health Perspectives* 113, 7 (July 2005): 894–99.

Information on Mealey's Lead Litigation conferences is available at www.lexisnexis.com and www.mealeysonline.com. (See introduction for more information on lead paint litigation.)

# Index